MIND
TREK

MIND TREK

Exploring Consciousness,
Time, and Space Through
REMOTE VIEWING

Joseph McMoneagle

HAMPTON ROADS
PUBLISHING COMPANY, INC.

for the evolving human spirit

Cover design by Grace Pedalino and Quintin Parrish

For information write:

Hampton Roads Publishing Company, Inc.
1125 Stoney Ridge Road
Charlottesville, VA 22902

434-296-2772
fax: 434-296-5096
e-mail: hrpc@hrpub.com
www.hrpub.com

If you are unable to order this book from your local
bookseller, you may order directly from the publisher.
Quantity discounts for organizations are available.

Call 1-800-766-8009, toll-free.

ISBN 1-878901-72-9

15 14 13 12 11 10 9 8 7

Printed on acid-free paper in Canada

This book is dedicated to my wife Scooter,
for all her efforts in support of my curiosity,
as well as always standing by me
when no one else would.

Contents

Introduction

by Charles T. Tart, Ph.D.
University of California
Davis, California
and
Institute of Noetic Sciences
Sausalito, California

For more than thirty years I have studied areas of the human mind that have not always been considered respectable for a psychologist to study. These have included altered states of consciousness such as hypnosis, dreaming, meditation, and drug-induced states, as well as parapsychological phenomena such as telepathy, clairvoyance, and out-of-the-body experiences. My studies have convinced me that so-called "ordinary" or "normal" experience is just the tip of the iceberg and that we have possibilities that are not only exciting but which make more sense of the human condition than ordinary knowledge does.

As you might imagine, I have met, sometimes studied, and sometimes befriended some very interesting people: psychics, meditators, healers, spiritual teachers, martial art masters, and Nobel Laureates, to name just part of the range. Some have been quite wise, some a little mad, many a mixture of both.

Joe McMoneagle is one of these very interesting people who have a lot to teach us. He does not fit our culture's stereotype of a "spiritual" person or a "psychic." Indeed, he would probably be embarrassed if anyone pigeon-holed him in one of these categories. Joe is friendly, bluff and frank, and his appearance is muscular, self-assured and tough. When you get him talking about his service in Vietnam, you're glad he is friendly. I can't imagine him wearing robes or turbans, sitting in contorted meditation postures, claiming mysterious "powers," or preaching sermons.

Yet in 1970, Joe McMoneagle "died," was "united with God," and has since learned how to regularly and practically use what might seem like magic to many people.

Like a lot of other modern Westerners to whom this has happened, the result has been not only exquisite happiness but embarrassment, feelings of going crazy, isolation from others, and a shaking of the foundations of life; and, eventually, a greater happiness and feeling of purpose than most of us ever find. Joe is smarter, tougher, and more together than before his experiences started.

What can we make of this?

In my psychological and parapsychological studies of the human mind, I've found that we humans have an overwhelming need for meaning. Just as we need vitamins to maintain bodily health, we need beliefs and experiences that show us that the universe makes sense and that we personally have a part in it. If we don't get enough vitamins, we get deficiency diseases, like scurvy. If we can't find or create enough meaning in our universe, we get psychological deficiency diseases, such as an insatiable greed for material things that we hope (uselessly) will distract us enough so we don't feel the pain of living in a meaningless world.

For most people for most of history, religion provided a framework of meaning. It provided an explanation beyond the individual's limited horizons about why the universe existed (such as God or gods or Universal Love creating and maintaining it), a rationale for the problems of life (the struggle between good and evil, for example, or losing contact with our own higher nature through ignorance and desire), and a set of guidelines for living a meaningful life (morality, duty, and various spiritual development practices). The religious-meaning framework could, to some degree, lift us beyond our isolated individuality and struggles and make us feel part of something greater and worthwhile.

I speak of religion at its best, of course, for religion almost invariably becomes corrupted to various degrees by politics and other mundane factors and can end up creating more psychological and social problems than it solves. All human institutions—religion has no monopoly here—are created with some knowledge and much ignorance and prejudice. With the passage of time, living knowledge tends to harden into dogma and superstition.

What is the "living knowledge?" If you look at the history of the great religions, you discover founders who had profound experiences of an extraordinary sort, experiences that we could describe from a modern psychological perspective as occurring in altered states of consciousness. These "mystical" experiences gave deep insight and certainty and drastically changed the lives of the founders. Although the meanings revealed were often only fully understandable in an appropriate altered state, the founders struggled to express them in ways that made sense and were helpful to as many other people as possible.

To oversimplify, as religions continued beyond the life of their founders, we can see two broad paths of development. In the more common one, the disciples of the founder had no or only partial direct experiences of what the founder taught and so tended to focus more on "doctrine," on the inherently inadequate verbal descriptions of the deep knowledge the founder had experienced. As generations went by, the religion become more and more one of rigid doctrine, uninformed by living experience. Believing became stressed as essential. This kind of religion can be verbally taught to people and emotionally indoctrinated into them by manipulating emotions such as hope and fear. It provides some meaningful framework, but it is shallow, more like conditioning than genuine education, and does not hold up well in crises.

The other broad development path stressed experience, not belief. The founder didn't expect people to simply believe, but to practice the methods the founder had practiced, such as meditation, and so eventually know the truth directly by having similar, deep experiences. We might call this path "spirituality," as distinct from "religion," since the term religion usually implies institutions, hierarchies, doctrines, dogmas, and belief.

Our culture knows a good deal about religion, and little of spirituality. We also know much about the corruption, folly, arrogance, and ignorance that goes on in the name of religion. Combined with the immense success of science, it is not surprising that formal religion is not a vital force in many modern people's lives, and that we look on "religious experiences" with suspicion.

And yet. . .we too readily throw out the baby with the bath water. We automatically dismiss unusual experiences as crazy. Some are indeed "crazy," but not all of them. We practice a kind of dogmatic, fundamentalist "religion" that sociologists call scientism, a belief system masquerading as science that claims that only what is material is real, that all spiritual or religious ideas and experiences are per se impossible and crazy and must be stamped out if humanity is to progress. Yet a "meaning" system that says life is just a meaningless accident of molecules bumping around for endless eons, that consciousness, including all of its highest aspects, is nothing but a by-product of the brain, that all dies and comes to nought, is not an inspiring meaning system. Indeed, I think it causes a lot of the suffering of modern life, suffering which could be avoided.

But science has given us enormous amounts of useful information about the world and ourselves, and we can't ignore it just because its manifestation as scientism is depressing. One of the unique things about Joe McMoneagle's book is the way it bridges science and the spiritual.

In July of 1970, Joe McMoneagle died. He was delivered to a German hospital with no detectable respiration or heart beat. When he revived, though, he reported an incredible and life-shaking experience, what we now call a near-death experience (NDE). He wasn't really dead, of course, since the term has a finality to it that didn't come about, but no one in their right mind wants to come as close to death as so often occurs in NDEs: most people who come that close don't tell us an interesting story later; they get buried.

There is another way to describe what happened to Joe McMoneagle. Recall the distinction between two broad paths that religions follow, the path of belief and the path of experience. While much is made of one's own efforts on the experiential path, there is frequently a tradition of initiation, in which someone of high spiritual accomplishments, or "someone" who is a spirit (adequate words are hard to come by here) can sometimes temporarily lift a student up beyond their current level of development and give them at least a transient glimpse of higher spiritual possibilities. This is grace.

We proudly trace our rational, Western civilization back to ancient Greece, with people like Socrates and Plato building the intellectual foundations of our culture. What we usually forget is that most of the great Greek philosophers were also members of various mystery religions, long since stamped out by Christianity. A crucial element in some of those mystery religions was initiation. Not a mere formal ritual, as we have come to think of initiations, but trials, vision quests, undertaken only by the most serious seekers and aided by prolonged periods of fasting, purification, isolation, and drama. The highest kind of initiation involved inducing an NDE, such that the seeker knew from personal experience that the human mind was more than the body and would survive death.

While the details of these procedures have been lost to us, a strange historical development has occurred. Modern medicine, not generally known for its spiritual bent, has developed resuscitation technology that has effectively "initiated" many people into the Mysteries!

So we can say that Joe McMoneagle was given the highest mystery initiation of the ancient world! Without any cultural preparation or subsequent support!

The NDE has happened to many people now. A few have written and lectured about it. The vast majority of them are pretty quiet about their NDEs, but their lives have been transformed. Their "initiation" has provided a new, deep, and vital framework of meaning. Most, for instance, would deny they *believe* in life after death; they would say they *know* this is true from direct experience. Most would talk about the importance of learning to appreciate the wonders of the here-and-now and of learning how to love. We can learn a lot from them, regardless of what we think about the ultimate meaning or validity of the NDE.

Joe McMoneagle is unusual among those who've had an NDE, though, for he has not simply ignored science and scientism as meaningless in the light of his new meaning system; he has worked hard to find out how this way of knowing fits with genuine science. This led him to become a subject in experiments on one of the most interesting kinds of psychic phenomena, remote viewing, and to become an expert remote viewer. In the classic remote viewing experiment, one experimenter goes away from the laboratory and hides, i.e., goes to some location know only to him or her. Meanwhile back at the laboratory the remote viewer, the subject, is asked to use some kind of psychic ability to describe the place where the first experimenter is hiding. Refined techniques have been developed, and are described in this book, to objectively decide whether you do indeed get psychic perceptions of the remote target site or just random musings. Quite often you do get startling accurate psychic perceptions.

From the point of view of scientism, the supposedly scientific belief that only what is material is real, doing a remote viewing experiment is nonsensical. Someone in a closed laboratory room can't see where someone else is. Light waves don't pass through solid walls.

A once-in-a-lifetime NDE makes the materialistic, scientific position obviously wrong. But you don't want to come that close to death in order to appreciate the NDE point of view. It's too tricky to make sure it's a "near" death experience! Repeated remote viewing, often done in accordance with the best scientific standards, give something like the NDE perspective to the rest of us who understand the value of good science but hope for some meaning in life beyond scientism.

The story and the information in this book are a fascinating read and should open up some important new views of life.

Preface

A lot of literature about the paranormal has been published since the turn of the century. A small percentage of what has been published could be called *scientific research*, with the larger portion being termed *subjective reporting*. This does not imply that subjective material is of less value; it simply means that because of the difference in their nature they shouldn't be mixed. Mixing usually results in a disservice to both.

One of the most interesting fields of the paranormal that has been recently brought to light is called *remote viewing* (RV), a term selected and used to represent cognitive mental functioning as it was being studied by Harold Puthoff, Ph.D., and a team of other scientists at SRI-International, Menlo Park, California. They chose the term *remote viewing* ". . .as a neutral, descriptive term free of past prejudice and occult assumptions."

Historically, research into remote viewing by SRI-International was initiated at the request of the Central Intelligence Agency (CIA) in 1975, under a program called SCANATE (Scan by Coordinates). As a direct result of the preliminary successes demonstrated under that program, the Army Intelligence and Security Command (INSCOM) initiated a project called GRILLFLAME in mid-1978 which was successful in utilizing military personnel to perform as Remote Viewers against hundreds of intelligence targets. This program became subsequently known as project CENTERLANE, STARBURST, and eventually STARGATE. Its long-term secretive and compartmented operation was finally revealed as a result of information released by the CIA and The American Institutes for Research (AIR), just prior to the project's termination in November of 1995.

I hold the honor of having been the only remote viewer to have participated within this project for the entire period of its existence (18 years), as viewer #001. I and one other participant, who currently desires to remain in the shadows, we are the only two remote viewers who contributed both to the intelligence collection side of the effort and the research and development side at the Cognitive Science Laboratory, SRI-International and Science Applications International Corporation, Inc., throughout that same period.

Since 99% of the data, files, missions, and methods utilized by the project are still classified and sealed within boxes at the time of this writing, these will not be discussed within this book, nor should they be. However, there is plenty we have come to understand about remote viewing from the research side of the house which is available. So it is primarily towards this focus which the book is directed.

While it is also not my desire to defend remote viewing against many of the less than enlightened comments arising from the AIR review, it did result in the project's termination. Therefore, I have addressed this report within Chapter 21. Let it suffice to say that most of the materials sealed in those classified boxes was never shown to the reviewers either. Given AIR's pre-existing attitude toward remote viewing or anything psychic, and its obvious shifting of the "goal posts" during the game, I would have to say its review was bogus from the outset and has no merit.

Unfortunately, while this research and the secret Army project brought a large degree of notoriety and legitimacy to cognitive mental research in the overall sense, it has done nothing to relieve many of the old prejudices or occult assumptions that are made by those ignorant of the facts.

As a remote viewer or subject, I have dealt with these prejudices and assumptions for more than eighteen years. I know these negative feelings are just as strong today as they ever were. We may have come a long way, but there is still an overwhelming percentage of closed minds bent toward preventing any growth or learning within this area of research. I like to view them as *those threatened who never sleep.* However, in spite of such efforts to sabotage good science, the research and development as well as the more subjective applications continue to thrive.

There is another truth which quickly became apparent to me many years ago. It is highly likely that I will never have any effect on the defenders of *normality* because their position of strength is a position of fear. What kind of fear? Fear of change. The harder one tries to present an open and convincing argument for the existence of paranormal functioning, the more resolute in their belief these defenders of *normality* become. Why? Most think the answer lies simply in the first-impression interpretation, that the paranormal represents the occult or something just plain weird. So perhaps we should do just the opposite. Do away with the term *paranormal* and substitute the term *cognitive talent* (CT), and perhaps it will become somewhat less terrifying.

So, if a large majority out there won't temporarily suspend their disbelief long enough to let in some light, why write the book? Well, there are a number of reasons, three of which I will list here:

My Friends. My friends and members of the various RV classes which I have run for a number of years have requested it. Many of them feel the information which I would put into the book would be useful and helpful to others. At the very least it would provide a somewhat limited compendium which may prove of value as a reference for those interested.

The Public. Many of the people for whom I have given lectures and presentations have said that they've wanted more than what they could obtain in a two- or three-hour period.

Expanded Understanding. The most important reason for this book is that there are things to be said about being a remote viewer which have not been publicly stated before. There is information, both good and bad, which must be shared with others, in the hope that it will expand human knowledge and understanding about remote viewing.

Is that possible? There are hundreds of books out there which address the psychic function in humans, and they give thousands of examples and descriptions of psychic laboratory experiments, protocols, statistical evaluations both pro and con, major successes and failures, exposés, etc., etc. So. . .what am I going to write about that no one else has already covered?

Well, I'm not going to write about remote viewing or being psychic in a way that is intended to convince anyone of anything. I don't *want* to convince anyone of anything. I don't want to stagger anyone with Herculean miracles and tales from the legendary past. However, I do want to address how being a remote viewer has affected me as a *normal* human being: how it has affected the way I think and the way I feel and changed the things in which I believe. Over the past fourteen years, I have integrated or at least attempted to integrate my RV experiences, to make them an integral part of my everyday life. I made a lot of mistakes during that period, but I also discovered something which I now cherish. I found the edges or boundaries of self.

Many of the psychics who have gained some notoriety have talked about how good they are, how accurate, how statistically significant their results might be. This has become a matter of contention, a sore point, between the psychics and the public. It doesn't take a CRAY computer to understand the egotistical chord this strikes in most people. But, if you step back a few yards and view it openly, you will find that it's probably not only necessary but a virtual requirement that psychics, all psychics, must validate their credentials right out of the starting gate. Having to validate credentials is a direct response to a demand made by the same society or culture who resents it. Psychics, like other professionals, must first prove they have validity before giving advice or speaking with authority on the subject. Not just validity in the dictionary sense of the word, but validity in a scientific or an evaluated and culturally approved sense. There is nothing wrong with that, I suppose, except that there are literally millions of other *professionals* in thousands of other job categories who don't have the same requirement.

There may be places that exist to train a person to be psychic, but they cannot validate the individual in terms which are acceptable to culture. So most of the books written usually wind up talking a great deal about the psychic experiments and why they are valid, but few go into what might be going on inside the person, to whom we usually refer as the *subject*.

What about the paranoia psychics suffer? The doubts? How do they deal with spectacular failure in the face of changing reality, or what do they do with observations, perceptions, and experiences that differ radically from the cultural norm? How many have described what a change in perceptive reality has done to them philosophically, or what kind of impact it has had on their relationships with wives, husbands, or friends? This seems to be an area which is only lightly touched, if touched at all. Why hasn't there been a lot written about what goes on inside the mind of a psychic person? Perhaps it has not been addressed because psychics, especially culturally validated psychics, have their own fears with which to contend.

As fears relate to writing about oneself, there are two which immediately jump to the forefront of my mind. These I will address now. There are others, of course, but they deal with other issues and will be addressed later, within other chapters of the book. The two most apparent are:

Fear of Losing Credibility. This one is easy to sum up. I have spent over eighteen years of my life striving to be validated, trying to have my efforts accepted by culture. In other words, I've subjected myself to thousands of laboratory-approved, controlled, and accepted research protocols. Now, after thousands of judgments and rehashes, with evaluation heaped upon evaluation, I feel I have the right to say that I've been declared a remote viewer of some worth: dependable, able to replicate within the confines of an approved protocol, sometimes sufficiently accurate, and (most importantly) not crazy.

Because I've developed and protected my abilities through anonymity, talking about what really has been going on inside my head is a risky business. It could shatter all that I have spent enormous energy to build.

So, at the outset, I can and will say quite frankly and unequivocally that in order to do something paranormal with any dependability or consistency in a lab, my concepts are not going to be, nor will they ever be, *normal* as others may judge them. In fact, they are, and will appear to be, quite threatening to some of the culturally *normal* people.

Fear of Failing To Be Good Enough. This one is more difficult to address, since I can say that it is a very real fear which I find in myself but appears to be somewhat hidden in others who may be psychic. Perhaps it is the one fear that most psychics really share but try so hard to bury. There are innumerable methods of presenting this fear in context, but they all are pretty much the same in the way they represent the issue. One that might be used is: "I fear that I have not paid enough dues to have sufficient authority to speak on psychic matters. I know that no matter how good I may think I am, somewhere out there will always be another human being who is better and/or more qualified."

In spite of this fear, I am going through with the writing of this book. Maybe it will provide some tidbit of information which might prove helpful or supportive to someone out there, someone who can benefit in some small way. One of the truths I've learned over the years is that psychic functioning is far more prevalent than it appears to be. There are thousands who are, or could be, as good as anyone else at psychic functioning.

I should also make very clear that in October 1978, when I was first exposed to remote viewing, I was an entirely different person from who I am today. I grew up in some of the toughest neighborhoods in Miami, Florida, and joined the Army right after high school in 1964. Immediately after Basic and Advanced Individual Training I went overseas where I literally stayed, except for the occasional leave, for just over twelve years. I served in Vietnam in 1967 and 1968 and experienced the ferocity of the TET Offensive, as well as other one-of-a-kind events, easily imagined. I spent a great deal of my time living up to the reputation expected of an Army Senior Non-Commissioned Officer, and later as a Chief Warrant Officer, both officially and non-officially.

I was married and divorced twice during my Army career. I think now it easily could have been said that, in all ways, I was as far from having an interest in the paranormal as one can be. At the time, my employer, friends, religion, and family were no more open than I was to any of those "flaky and weird" possibilities. Of course, it all begins to happen when you least expect it.

I have discovered a rule of thumb which I believe exists in the paranormal world in which I live:

Everything is subject to change,
and it will usually be. . .at a moment's notice.

This is one of those unique rewards one gets for becoming more aware. For some, such changes are feared. For others, they represent an adventure which is difficult to turn one's back on. I feel that I have always been, and will always be, one of those adventurers.

Joseph W. McMoneagle

1
The Beginning

Somewhere in my past (this lifetime!) I began a search by stepping off in what now appears to have been the right direction. In the beginning I called it a search because at the time I was not certain what it was that I was looking for. I should also make clear for the record that I did not initiate the search on my own accord. It just happened.

Somewhere in this trek toward the present, a transformation took place which has profoundly affected my deepest concepts of reality and helped to create my current philosophy. The effects of this transformation have now cascaded down through all the important areas of my belief, to the core of my being, and have irrevocably changed my perceptions as well as my attitudes toward organized religion, society, culture, ethics, morality, and even the meaning of death, to name just a very few.

I like to think that most, if not all, of the changes have been positive and have left me with a substantial increase in personal awareness, the results of which have generated a plethora of personal experiences, especially those which are paranormal by nature. This is especially so over the past fourteen-plus years. These experiences or acts within the play of my life have only underscored the veracity of my new-found concepts.

Throughout this book, the term *remote viewing* will be mixed quite frequently with the taboo word, *psychic.* They will mean approximately the same thing. The primary differences lie in the word origins and the specific protocols in which they are usually found or used. These will be pointed out whenever necessary. The most important difference you should know is that *remote viewing* or *RV,* as it is called, is always done within scientific or approved research protocols. *Psychic,* on the other hand, usually implies the information came to someone paranormally, without any specific controls applied. To say that either is the same as the other would do a great injustice to the many years of valid research that a great number of people have spent a large portion of their adult lives pursuing. In brief, *RV* represents the scientific or research side and *psychic* stands for the experiential, subjective, or that which has been observed through application.

Of course, the use of *psychic* will be threatening to some of the readers, but then so will the term *remote viewer*, when those threatened have finally come to understand its fullest implication.

Within the pages of this book, I intend that both methods of identification should mean *knowing details about something which could only be known through extrasensory perception or ESP.*

Examples of numerous controlled and uncontrolled experiments will be used throughout the book, not for validation of psychic or RV functioning, but in order to underscore and elucidate points which I am trying to make regarding my beliefs, concepts and perceptions. I have chosen to use both the controlled as well as the uncontrolled experiments because:

1. Both have had a profound and equally important effect on my concepts and beliefs;

2. In my perception, both experiences are just as valid from an experiential or learning point of view;

3. Finally, I cannot deny the effects from both any more than I can deny anything else that has happened to me in my life.

What must be remembered is that I am not writing this in order to prove that psychic functioning or RV exists. I already know this to be so. I am writing this in order to address what effect that knowledge has had on my mind and in my life and to share that information with others. It is in this act of sharing that I hope to show the others who may be dealing with the same difficulties that they are all right, that they really aren't crazy. Therefore, my experiences, whether occurring in a controlled or uncontrolled environment or protocol, are of equal importance.

Somewhere out there in the world, there are at least a few people who are now asking, "How good a psychic are you?" This is an honest query, which creates an immediate obligation for me to at least establish some level of credibility for those who would ask such a question. There are always some who still require proof in one form or another. Most will be convinced after reading about the examples presented here, but in this early stage of the book there should be something, a portion or section, that will attend to helping maintain what I call *a temporary suspension of disbelief.*

This temporary suspension of disbelief is important because it opens the window of the mind's eye just long enough to allow an experience to crawl in and shake an otherwise complacent and normally non-changing belief structure off its foundations.

So, to meet this requirement, I suggest the following three books on remote viewing and ESP if a need for proof of extra-sensory perception is still necessary. I believe these three publications will provide more than ample descriptions and details with regard to remote viewing as might be required by the average person.

Mind-Reach, Scientists Look at Psychic Ability, by Russell Targ and Dr. Harold Puthoff, Delta Books, 1977. This is the original book on what remote viewing is and how it was outlined by those who performed experiments in the SRI-International Laboratory in the early seventies. There are abundant examples and considerable information regarding techniques and methods for designing and practicing remote viewing as an art.

Mind-Race, by Russell Targ and Dr. Keith Harary, Villard Books, 1984. This is a follow-up book, very much like *Mind-Reach,* which provides some additional information on remote viewing not found in the first book.

Natural ESP, A Layman's Guide to Unlocking the Extra Sensory Power of Your Mind, by Ingo Swann, Bantam Books, July 1987. Reprinted as *Everybody's Guide to Natural ESP. Unlocking the Extrasensory Power of Your Mind,* Jeremy P. Tarcher, Inc., St. Martin's Press, New York 1991. This is an excellent book that presents a psychic's viewpoint as regards remote viewing and is a rich resource of information as to how the author believes the psi-functioning mind operates.

Some of the successful and partially successful drawings and psychic efforts referenced in *Mind-Race* and *Natural ESP* are mine. I am not identified by name, however, because until now I've requested anonymity and my friends have honored that request. The reasons for anonymity were enforced by my participation for eighteen years in the classified Army Project (now known as STARGATE) and are a direct result of my having signed various security agreements associated with that project. Wherever I have been referenced in those books it has usually been as an *engineer* (which I am not) or a *technically qualified individual* or a *number.* The numbers by which I have been most known by over the years have been #001

(Project STARGATE) and #372 (SRI-I and SAIC). There are hundreds of you out there, perhaps thousands, who will recognize these numbers. I can hear the collective "Ah ha!" It is unfortunate that I was required to use identification numbers in the first place, but at least now you understand why.

I worked with the Psi-lab at SRI-International as a full-time consultant for over six years and have participated in remote viewing experiments at the SRI Radio Physics lab for somewhat in excess of thirteen years. I worked for the Cognitive Sciences Laboratory of Science Applications International Corporation, Menlo Park, California for three years, and am currently a Science Associate with the Cognitive Science Laboratory, Palo Alto, California. In addition, I have lectured at seminars, acted as a consultant, and participated in RV experiments at The Monroe Institute and elsewhere since 1978. Some of the experiments which will be described within the book were done in one or all of these places, as well as other locations and labs, to include my home, with various assorted learning groups and people. The specific locations are noted wherever or whenever appropriate.

Where does someone begin to recognize significant changes in his perceptions and attitudes?

This is a tough question for anyone, and it is certainly one that has driven me to much reflection over the past years. There are thousands of significant experiences, both psychic and non-psychic, which have affected my life, decision-making ability, beliefs, and concepts. How and where can I find the one spot where I began to drift from the norm?

As a first guess, one would have to say that it's obviously got to be where the first *abnormal* experience occurred. Or is it?

After thinking about it for some time, it became clear to me that the experiences a person endures throughout a lifetime seem to fall within two categories. These are, as we *first* recognize them, voluntary and involuntary. One might say they are those experiences one chooses to have and those which one has but can do nothing about. (Note: this understanding of definition will change radically later on in the book.)

I am now talking about significant experiences, or those which will have a major impact on our personal make-up or our belief concepts. These are usually experiences that permanently alter or change our reality.

Think of facing these experiences as approaching a doorway. In the first category—that is, experiences we control—we know we've opened a door and the door goes somewhere we've not yet been. The door stands open, but we still can't see into the next room. Walking through the door will give us a new perspective; it will also alter what we know. In this first case, we still have a choice either to enter or to close the door and walk away. Therefore, we have a personal control over how open or closed we might be to a possible new experience. Making the decision to walk away would be like closing one's eyes to a new perspective, a closing of the mind.

The first category is not where the beginning is usually found. It takes a lot more courage than most humans possess to charge into the unknown, slamming doors behind them. Once you've gone through a door and viewed the other side, it's most difficult if not impossible to forget what you've seen or experienced. So backing away from a new reality is a choice that must be taken *before* you go through the door, not after.

So, for most of us, the beginnings of a really major change usually come out of the second category—what we believe to be an involuntary experience. Those experiences that you find you're subjected to, but which are outside the bounds of personal control. This is where I concentrated on locating the beginnings of my own life's changes. This is where I knew I would find the original impact craters, the beginnings of my understanding of the paranormal.

My first discovery about self was a remarkable surprise. I found that within those second category experiences there were very few that I had accepted, processed, or integrated. Almost without exception, the majority had been denied and buried, sealed off from the rest of my normal thought processes. I had ignored vital input and continued to live by concepts and standards of reality shielded with blinders, not unlike the kind they used on the fire-house horse in the good old days.

In my own case, I could describe my mind as being nothing more than a wonderful and complex cloud. When faced with a change it didn't like, it just didn't process it. I found a region where I had been storing all of the phenomena of life which didn't fit anywhere else. Where all of the experiences thrust upon me, forced on me against my will, were simply placed and unconsciously ignored. Instead of placing myself in a defensive mode with regard to my philosophic beliefs, I just simply ignored the threats to my consciousness as something I was unable to process and filed them neatly away in an area I would have to call *not real*, a sort of nebulous territory.

That is where I found the first experiences. They were experiences that opened doors to a different reality and I had been propelled through to new perspectives. They were philosophic doors that had shattered the foundations of my normal world. But, strangely enough, I had buried these experiences rather than deal with them.

Why? I'm not sure. At that time in my life, maybe I just wasn't ready to make the changes these experiences required of me. Or, more frankly, I was afraid.

The first experience was one of two significant time periods in my life which ultimately have become tied together. These two time periods were actually nine years apart, but, since one interacts so well with the other, I believe both events were in some way connected—if for no other reason than to underscore the effects of each within my conscious mind. I will call these experience **A** and **B** for writing purposes. The events contained within these two time periods dovetail very well together, specifically in the combination of effects as represented by changes in my philosophy or, at that time, my expressed reality.

The **A** experience was an event that occurred around July of 1970. It was one of my deepest and darkest secrets for a nine-year period of my life. I went to great lengths not to talk about it, particularly with anyone in the Army, my principal employer at the time. The experience occurred while I was stationed with a small unit in southern Germany—it was a classic near-death experience (NDE) associated with an out-of-body experience (OBE).

The **B** experience was actually a series of two events, one of them occurred in July of 1979 **(B1)** and the other in October **(B2)** of the same year. These two events marked the change in how I would deal with the subject of the paranormal. I met Dr. Hal Puthoff and his colleagues at SRI International **(B1)** in July of 1979, and was introduced to Mr. Robert A. Monroe **(B2)**, the author of *Journeys Out of the Body* and *Far Journeys*, in October of the same year.

So, the real beginning of my own journey was a near-death experience in 1970. Therefore, appropriately, that is where my story will begin.

2
The NDE

Many readers are probably wondering why I would keep an NDE a secret, since it is now quite openly talked about. The reasons I chose to do this are fairly complicated but have a lot to do with what *my* perceptions of an NDE and an OBE were at the time.

It is one thing to look safely back and view the experience with hindsight, but in 1970 my views and perceptions were quite different from what they are today. Back in those days, a near-death experience or NDE was viewed as an abnormal experience, something someone suffered as a result of damage to the brain, hypothetically a result of loss of oxygen to the brain cells. At least that was the official medical view at the time, one which I quickly and comfortably shared, I might add, since it made the totality of my experience ok and not as crazy as I felt I might have been at the time.

I distinctly remember that at the time the doctors were constantly cautioning me to try and stay with the program, to understand that all the effects I had been and was experiencing were simply induced hallucinations. They didn't want to hear about white lights and small energized light-beings. I remember trying to tell one of them (while undergoing bi-lateral brain testing) that I could read the mind of the nurse in the next room. I don't remember his exact response, only that it was negative in the extreme.

I think any reader would agree that if you are lying flat on your back in a hospital and the best medical minds available are investing twelve to fourteen days evaluating the extent of your brain damage, you are apt to believe whatever they say is happening or true. This was essentially the circumstance at the time.

The A Experience
July 1970

One July evening, fate provided me with an experience which remains just as vivid today as it was the day on which it occurred. I remember with exceptional clarity and detail all of the things that happened during the experience and most of what followed but, for some reason, cannot remember much about what led up to it. There may be psychological reasons for that, but lacking memory of the detail before the event has never seemed to be very important to me. I will report what I can remember of the event itself.

* * * *

It was a miserable day with dark overhanging clouds, and it had been raining off and on throughout the afternoon. It was a Friday, and I had developed a habit of taking a few friends out to dinner in the early evening on most Fridays. On this particular occasion we had chosen a restaurant just across the River Inn, southwest of Passau, Germany, in an Austrian town called Braunau am Inn, which means Braunau on or by the River Inn.

The name of the restaurant is lost forever in the clouds of my mind, but I distinctly remember how it looked. It was old and narrow, situated on a cobblestone side street very close to the edge of town. Inside, the air was choked with cigarette and pipe smoke, and the tables and chairs were jammed very closely together. I remember it as being a loud and happy place with people who recognized us as Americans and welcomed us happily to share in their usual end-of-week celebration. It was a bit warmer than usual, but comfortable.

As was also habit, we all ordered before-dinner drinks. Normally this meant a Weissen beer, which is a combination of light beer and sparkling wine with a twist of lemon. This particular evening, however, someone suggested that I might try a Strohes Rum, which is a very heavy and dark rum that has the flavor of butterscotch. So I conceded and ordered a rum and Coke.

The conversation I don't remember as being remarkable in any way, just congenial.

After sipping on the drink for about ten minutes, I noticed that I was beginning to get extremely hot on the back of my neck. I asked my friend sitting to my right if he had noticed anything peculiar with his drink, thinking that perhaps the drink had something to do with the way I was beginning to feel. But he commented no. So I tried to ignore the discomfort and to get more involved in the conversation. It seemed, however, that the harder I tried to relax, the worse I felt. After thirty minutes of progressively increasing misery, I finally told my friends that I really didn't feel very well and felt that I should leave. They suggested that some fresh air might help and I quickly agreed. By this time, rising from the table seemed to be an effort, but I managed to extricate myself from the tightly packed chairs and make it to the front door of the restaurant.

I remember that at this specific point in time things appeared to slow down. My perceptions of time seemed to be altering, going into slow motion. My mind would send a command to my right arm to push open the door, but it seemed like the command took forever to reach my hand. Once it did, my observation was that my right hand then moved in a slow-motion arc toward the handle. The sounds and colors of the restaurant foyer began to slow and intensify as well, much like a record being slowed down on a turntable, while the volume was being turned up. The voices around me became louder but remained unintelligible, like words played through a tape machine at half-speed. I remember suddenly being intensely frightened by what was happening to me but hopelessly unable to do anything about it. My last blurred memory was the door opening and my body falling through it from its own momentum. I distinctly remember fearing that I would break the glass with my fall and then heard a horribly loud *pop* and thought that it might have been my face striking something as I was falling.

Expecting to feel the cobblestones smack me in the face, I found myself catching my balance and then standing in the middle of the street. You can imagine my wonderment. I was no longer falling but felt very light and was standing there calmly looking at my right arm, which I was holding out in front of me.

It was like waking up and finding oneself already doing something. I suspect it would be very much like waking up suddenly while sleepwalking—becoming conscious and realizing that you are standing at the front window of your living room, watching the wind blow through the trees in the moonlight.

I must also interject here that I was no longer afraid. The intense fear which I had felt momentarily as I was falling through the restaurant door was completely gone. In fact, I was so comfortable that I remember quietly chuckling to myself that my initial fear was only a stupid reaction.

The first interesting thing that I noticed was that it was gently raining but I was not getting wet. In fact, the small water droplets were hitting my arm—I could feel them doing so—but then they would slide down through my arm and fall to the street at my feet. Yes, that's precisely what I said—slide *through* my arm. The excitement was overwhelming and I felt as though I should show someone else what was going on, to share the wonderment of it. I looked at my clothes, which in my perception were exactly the ones that I had been wearing, and they were not getting wet either.

It was at this same time, while looking down, that I noticed that I couldn't see my feet. It was also when I realized something was happening, a major event was going on, and I was part of it.

My first intent was to return to the restaurant and tell my friends. Tell anybody. Tell somebody! It was that thought which gently propelled me forward toward a crowd which had begun to gather at the front door of the restaurant. I noticed that I was drifting and not walking, which added to my wonderment. When I stopped, my eyes settled on a body lying half in and half out of the gutter by the front door. The shock at what I saw sent a huge shudder throughout my being. Lying in the street was my body, face up, with eyes and mouth open.

By that time, one of my friends had sat himself down on the curb and was jerking me violently up and into his lap. It was at that point I knew that I was dead, or at least that was my perception at the time.

After recognizing that it was my body in my friend's lap, and assuming that I was either dead or dying, a lot of things quickly began to happen. My friend, I observed, was jamming his finger down my throat and, while I could watch it being done, I couldn't feel it. Many days later he told me that I had gone into convulsions and had stopped breathing and that he had been trying to pull my tongue, which I had swallowed, forward. From my vantage point, hovering over him, I could even see the blue forming around my lips and beneath my eyes.

He almost lost the end of his index finger because the physical me had clamped down on it hard enough to cut through to the bone on both sides. I don't recall seeing that happen, but that is what he told me later.

After unsuccessfully trying to retrieve my tongue, he then slid me off and onto the pavement and felt for a pulse. Not finding one, he began to violently strike me in the chest, cursing me to breathe with each punch.

The interesting thing I experienced through all of this was that every time he struck me in the center of the chest, I would feel a *click* and find myself looking up through my physical eyes into his. This would immediately be followed by another distinct *click,* and once more I would be out of my body and looking down at him from above. After ten minutes of this I was beginning to feel like a yo-yo. *Click*—pain, *click*—no pain, *click*—pain, *click*—no pain, *click.* . .and so forth and so on.

As he continued striking me in the chest, I began screaming at him with my mind while in the out-of-body state to *stop this nonsense, can't you see I'm dead, leave me alone!* Until eventually, he did stop and I remained outside of my body. I remember him looking up at someone else and shaking his head.

I then watched them move my body down to a bench along the edge of the road and then they were asking someone to fetch a car. I rose approximately fifteen feet up into the air so that I could get a really good view. It was just like being a little kid again. I was really excited by all of the lights and the crowd of people who kept trying to see what was going on, and I was quickly becoming used to being free of physical restraints for the first time. There was sadness that I felt for the people who were obviously suffering emotional pain because of me, but I understood very clearly by that time that I couldn't really die, and the new-found freedom and joy which that offered was far and away the overwhelming emotion. It was exhilarating. So, I gave full rein to my curiosity.

I watched as they loaded my body into an automobile and took it back across the border to Germany and the local hospital. The entire trip was spent cruising just above the car, zipping up, down, and through the overhanging telephone and electric wires. When the car arrived at the hospital, I watched my friend kick at the door in frustration. I didn't know until later that German hospitals usually lock their doors after 7:00 or 8:00 P.M. I watched as they loaded my body on a stretcher and rushed it down a long corridor to the emergency room, where they shifted it onto the table and proceeded to cut away the clothing.

I watched from the ceiling as the doctor inserted a long needle into the center of my chest while a nurse rubbed some kind of ointment on both sides of the rib cage. I watched with great curiosity as they placed the small white paddles on each side of my chest and began jolting my body. It was at that point, for some reason, that I began to quickly lose interest in what was going on with my physical body. I began to wonder what was going to happen to the real me. Wasn't there a God? Didn't something happen when you died?

Almost as if the asking of the questions were a notice or announcement, the voices in the room began to fade, and I felt as if I were slowly beginning to pull away from the emergency room. I was moving backward, and the view of the room was beginning to grow dimmer and smaller, as if I were falling upward through a tunnel. As seconds seemed to pass, I began to accelerate, but in reverse. It wasn't that I was afraid to turn around and see where I was going, because I knew that I was safe and that I could not die, or at least cease to exist. It was more of a mild curiosity in every new thing that I was experiencing. I was enjoying the ride, its feeling; I was becoming one with what was happening to me. After a time, which I couldn't estimate then—nor can I now—I became aware of a gentle warmth on the back of my neck. It began at the base of my skull and spread down and through my entire being. It wasn't the kind of warmth we associate with a heater or a radiator; it was more like a warmth of feeling, of being. It made me tingle all over, everywhere. It began growing in intensity, and I began to feel really good all over. Soon it even exceeded the definition of good—then better—then great—then glorious. On and on, through definitions that don't exist to describe it, the feeling continued to grow in intensity and completely filled my being.

Now, a lot of people want to know what *exceedingly-outrageously-fantastic* means, and I find it a difficult question to answer. The closest that I can come to giving an example that most people will understand is that it was like the peak of a sexual climax times twelve times ten to the thirty-third. That would be a twelve with thirty-three zeros after it. (Sexual peak times 12×10^{33}, or a normal climax times 12,000,000,000,000,000,000,000,000,000,000,000.) It was the most overwhelming feeling I have ever experienced in my life.

I turned to look for the source of this feeling and was immediately engulfed in the most brilliant and softest white light imaginable. At the time, my first and only assumption was:

"So this is what God is like!"

I knew immediately that I had been absorbed by a Being of Light, with unimaginable qualities and quantities of power, goodness, strength, and beauty.

There is no comparable place in physical reality to experience such total awareness. The love, protection, joy, giving, sharing, and being that I experienced in the Light at that moment was absolutely overwhelming and pure in its essence.

The downside was that I could also see the best of me. In comparison, it was the clearest picture of all my failings, wasted energy, lost time, useless actions, and stupidity that I have ever seen displayed or have ever experienced in my lifetime. It was a horrible feeling, just seeing how I matched up against the Light. But understand that there was no condemnation or judgment for any of my past actions. It was more of an allowance, or enabling. It allowed me to clearly see the non-constructive and non-creative aspects of self, those moments of lost focus or inattentive awareness. Which, judged from my own view at the time, were far more frequent than they should have been.

In the midst of this total wonderment, I then began hearing messages in my mind. I've been asked many questions regarding the messages, how they were perceived and what they were about. It's difficult trying to put into physical-reality words or expressions what is going on in an altered state, so the best that I will ever be able to do is approximate what the experience was like.

The voice of Light was crystal clear and embodied the purest form of warmth and love. The kind of warmth and love that I am talking about is not the kind we think we know about here in the physical. Instead, it is more a giving or unconditional sharing, it's an *in love* feeling. The emotions delivered by the voice were those of a brother to brother, sister to sister, mother to mother, or father to father. One entity speaking to another, with the understanding of perfect balance and harmony, a total giving without actually giving anything up, a total sharing without expectation of recompense. All of it, with a perfect understanding that there was no judging or evaluation being done.

I am using the term "perfect" here to imply absolute, or what one would call beyond-the-shadow-of-a-doubt clarity. There were no mistakes or room for misconceptions within the communication. In either direction, I might add.

The voice in the Light said within my mind, "Go back. You are not going to die."

I, of course, argued with it.

I can feel the shudders running through many of my readers at this point. *You argued with it? You argued with God?* That is a normal and reasonable question, one that is usually generated at this point in many of the presentations or seminars that I've given. Yes. I argued with it. I was so intensely comfortable and at ease in my new state of consciousness that I could quite easily have embedded myself within the Light and just *existed* there for the rest of eternity. Right there, in the folds of the Light, was where I wanted to be. But such wasn't to be the case.

Fade...*pop!*

I sat bolt upright in the hospital bed and looked around at the non-comprehending German patients watching me from the other beds within the room. I immediately began to cry and had tears flowing down my cheeks. The other patients had no idea what was going on and became very agitated. One of them hobbled down the hall to look for the doctor and I tried through my confusion to explain that I had just left God.

Guess what? You're right—bedlam.

Almost without exception, everyone who was within earshot thought I was absolutely round the bend, over the rainbow, wacko. Things became more confused as I continued to try and communicate the experience in half English, half German. The last thing that I remember was a needle in the arm and fading off to sleep. Thus ended part of my first experience.

* * * *

Looking back at my experience, I have often wondered why it has remained so clear in my mind for so long. I believe it might have something to do with our emotional investment in reality. It has now been over twenty-seven years since the experience, but the huge amount of detail still resides in the forefront of my memory, just as clearly and cleanly as the day that it happened. The specifics of the trauma remain vague in my mind, but the actual NDE and OBE remain pristine and clear for some reason. Of course, I've developed a number of concepts and conjectures as to why, but I've reserved those for further on in the book, where they might be more helpful or more easily understood by the reader.

3
Aftereffects

What happens after an NDE? What happens when you wake up? Since 1970 there has been a lot written about the near-death experience.

When I began working with Hal Puthoff and Russell Targ at SRI International in 1978, they gave me a gift of the book *Life After Life*, by Raymond A. Moody, Jr., M.D. In the book, Dr. Moody presents a compilation of material on the NDE phenomenon. In it there are reports from a number of people on what they felt at the point of return. These accounts vary from one person to another—some are even diametrically different—but they all address the same thing. The impact is shattering on the person who has had the experience. I've always felt that mine was a major trauma.

Back in 1970, waking up and still being in my physical body was the most depressing experience of my life. At the time, I wrote in my diary that it was like being torn swiftly and unemotionally from the cradle of one's life's beginnings. . .that it was the cruelest and most vicious act a human being could ever experience. My anguish was intense, my depression was like a bottomless ink-filled well.

Of course, no one in the hospital could be aware of the full impact and extent of what I had experienced or imagine the emotion that I was going through. On the contrary. Everyone in the hospital, the patients in the room, nurses, and doctors, were elated that I had awakened. As far as my wife, our friends, and the United States Army were concerned, I was alive and that's all there was to it.

I had cheated death, I had survived. But inside, I was an absolute basket case. Without exception, my opinions and convictions concerning God, life, death, and reality all lay in a huge and broken heap at the foot of my hospital bed. My depression at having severed the connection with the Light Being was extreme. I was once again floundering in the sea of reality we call a physical world—but this time adrift, without rules. Anger quickly overcame depression. In my case, anger began to overrule my other emotions as well.

There are great number of immediate changes that someone experiences from an NDE after returning to the physical world. In my own case, these changes probably didn't differ from those of many others who have had such an experience.

The first change is an attempt to communicate what happened during the NDE, creating some very interesting reactions. What I wanted to communicate to those around me was what happened, not what I dreamed, not what I imagined, not what was expected—I just wanted to tell everyone what happened.

Those closest to me listened. To their credit, they even nodded once in awhile, as if in affirmation. Their eyes said, *I think you've suffered some kind of mental damage, but don't worry, I'm here for you.*

Those tasked with caring for me, such as doctors, nurses, and the like, were even more solicitous. Their eyes said, *Yes, we know. Now let us help you to recover from this illusory fantasy.*

Those with no investment, well, their eyes didn't have to say it, they were saying it out loud: *You've suffered a trauma that cut off the oxygen to your brain, and these are illusions which you are suffering as a result. Don't believe everything you're feeling right now, etc., etc.*

It doesn't take long for a sane person to realize what is going on, so I did what sane people do—I shut up. I listened to the doctors and tried to deal with the depression on my own. Who was I to rock the boat?

I've debated about saying what I'm going to say next because I don't want any of my readers to misinterpret the information that I'm sharing. I've decided that it's important to talk about the entire experience, since it may help a few of the readers out there who have had the same feelings and don't understand or know what to do with them.

There were three aftereffects that continued happening after the NDE and they were, for the most part, very intense for a period of almost six months. As a result of those effects, for the first time in my life I actually considered suicide. I seriously contemplated taking my own life.

The First. The first and most overwhelming effect was depression. I felt as if I had been brought back into the most primitive human culture a God could have contrived to create. I use the term *primitive* because it was like swimming in a sea of humans who hadn't learned the simplest of truths. It depressed me even more because in comparison I felt that I was as bad or worse than anyone else. It was true that during that period of time I was very confused and disoriented. However, my perception was that much of what had previously been a reality for me had been stripped away. It was as if all the false motivations and reasons for human interaction had been peeled back, exposing the bare-bone facts beneath. And the bare-bone facts weren't fun to look at.

The Second. The second effect was spontaneous knowledge. Knowing what someone is *thinking* when they are talking to you. Knowing things about people which they have not openly shared. I would later come to understand this new-found sensitivity is called psychic functioning. But at the time I didn't know what to call it. Without going into any detail, there were things I suddenly and quite spontaneously knew about people very close to me, that had been closely guarded secrets prior to my NDE. These thoughts would just come into my head when I least expected them. Most were shocks to me emotionally, especially the information relative to relationships. If you can imagine—it would be like suddenly knowing your mate is sleeping with someone close to you, a friend. Or knowing your best worker is trying to take your job. No warning, just—*pop*—and you know what's going on.

Most doctors want to classify this as paranoia because they don't understand it. But that isn't what I am talking about here. It was like suddenly tapping into a completely new information line, one over which you have no control.

A friend of mine at the time, a psychologist, suggested that coming out of the NDE made me more sensitive to other forms of detail. He said the close brush with death opened a new modality of perception which was just more sensitive to those around me and the messages they were giving off. He suggested that, in this newly developed mode of sensitivity, I was probably processing more information and arriving at more detailed and previously less obvious conclusions about people and relationships. These details had always been there anyway, but they were ones to which I had not previously been paying much attention. In other words, I had opened myself up to a greater sense of awareness.

I wasn't sure, but at the time his comments seemed appropriate. Now, knowing what I know, I think I hung onto his hypothesis as a way of maintaining my sanity or maintaining what I believed and understood to be as normal.

The Third. The third effect was that I began having spontaneous out-of-body experiences or OBEs. I'd try to nap in the middle of the day and would suddenly find myself relocated to a temple in Japan, floating through the trees and listening to the creaking sound from the wheel on a wheelbarrow being pushed down a dirt path. Or I might pop out and find myself hovering over a section of ocean shoreline in a place I couldn't recognize.

All three of these experiences were happening while people around me were looking desperate and hoping that I wasn't suffering serious mental damage. I felt very much alone. What they weren't saying was how much they hoped I would quickly return to normal. Needless to say, I didn't, and they quickly progressed to what I call a stage-two response.

A stage-two response occurs when someone you know begins to act crazy, but you know he can't really be crazy, so you figure there must be some other medical reason for it. Usually, arrangements are quickly made to determine what form of brain lesion the person is suffering from, or how much brain cell damage had been done during his close brush with death.

Because these effects occurred spontaneously and because of the treatment I was receiving, I was faced with a very compelling reason to believe that I actually was going crazy and that I needed to become well.

The United States Army's reaction was to move me to a special hospital in Munich for extensive brain testing and analysis. They wanted to determine the extent of brain cell damage which might have taken place as a result of my being delivered to the hospital without heartbeat or respiration. As I found out later, when I was delivered to the emergency room I had not been breathing and there was no pulse for some minutes.

They kept me in the rest home in Munich for just short of two weeks. Brain specialists connected wires to my head and ran me through extensive studies to determine the amount of damage. The results were all written in German, but even with my rudimentary knowledge of the language, I could understand they had found nothing wrong or out of sorts.

This wasn't good news. The thoughts that maybe I really was going crazy quickly returned and I withdrew inside myself, refusing to further address any of my experiences. From that point on, it was an exercise to forget.

I developed a tentative conclusion that society (and the Army was my society at the time) had only two choices from which to formulate a conclusion. They could either decide from what I was telling them that I was ok and sane or, if the results of the EEG studies were positive, decide that I had somehow damaged my mind. Whatever they decided, it would most assuredly be based on what I was saying since nothing was turning up from the EEG studies. Since it became obvious to them that it wasn't the latter, I stopped pressing it. Hence, only I knew that I was crazy and I wasn't telling anyone.

An interesting thing happens when you've made up your mind that you are probably crazy and losing touch with reality. You drag up all of your old and stable concepts of belief in God, the earth, and what makes things go around. You gather them up and then try to invent reasons why such concepts shouldn't change, and you cling to them like a life raft in a sea of confusion. In short, you deny, deny, deny! You lie to yourself about how sane you are and how close your brush with insanity really was. You patch and Band-Aid your philosophy, stretch your concepts to fit, and whatever works you use to re-stabilize your ability to cope with your environment. The problem is, nothing ever really goes back together again the way it was.

Everybody knows how difficult it is to put Humpty-Dumpty together again. There are large, gaping holes that you continually find yourself tripping over. There are little chunks of buried experience you try to ignore but are always stumbling into. You suddenly find that you are always on the watch for a slip of the tongue, an errant comment, anything which may give away the fact that you are crazy or, more accurately put, not normal. After a while, an interesting side effect begins to occur. You're not conscious of it; it just grows quietly around you. Your new-found awareness slips away. Over time, you begin to cross-file and index reality information in two parts. There is the normal (that is, culturally normal) pile and the abnormal (or crazy) pile. In most cases, you aren't even aware that you are doing it. You've soon built the cloud chamber for your mind, in which to place those phenomena that no longer work or make any sense anywhere else.

There are a number of reasons for this, some you will recognize as they happen and some you won't. What is important here is to note that it happens. Soon, you'll find that you are once again operating and interacting in the cultural norm without any problem, which is then translated to mean that you're getting better. This, of course, induces a false sense of security.

So, on the conscious level, everything has smoothed out and your culturally normal philosophy and concepts of reality operate along in a very non-threatening way and you are able to suppress abnormal input.

On the unconscious level, however, your subconscious awareness is screaming out messages and they are going straight into a dead-letter file (cloud) because your conscious mind is ignoring them or, worst yet, egotistically altering the message into something less coherent.

This may equate to a period of time in most people's lives when they are dreaming heavily, but none of the dreams make any sense at all. So you ignore them. What is also going on? The conscious mind is getting its way so much that it begins to forget how much of a threat the subconscious really is to reality and the conscious mind becomes lazy. Messages, albeit small ones, begin to filter up and through the conscious. When you notice them, you ignore the source or ignore the message. This is how I spent the next nine years, from 1970 until 1979: aware, but totally asleep.

It is at this point, in 1979, that two very significant events occurred, both in Washington, D.C. The dates of their occurrence were nearly simultaneous, once again underscoring a very interesting coincidence.

The first occurred while I was visiting a bookstore at Tysons Corner Shopping Center. I turned down an aisle and found a book lying in the middle of the floor. Wanting to put it back in its appropriate place on the shelf, I naturally looked at the cover and read the title: *Journeys Out of the Body*, by Robert A. Monroe. I felt an electric shock run through my entire body and quickly glanced up and down the main aisle to make sure that no one saw me reading the cover. I hung around the book store for what seemed an eternity but finally found the courage to buy the book.

At the time, I don't think that I was afraid of the subject matter. Hadn't I experienced the exact same things and weren't there a lot of people out there in the world who professed to believe in it? I think my real fear was that the section or portion of culture which I had chosen to live in (specifically the Army) couldn't deal with it. I had already suffered from the extreme prejudice I experienced as a result of my ND/OBE, so I didn't want to generate any new ill will. In any event, I found the courage to buy the book and take it home with me to read.

It was only days between having taken the book home to read and the second event. It was a very mild day for early fall, and the trees were right in the middle of their prime color change, so I took a lawn chair out to sit in the sun at the rear of my apartment in Reston, Virginia. My particular apartment building, like many of the others, housed a number of people from all walks of life whose ages were pretty close together. Since I lived on the second of three floors, where I put my lawn chair was directly across from the deck railing of the lower apartment. Living there was a young couple to whom I had never been formally introduced. They were also enjoying the beautiful day and were in the process of removing some of their more prized plants from outdoor planters in preparation for winter. We exchanged only a cursory hello in a passing greeting as I moved over to the brightest sun spot with my chair. I made myself comfortable and for the first time opened Bob Monroe's book.

Not more than fifteen minutes had passed when I was interrupted with an inquiry from my neighbor. He wanted to know if I believed in the *stuff* I was reading.

Now, as I think back about it, my response was probably a shade short of civil. I don't remember specifically what I said in return, but it was something like, "I don't know; how can you validate stuff like this," or something of that nature. In any event, my neighbor smiled and quickly went indoors. I began to get cold very early on and didn't sit in the sun for very long. I felt somewhat embarrassed even though I shouldn't have been. I was so afraid they would find out that I was the crazy guy who lived upstairs that I tried to avoid them going to work the next morning; but they sought me out.

As I was climbing into my car at 6:00 A.M. for the commute into Washington, D.C., my neighbor walked over, smiling, and handed me a folded paper which he suggested I read at my leisure. I opened the paper and found that it was a copy of an article written by Harold Puthoff, printed in the journal of the Institute of Electrical and Electronics Engineers, Inc., or *IEEE Journal* in 1975, which addressed something I had never heard of called "remote viewing."

By 9:00 that evening I was faced with a real dilemma. I was dealing with all of my memories from my experience in Germany, but, even worse, I was beginning to think the experience was *real!* Concepts that had protected me and kept me comfortable all those years no longer made any sense. What should or could I do about it?

My job in Washington, D.C., had much to do with sub-contract management for major ongoing projects in military research and development. Consequently, as a normal course or function, I was required to fly out to the West Coast on numerous occasions in order to coordinate or check on the projects with which I was involved. Much of the work was being performed in the Menlo Park and Mountain View area. I didn't know where Robert A. Monroe lived yet, and besides, he was just another guy like me, or at least that was my thought at the time. That left Dr. Puthoff at SRI-International.

Now here is where I could get answers: proven, officially stamped, scientifically developed, rational, and non-threatening answers. I decided that on my next trip to the West Coast I would try to look up Dr. Puthoff and find out what I could about my particular type of experience, and that is what I did.

Events subsequent to November, 1995 now allow me to add the following:

While the events I've described up until this point are essentially true, there is the following exception. While I was visiting numerous facilities on the West Coast in support of my assignments up until this time, the actual reason I was able to meet with Hal Puthoff at SRI-International was a direct result of my having been recruited into the Army's secret Remote Viewing Project GRILLFLAME.

Over the course of a number of weeks, I was interviewed extensively by Army personnel who were tasked with assembling a group of Intelligence personnel for exposure to Remote Viewing. I volunteered to become a member of this unit and to be tested by SRI-International scientists for any psychic talent that I might possess. One of the requirements for membership within this unit was that I sign numerous security agreements which forbade my speaking about either the existence of the unit, or its assigned mission. I was not aware at the time that how I performed during those remote viewings would actually determine my continued or permanent assignment to the unit.

Until release of the unclassified American Institutes for Research report in November of 1995, and subsequent information releases by the CIA and others responsible for the project at its termination, I felt it was my responsibility to protect this connection.

I apologize to previous readers for this slight mis-direction. I wanted to provide the public with information about remote viewing and what it could do, but at the same time respect and honor my commitment to the Army and my Nation. I feel that I was able to do both within a positive format. Thus began experience **B1**.

4
The SRI Experience

In October of 1978, the Army solved my problem. Following extensive secret interviews within the Headquarters of the Army Intelligence and Security Command, I was recruited for participation in the then secret project GRILLFLAME—later referred to as CENTERLANE, STARBURST, and then, STARGATE.

GRILLFLAME was created with the intention of exposing selected Intelligence personnel to the methodologies and protocols of remote viewing to determine if these same personnel could then utilize these talents for collecting information pertinent to both our own, as well as enemy targets of interest.

My first meeting with Hal Puthoff, the scientist in charge of the research side of the project, took place on a Monday morning. With only a brief introduction, I talked a great deal about my interest in remote viewing and the IEEE article that I had read. My memory is that I probably made absolutely no sense whatsoever and pretty much stammered through the conversation. We spoke only a short bit about my own personal experiences and how I felt about them at the time. We scheduled my first exposure to a remote viewing experiment for the following morning.

Early the next day I arrived at the designated reception area and met Dr. Puthoff.

There are a number of things that you immediately notice about Hal the first time you meet him. He is just as warm and friendly with a stranger as he is with those he knows well. One is struck at the outset by how easy he is to be with. There are other things about him you come to know over time.

He is quite unconventional in his approach to unique problems, but still very much the scientist. Very open-minded in his thinking but very demanding in the scientific methodology he uses for his scientific research, especially within the paranormal arena.

Over the years there have been numerous assaults on his research.

But throughout those years, I have always known him to be quite open in discussing his material wherever or whenever honest criticism has been made.

It was not long before I found myself telling him all about my OB/NDE and asking him the most absurd questions. It is much to his credit that he didn't just throw me out.

The method of Remote Viewing they were using at the time consisted of using an actual person or team of persons as *outbounders*, for the remote viewer to target on. In other words, the remote viewer stayed at the lab and tried to report on the location of the out-bounders without having any information about where they were going.

The targeted location, or where they went, was selected from a target pool consisting of approximately one hundred specific places within a thirty-minute drive of Menlo Park. This pool was constructed by someone from another lab who was not a participant in the remote viewing experiments.

Anyone who has ever been in the Stanford University area of Palo Alto/Menlo Park can attest to the richness of the target environment. Within fifteen to thirty minutes of the intersection at El Camino Real and Ravenswood Avenue there must be at least six hundred significant buildings, playgrounds, parks, fountains, shopping centers, schools, pools, and sculptures. It was from this diverse morass of targeting possibilities that someone had constructed a target pool.

In creating the original pool, each target location was written out on a 3x5 card which was then sealed in a double-wrapped and opaque envelope. These envelopes were numbered with non-sequential three-digit numbers, no two sets of numbers alike, and they were then stored in the SRI Radio/Physic's Division safe until called for. Only the creator of the target pool had access to the individual envelopes.

The participants for an out-bounder experiment were always a remote viewer and a interviewer, who would be together throughout the experiment, and the out-bounder team. The team consisted of a person or persons who would actually travel to the target location. All participants would meet in the remote viewing room prior to beginning the experiment.

The remote viewing room was an interior room without windows. It was chosen in order to preclude any possibility of the remote viewer or interviewer determining anything about the target, even the direction in which the out-bounder team might depart from the area.

In the viewing room was a couch, on which the remote viewer could either sit or lie down, a small coffee table, and an easy chair for the interviewer. A stopwatch, a tape recorder, and a stack of white bond paper with felt-tip pens, number-two pencils, and ball-points were on the coffee table. Usually the lighting was kept low, but it could be turned up or down to fit the desires of the viewer.

Once all three people entered the room, the out-bounder or target person would use a single nine-sided die to determine a three-digit number. This was accomplished by simply throwing the die three times to produce three numbers. Once the number was obtained, the specific time the out-bounder team would be on target was coordinated. Usually, this would be thirty minutes from the actual time of departure. Whatever the target was, they would agree to stay at the target for a minimum of fifteen minutes from the specified target time.

After departing the remote viewing room, the out-bounder team would report to the keeper of the target pool and present the three-digit number. They would be handed the double-wrapped, sealed, and opaque envelope with the identical number and would then depart the building, going directly to the parking lot. Using their automobile, they would leave the SRI-International compound by driving away in any direction, but without opening the envelope.

After driving around the local area, but not earlier than thirty minutes prior to the specified target time, the out-bounders would then open the envelope and read the instructions written on the card within. Following the instructions, they would proceed to the specified target identified within the envelope, trying to arrive at the target as close to the exact time agreed-upon as possible.

Meanwhile, in the remote viewing room at the lab, the interviewer and remote viewer would pass the time of day discussing remote viewing or related paranormal topics, with a break in conversation and "cool down" period of five or ten minutes prior to the agreed-upon target time.

I didn't know it at the time, but the pre-session discussions were a normal procedure to assist a new remote viewer in dealing with the concept that remote viewing was possible and culturally non-threatening. In retrospect, I must say that it worked exceptionally well with me. By the time I began my first target session, I was totally open to the possibilities, whatever they may have been.

After the break in conversation and at the agreed-upon target time, the interviewer would turn on the tape recorder, start the stopwatch, and simply ask the remote viewer to describe where s/he thought the out-bounder was currently located. The remote viewer would then give a verbal response, which was taped, or draw pictures of what s/he thought the target looked like.

After fifteen minutes on the target, the experimental session was terminated in the lab. At the same time, the out-bounder team would depart from the target, returning to the lab as quickly as possible.

Following their return, the remote viewer, out-bounder team, and interviewer would travel back to the target and spend ten or fifteen minutes together debriefing the viewer on the target. This was done in order to provide the remote viewer with immediate feedback on how well or poorly he or she had done.

This is essentially as it was explained to me, just prior to my first experience. Unfortunately, it says nothing about the way in which the information is obtained or how it is experienced. For me, my first actual experience was overwhelming.

In order for the reader to understand how I was dealing with the perceptions during the experience, I have chosen the first of the original six targets to present as an example. The statements that follow are taken directly from the tape transcripts and refer to the drawings provided. The photograph of actual targets was obtained at a later date for historical purposes and was provided for use in this book. It would be impossible for the reader to understand what was actually going on in my mind without some form of explanation. Therefore, inserted between the lines of transcript is some of what I can remember, also of what I was mentally dealing with at the time. There was no way anyone could tell me beforehand what I would sense during the experiment. As I look back to this fragile beginning, I still find myself impressed by the early results. As best that I can recall, this is what happened during my first remote viewing, number one of my original six experiments.

Target #48

Remote Viewing Experiment with Russell Targ as the interviewer.
Subject: #372 (Joseph W. McMoneagle)
Time: 1:47 P.M., June 4, 1978

Outbound: Dr. Ed May and Dr. Hal Puthoff, expected to be at the target site at 2:15 P.M.

Russ Targ: It is 2:15 now and we will assume that Hal and Ed got to their remote site by now. You have plenty of time. Tell me about your mental pictures, with regard to where they might be.

My first impressions were a jumble of every conceivable building that I could remember seeing in the Menlo Park area. So, having to settle on something, I closed my eyes and tried to imagine opening them at the target area. I remember thinking at the time that my first impressions were really dumb. How could I know they had anything to do with the target area? It was like listening to my imagination, only it was running rampant.

Joe: I see sort of a defined circular area with a tree in it. There's some kind of bench-like affair, three sections. I see some angular tepee-like objects, only with a long sharp edge, like-inverted V-shaped objects. Say it is part of a corner of a structure or something, has unique bands going around it.

Whew. I really didn't think I would get to the end of the sentence. I knew everything that I had said was pure imagination. But at the same time, the thought that it was a building felt sort of different. A sort of strange building. I kept imagining it with bands or stripes around it.

Russ Targ: Can you see what this tepee-like structure is made of?

As a result of his question, I remember thinking, hey, he likes this information. Maybe I'm doing ok. But I still didn't have any idea what I was really supposed to be doing. So I tried to put my mind back in the same position it was in when I thought of the tepee-like structure. I found it was really very easy to imagine my mind being there once again.

Joe: It is apparently some kind of stone that looks like it's poured stone; it's natural but it's poured stone, some aggregate stone that has been poured into a mold. It does not have a real coarse texture, but it does have a rough texture to it. It appears that I am on the top edge looking down the face of this and there is a barbell-type shape that's rounded on each end. It is almost as wide in the center as it is on the ends. It appears to be associated with the face of the building in some way. Either on the ground before it, or standing behind it, whatever the perspective might be. There's a white and black pattern, a white-black-white-black striped pattern. It's not a full stripe, it's just like it's a keyboard on a piano, black keys and white keys. I see the corner of some square stone that has a shadow on it like from a tree, overhanging trees. I see a high wall, a high wall of concrete that goes in the opposite direction of where the tree in the center is. I had the feeling that I went through strips of glass on the face of this building, this ledge I was looking down.

I had no idea if what I was perceiving was right or wrong. I do remember feeling like I was picking up on tiny little bits and pieces, struggling to put them all together into some overall format. The general gist of how the information was stringing together felt somehow right. So I continued to build on what I envisioned to be a structure. I actually began to feel more like I was at my imaginary building than in the room talking with Russell Targ.

Russ Targ: Can you pull away from this building a little bit and get a general idea of what its shape is?

I imagined floating up in the air over my structure and pulling away some distance. My impression of what I could see immediately changed.

Joe: It's like an inverted rectangle with a square fastened to the back, or a rectangle laid down behind it. Like it's two buildings in one. . .one building. I seem to sense that there is dirt by the walls that has flowers in it. Not real high ones just with a big hole in them for flowers. I see another variation of the dumbbell; the rounded ends are the same but the square is wider in the center.

Suddenly I got a surprise image of something I didn't expect to see.

Joe: I see bicycles. It's like bicycles there. Wheels and spokes. A blue one and a red one. Like in a stand. I see overlap stripes; I'm going to have to draw that. I get the sense that it is like a patio, but it has lots of trees in it. Like there're holes cut for the trees. Holes for the plants.

It was as if, all of a sudden, there was one surprising element after another. I hadn't expected the bicycles, or the patio, or the trees planted in structured holes. These images were coming out of nowhere. I was beginning to feel different about the information that was pouring in even more rapidly.

Russ Targ: Can you sense what the focus of this place is? You look around, what do you see that is interesting?

I imagined spinning in a circle in front of the structure, having no expectations.

Joe: Just the dumbbell pattern. It's like there is a whole profusion of dumbbell patterns.

The dumbbell pattern had taken over my mind completely. It was almost mesmerizing. I felt as though I were trying to pull my view away and look over my shoulder.

Joe: And I sense some kind of a metal scallop, like it does this three times.

I sketched a triple scallop design in the air with my finger.

Joe: It's thick, there is glass associated with that. Like you get in a glass wall. It's either inside or outside the glass wall, or maybe a little of both.

Russ Targ: Is there any color associated with the dumbbell pattern?

Joe: White. It's almost all white. Maybe a bluish gray. The metallic scallop pattern is a shiny substance like aluminum or stainless steel, something that reflects a lot of light. Across from the building there is some kind of well-manicured hedge-type things. . .the dumbbell shape keeps sticking in my mind for some reason.

Again, I felt as if I were being overwhelmed by the dumbbell pattern but could not seem to determine exactly where or how it related to the target.

Russ Targ: What is the orientation of that?

I really concentrated on the dumbbell pattern, asking over and over in my mind—What does it mean? What does it mean? I started getting two distinct connections, or so it appeared in my thinking.

Joe: There are two forms of dumbbell patterns. This is the perspective of one, where the sides are larger than the ends.

I found myself imagining a sort of rectangle with rounded ends.

Joe: It appears it is on the ground, but I don't know exactly how it is on the ground. I don't know if it is a pattern in the patio, or the walkway, or an outline.

I turned my mental attention to the second pattern and it had an entirely different feel to it.

Joe: I see a lot of dumbbell shapes and archways. There's an arch that is not a. . .it's not a live arch. . .but there's leaves in the arch, I don't know if it's live or not, but there are leaves in the arch. There are dumbbell patterns.

Try as I might, I couldn't separate the second dumbbell pattern from arches and the strangest feeling of not-live leaves.

At this point Russ terminated the verbal portion of the experiment and asked me to render as much as I could of my perceptions in drawings.

This is done for two reasons. Drawing is thought to be a right-brain or a less logic-oriented function. What they knew about remote viewing at that time, which I didn't know, was that some subjects who do very poorly in the verbal do exceptionally well in the artistic; or vice versa. So I drew as much as I could remember of my perceptions.

By this time, I was really into second gear. I had stopped worrying about what might or might not be correct and had really let go of my inhibitions. I was convinced there was a good probability that everything I had described was pure imagination, but I also knew that what I was doing was fun. So, regardless of outcome, I threw myself into the drawing *(Figure 1)* with an enormous amount of enthusiasm.

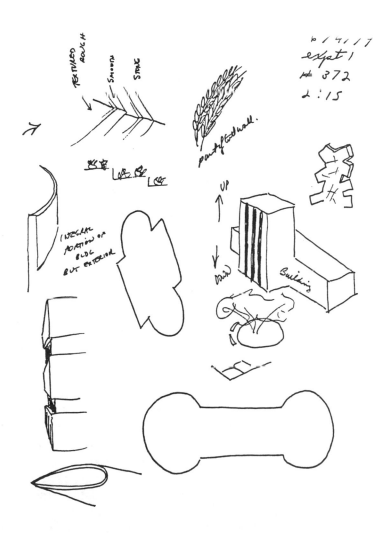

Figure 1. (Provided by Dr. Edwin C. May from original transcripts.)

In my drawing, I clarified that there were two different sets of dumbbell shapes. One was clearly a pattern on the ground and the other had something to do with arches. I went on to further clarify the V-shape or tepee image as being the corner of the building, which had a form of banding: rough-smooth-rough-smooth stone. For some reason the overall perspective felt really good and I said so. Then I drew the overall shape of the building and described the interchanging shadows or stripes on the face of the building. I went on to describe some sort of sculptured-type objects (although incorrectly identifying them as wood). The leaves were part of an archway or overhang-type of area on the building.

When asked if I had an overall feeling for the specific type of building that it might be, I stated that I thought it could be a hospital of some sort. I re-capitulated the very straight-line architecture, the very low-hanging trees, the dumbbell shapes, the bicycles, and the overwhelming feeling of shiny metal in front of or behind plain black glass. I finally stated that I kept wanting to search the front of the building to find this decorative black glass. We terminated the information collection portion of the experiment at 2:38 P.M., with a statement that the building was probably five stories tall. The entire psychic portion of the experiment lasted just eighteen minutes.

While we waited for the return of the out-bounders, Russ and I continued to talk about the remote viewing experiment. I was admitting more to myself than to him that I was really surprised at the simple approach they were using to do psychic research. I had unfortunately expected to see a lot of strange and bizarre behavior and had wound up experiencing what appeared to be flights of imagination. . .my own!

Russell explained that remote viewing, as they were studying it, was very simply one more *normal* capability of mankind, albeit one that had probably fallen into far less use than it might have been at one time in man's history. As I look back now to that first experience, I realize that I came out of the first part of the experiment with a sort of elation. I felt good because my first exposure to psychic functioning was as mild as daydreaming. More than that, I "knew" it was only daydreaming, and all my concerns and fears that it was weird and threatening to my belief structures were going to be unfounded. We continued to pass the time with idle conversation, discussing weather and food, as they were two safe subjects.

Ed May and Hal Puthoff returned to the lab and met us with sober expressions. I was directed not to discuss the target as we all loaded into the car for our return to the target. I knew they would be pulling up to arches in front of a McDonald's, or possibly a baseball field, and I would feel very foolish when they did. We drove around for almost twenty minutes, re-tracing the exact route the out-bounder team had taken in order to reach the target. Finally, we entered the Stanford University campus and I began to feel relief as I noticed the large tower and Spanish-style buildings. I was not prepared for our arrival at the Stanford Art Museum *(Figure 2)*.

Nobody said a word as Russ pulled photocopies of my drawings out and passed them around.

It is very difficult to explain the type of excitement one feels when you suddenly see your imagination displayed before your eyes. I had never been to the Museum before. But at that moment in time, I knew that it was the very building I had laboriously constructed in detail within my mind. I found that I wanted to kick myself for having not paid attention to all of the minor details which were now flooding through my mind that I remembered seeing during the session but had failed to speak of or draw.

My attention was immediately riveted to the dumbbell-shaped forms at the tops of the columns in the arched area. I looked around the grounds and quickly found the other shapes which had been so clearly in my imagination. The low, droopy trees bracing the entry, the small bicycle rack in the front right, which had only the red bike still in it. There was the black glass behind the decorative iron work, the Rodin sculpture garden to the left side of the building in the patio, the many circular containers with tall trees spread throughout the patio area. There was even a white-black-white-black shadow effect

Figure 2. Photo of Stanford Art Museum.
(Reproduced with permission of Dr. Edwin C. May.)

between the pillars and darkness under the arched entry. The round planters, everything, as I had imagined it to be. The overwhelming closure I experienced standing in front of the building was a traumatic shock to my belief system. My mind was spinning, and I didn't say much as we loaded back into the car and returned to the lab. Before I departed that afternoon, Hal convinced me that I should participate in a full series of six experiments. He explained that they required a full series of six in order to properly judge them against one another, to determine how much beyond chance expectation the results might be. Chance expectation, I quickly thought. That's probably what happened. Regardless of the odds, I had obviously hit the exact target by chance. Fate had produced the one-in-a-million probability that my guesses equaled the actual target. When I departed the lab, I was feeling a lot better knowing that in all probability it was chance or luck. My thoughts were quickly dealing with the open wound to my philosophy of life, my concepts of reality. They were shaken badly, but so far it wasn't something I couldn't patch. Down deep inside I knew I was only putting on a lot of temporary Band-Aids. The best was yet to come.

5
Initial Efforts

Judging the results from a series of remote viewing experiments was rather simple in those beginning years. It became more complicated later when critics, unable to attack the actual process, decided to go after the method of evaluation. I should also note here, that evaluation of an intelligence collection problem is entirely different from that required by science. This is addressed in Chapter 20.

My position regarding this matter has always been a simple one. In the final outcome, what the judges think or don't think about a target series doesn't matter. When I've worked a target site, I know what my perceptions are. As I produce the different transcripts for each of the target locations, I remember what I was thinking at the time. When I visit them later I see there are portions of each target that look familiar and there are portions that don't. It's a fairly easy task for me to correlate my perceptions about a target after going out and seeing it.

Also, one has to remember that judging within a protocol is of extreme importance to the scientist. It would be bad science to collect data in a scientific way and then not judge equally as well. So, our motives are different. The scientist has his job and I, as the remote viewer, have mine.

In all of the experiments in which I've participated, there has been information pertinent to the target or there has not. When there has been pertinent information, it has ranged from low to extremely high. In fact, there have been remote targets which have been specifically named during targeting.

The target information I'm talking about now isn't the obvious, like there was grass, or there was dirt at the location. Anyone can take a crack at guessing things like that. And all they'll ever be doing is guessing. Everyone knows there are certain aspects about a target that are reasonably easy to guess, if you're willing to take a chance on it being an indoor versus an outdoor target possibility.

When I refer to information about a target, I am speaking about things like color in the correct percentages, curves versus squares as predominant patterns, water or no water, size and shape, or specific artifacts at the target location. As within the example of my first target presented in Chapter Four, I didn't say *a* building; I said it was like two buildings combined and drew a picture that quite closely resembled the Stanford Art Museum. The drawings for the other five targets in the series were equally different and stood out well in contrast, one from the other.

How does it feel, this collection of information?

The experience I had was like that of a feather brushing across my mind. The softest and lightest touch of information, that drifted in and out so easily that I couldn't quite grasp it. In fact, it's very much like a feather. When you try to grab it mentally, like the down from a pillow, it will always escape from your grasp just before your fingers are able to close about it. That's very much like the feelings that I remember having in my mind during those first series of remote viewing experiments.

What I experienced, I didn't need a judge to keep score on. I *knew* the parts of the target that I had right when I saw them. Instantly, I recognized those portions and parts that had deftly drifted across my mind. I also recognized the sizeable chunks that I missed and the gross statements of error also contained within each of the exercises. But, as we all know, hindsight is always a late teacher.

So, finding out how they had finally scored my first series of experiments eventually astonished me. It also underscored the truth of the experience, as it had felt to me. What it meant to me was that everything I knew regarding how we are made up and how we think or gather information was somehow different from the way I had always pictured it to be. All of the past fears long buried from the NDE and the years that followed suddenly clawed their way upward and outward, into the sunlight.

At this point I must digress somewhat and describe how the experiments were actually scored.

In order to establish a measure of accuracy for any remote viewing experiment, the entire group of targets must be subjected to independent judging on a blind basis by someone unconnected with the actual remote viewing experiments.

So, the results of each of my six experiments were put together into separate packets. These were the transcripts, or unedited narratives of my taped interviews, as well as any drawings I might have produced. These packets were left unlabeled and were shuffled into a random order. They then marked the envelopes with a single digit, one through six. This is random and only provides a means of noting which random packet the judge might be working with.

Taking these packets, the judge then visited each of the actual target sights and placed the packets in rank order (1-6). The data they were most interested in was the summation of the ranks assigned to the target-associated transcripts. The lower the value, the better the result. Based on that number they could determine the degree of probability of attaining such a number against chance. At the end of judging there would be six columns of data with the six packets stacked, "best matched" to "least matched" judgments.

I returned to the East Coast after completing the six targets on my first visit. Hal told me that he would send the results after the independent judging. It was approximately a week before he called to relate the results they had obtained. I had scored five first-place matches and a second-place match. In terms of significance, statistically it was reported to me as being well beyond chance possibility.

I was stunned. I had actually *guessed* enough information correctly to permit a total stranger to go back to each of the target locations and correctly match the appropriate transcript (with drawings) five out of six times. The sixth target they had matched as their second selection. My intellect was saying that it was impossible. How could a person know that much about a place they hadn't yet been to? My mind was suddenly filled with concepts, probable and impossible.

The possibilities overwhelmed me. I was suddenly faced with the realization that there was nothing to which the mind couldn't gain access. People only had to open their imaginations and let them go to work.

I quickly shuffled through the papers on my desk and pulled out the IEEE report. I read through it at least four times. They had included a detailed description of the outbounder protocol we had used at SRI-International. It would be the same protocol we would continue to use within the Army project for training purposes. I instinctively knew that with practice, I could probably improve my own ability. I knew I could.

Completely unknown to me at the time, the Army had already decided that I would be a permanent member of the unit. My displayed skill had already exceeded their bottom line. I was assigned Remote Viewer No. 001.

When all this began, in 1978, I could not have guessed or imagined the size of the bucket of worms that I was so enthusiastically opening. What seemed logically simple at the time turned out to be one of the most complex and dramatic string of events anyone could have jumped into. Most of the changes I've experienced as a result have had profound effects on my way of thinking and just about everything that I believe about life or reality.

The first task was establishing a pool of targets. Setting up a target pool sounds easy, but it isn't. Back in those early days I thought it only required telling someone to go out and pick fifty or so spots in the local area that would make good targets, write out a detailed description on how to reach each of them on a 3x5 card, and seal the cards in double-wrapped and sealed opaque envelopes.

We were totally wrong. That was one of many mistakes and errors we committed through ignorance from the outset. The penalty was twenty-four straight failures. No, let me rephrase that; there were twenty-four *dismal* failures.

In any event, as I look back on that period of my experience, I am amazed that I doggedly kept at it, even when it never seemed to work.

We put together a pool of fifty targets. Included within the assortment was a plethora of things that were similar. Not to the naked eye of course, but to the psychic mind, the third eye, many of them looked the same. As an example, at least sixteen of the targets were fast-food joints.

At this point, I should give a quick description of what the term *gestalt* means. As I will use it here, it means *the representation of a whole based on the configuration of its parts, all being inseparable.*

In the preliminary remote viewing experience, the subject or remote viewer is usually dealing with a *gestalt* input. That means s/he is getting the target as a single overall or overwhelming representation. Translated, this means that a hamburger joint is a hamburger joint, is a hamburger joint, is a. . .well, you can kind of get the picture. So, you can guess the difficulty an independent judge might have had in those early days, never mind when sixteen out of fifty targets we put together were hamburger joints.

More to the point, however, I wasn't trying to do the remote viewing for judging. I was trying to do it to learn, to improve, to become better. Needless to say, the first twenty-four targets didn't help in that regard.

I called Hal on numerous occasions with long shopping lists of questions. How much? How long? How tall? He was a saint. He and his colleagues, Dr. Edwin May in particular, always responded in detail with the appropriate response at the time. I sometimes think they were being psychic, since it was entirely their support that kept me going in those early days.

So that the reader doesn't make many of the same mistakes that I did, I now provide the following information for properly selecting a target for remote viewing. Bear in mind that this selection process pertains to targets intended for entry-level training and that all recommendations made within this book are *subject to change*.

Selecting a Learning Target

1. All targets should stand alone. They shouldn't be crowded in with equally interesting objects or buildings. They should be kept as separate as possible from other targets or possible targets.

2. All targets within a target pool should be uniquely different from one another. They should not be conceptually the same (as in hamburger joints), nor should they appear the same, such as a swimming pool and a square garden pond.

3. There should be something specifically unique about each of the targets. The shape or perhaps a repetitive design in the architecture, an overwhelming color scheme, lots of glass, etc.

4. They should be simple in concept and function. For example, a waterfall would make a good entry level target, or perhaps a church steeple, or sewage plant.

5. They shouldn't be overly large or overly small in area. The target should be something the out-bounder team can stand in the middle of and see completely without a great deal of moving about.

6. The target should be interesting. It should capture the interest of the out-bounder team and not let their minds drift off to what they might be having for dinner that evening.

7. There should be a mixture of indoor and outdoor targets, at least fifty/fifty.

8. Target pools should be kept to a maximum of ten and should not be put together until they are ready to be used.

9. The person putting the target pool together should be someone who will not be involved in the remote viewing as either an out-bounder team member or an interviewer.

Selecting targets almost sounds too restrictive. If you are thinking the rules make it easier, you're half right—they do. But only in the psychic sense. They don't provide any helpful hints or logic on what the target might or might not be for the viewer of record.

It was difficult in the beginning to see what I can see now. The more you can do to isolate the target from any other information, the easier it is to pick out the accurate details psychically.

Initial efforts were very depressing. Surprisingly, I was to discover that it was my own actions and approach that accounted for most of the problems which I encountered. I want to share some of these with my readers so that you don't make the same mistakes.

6
Altering Beliefs

One of my earliest mistakes was to drift from protocol. In lay terms, I was very, very sloppy.

There are a number of people out there who would argue that this is ok. They would say, "You're not a scientist; you can't be expected to stick to protocols. You aren't trying to prove it works; you're only trying to learn to improve on what is going on. Leave the science to the guys with *Dr.* in front of their names and press on with whatever gets you there the fastest."

Some of this is right, but most of it is wrong. It is right in the sense that I am not a scientist, I lack the formal training, and my focus is more within the area of applications. My mistake was in not realizing that protocol does a lot more than support good science; it also provides the necessary structure and means for attacking a rock-hard-and-fast belief. Being able to alter your belief in what is real is critical in learning to RV.

The learning of remote viewing is not a single act or function; it's more like two sides of a coin standing on edge, or two sides of an argument. When you alter one side or perspective, you must change the counter side as well. One side of the coin or argument is the physical function (the act of remote viewing); the other is more a philosophic function (the belief that enables RV to operate). You cannot have one without the other. Either side requires that a *belief* in what you are attempting must always come first.

The fastest way I know to alter any fixed reality or belief is through experiential learning. However, the experience must be believable. If there is any room for doubt then there *will be* doubt. Sloppy protocol leads to doubt and is therefore of no benefit for changing a belief.

I can hear many sucking air in through their teeth and sighing great sighs. I've heard and participated in a great many debates regarding the differences between using scientific protocols to prove something and applications which aren't intended to prove anything. Many say if something works, use it. To hell with scientific protocols.

Well, they are right in a sense, but not while learning. Especially when learning to RV. For you to progress in RV, you must get from the *believing* side of the canyon to the *knowing* side. Any doubt allowed in the process will hinder crossing the canyon. It will be a long and arduous journey to start with, so there is no sense in suffering any more difficulty than is necessary. Stick to the protocols. Stick as closely as possible to them while in the learning stages. Later, when you *know* remote viewing is real, when you've gotten out of the *believe it's real* stage, then we can talk about pure applications. But, in the beginning, stick to the protocols.

A second reason for sticking to the protocols has to do with information processing. Protocols are structured. They give you an outline into which your notes can be written and from which you can make sense. They provide a framework for an experience to occur the same way time after time. Learning to RV requires hundreds of hours of practice. Protocols stabilize an otherwise difficult process. For those who wish to pursue RV further, I've included three simple protocols as an Appendix to this book. They may not be scientifically perfect, but they will provide ample structure for learning and altering your basic belief concepts.

By not sticking religiously to protocol, I probably added an additional year or longer to my learning-experience curve. It made it doubly difficult to root out many of my hardcore beliefs and added considerably to my list of target failures.

Failures

Speaking of failures, one of my earliest discoveries was to be one of the most valuable. In remote viewing there are failures for the scientists, there are failures for the judges, there are failures for the observers—but *there are no failures for the remote viewer.*

I hear the sighs again and it causes me to chuckle, because for a long period of time, in fact throughout the beginning, I believed there were failures. I was making them, wasn't I? They added considerably to my depression.

The reality of it is that the learning remote viewer, as well as the professional, is in a win-win situation. I can go to hundreds of places in my notes and files and show where this has been the case.

What the remote viewer is actually trying to do is to translate symbols and images from the mind into knowledgeable statements about a remote target. For example, if I am working a remote target and see a sideways < in my mind, I might translate it to mean the bow of a ship. Upon seeing the actual target, I will find out that it wasn't the bow of a ship; it was a church. The scientist sees a failure, the judges see failure, any observer sees failure, but what I *see* is that a sideways < is part of my mental picture of a church. I have learned something, so I have not failed. Right or wrong, I am learning and squeezing 100% from the experience.

It took me almost a year to understand this, and it's since made a tremendous difference in my attitude toward the results in thousands of experiments. I let others worry about the right and wrong as they are reported in journals; I pay very close attention to the details, the mental dictionary of symbols I've been collecting in my mind. References to failure from here on are purely semantic.

Reasons For Failures

Another major error I committed at the outset resulted from making too many observations that were not pertinent to the act of remote viewing. I began to create lists of things that were necessary to encourage good remote viewing.

Now, there is nothing wrong with this when these lists are properly assessed and the data is incorporated properly within the scheme of things. But making lists can sometimes become more of a hindrance than a help.

For example, I noticed in the beginning that I seemed to do better on targets when I was fully relaxed just prior to remote viewing. This has since become known as a *cool down* period. So, as item one on my newly developing list, I wrote "Cool Down period 15-30 minutes."

Item two, which I discovered over time, became "A low and gentle ambient light."

This was quickly followed with "No sharp noises in the area, early morning hours versus late afternoon hours, lying down versus sitting up, no more than one other person in the room, number-two pencils versus felt-tipped pens, must be wearing my favorite pair of socks, not on rainy days, not after driving a car, etc., etc." The list, as well as the remote viewing, became quite cumbersome. It didn't take long to realize that I was no longer paying attention to those things that aided and abetted remote viewing; I was creating lists of reasons why it probably wasn't going to work.

The human mind is ingenious. When faced with a major change to a concept in reality, it will resort to any means or devices necessary to thwart such change. In simpler words, it will do anything to protect the old beliefs.

I didn't want to let go of my belief that remote viewing couldn't work, so I created a long list of reasons for it not to. When I realized what I was doing, I crumpled the list up and threw it away. I decided that if I really wanted to learn to RV, then I would have to learn to do it regardless of circumstance. This turned out to be one of the best decisions I could have made at the time, and there is a simple, two-fold reason why. First, I became committed to learning how to remote view within any circumstance or under any condition; and, second, I was committing myself to whatever changes in belief might be necessary or might come along as a result.

The first reason has been extremely beneficial throughout and following my earliest learning years. Being open to remote viewing under any circumstance has allowed me to perform and perform quite well under extremely difficult and sometimes near-impossible requirements.

As many paranormally talented people will attest, it is very difficult to walk into a modern laboratory or clinical study environment and do what needs to be done on cue. Almost without exception, in most labs there is little done to cater to the subject. SRI-International was one of a few exceptions, and Science Applications International Corporation is another. But there are many labs which do not gear their study to support the subjects' views.

I have by now completed thousands of experiments under controlled conditions, or under the bright lights, in a number of labs. Many of these experiments were highly successful. The best ones were those in which I was processing and learning remote viewing the hard way—I was doing them under any circumstance.

The secondary benefit—acceptance of changes in reality—was a natural result of the first. Seeing it work under the worst of circumstances reinforced my *knowing* that remote viewing is real. I quickly overcame the necessity for *temporary suspension of disbelief.*

Since those days, I have come to understand there are a few things that can be done to make the task easier. There are obvious and logical reasons for them as well. At a minimum, attention should be paid to the following:

a. Remote viewing should be done in a room which is as

empty as possible. Not seeing a lot in the form of objects within the viewing environment helps to reduce the mental clutter. The short-term memory retains a lot of what you last saw before you close your eyes. The subconscious will mix some of those objects in with input from the target, thus creating mental overlay or jamming.

b. The ambient lighting should be soft and gentle. This also reduces the images that might otherwise remain on the backs of the eyelids when you close your eyes. Again, the idea here is to reduce overlay or outside influence.

c. You should sit in a comfortable chair, one in which you can become relaxed. Physical comfort has a lot to do with mental performance. I don't recommend lying down, however, as this can cause too much comfort, which will result in a nap with no remote viewing taking place. However, there are some who can operate this way, so all the more power to them.

d. You need plain white paper and pencils, and a tape recorder is recommended, since you will probably be thinking faster than you are able to write. It helps to not leave anything out. The paper and pencils are for drawing. Some people talk better about a target than they draw or vice versa. Some switch around, better drawing one day and better talking the next. This probably has something to do with the way your particular brain operates or has been trained to operate.

e. You should be well rested.

There are a number of other things that might be of benefit, but they are personally oriented. Some people do better waiting a while after consuming caffeine or other stimulants. Any degree of outside mental or physical influence will disrupt or make the remote viewing more difficult, such as consumption of alcohol, music, emotional upset, etc.

Symbols

There were many other problems which cropped up in the earliest portion of my learning. Most of them were minor, but they won't create the havoc they did with me if you pay attention and watch for them in your own efforts.

One of them was a presumption on my part: I assumed that once I learned a specific symbol, a gestalt image, or a sensed input, it wouldn't change. Well, they change all the time. The simplistic inverted "V" which might have represented church in the early targeting, would change to something far more complex in later stages. So I learned the language of my mind was a pulsing and thriving breeding ground for constantly changing symbols and signals. As quickly as I could figure them out, they would alter or change. There were, and still are, some archetypical symbols, but they are far and few between. By archetypical, I mean symbols which appear to be common to all humans attempting to RV. The following represent a collection of these as examples:

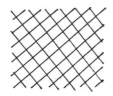

WALL, BARRIER

TUNNEL, ENTRANCE

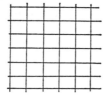

REFLECTIVE SURFACE

CHURCH, RELIGIOUS PLACE

OVERHANG, ROOF

DEATH

BUILDINGS

ARCHES

Why do the symbols occur early on and then change? I believe it is for two reasons.

a. Initially we are getting the gestalt, or most overwhelming or holistic perception of the target. Hence, simple symbols work. A single symbol will represent the entire target's gestalt.

b. Our conscious mind doesn't yet know how to play the game. I've hypothetically thought this might be an effect of ego. Our egos are in charge; they run the show. When you become conscious that the subconscious is communicating directly with *the mind*, the ego panics and does a change-up on the signals or symbols in order to regain control.

Also, the subconscious doesn't deal with physical reality using the same rules of logic which the conscious mind understands, so it will try to send messages in unique and sometimes totally misunderstood ways.

So, any presumptions of stability in the signal line must be let go of at the outset. This means constant practice and constant vigilance will be necessary if you intend to reach any degree of accuracy in the translation of your own mental language.

Finally, I would say that it is necessary to save everything. Keep copious notes and memos about everything you do and everything you think. I didn't do this at the outset and, as a result, lost a great deal of the valuable information which I then had to recapture at a later time. These notes are invaluable, as will be shown in a later chapter. They may unlock secrets which would otherwise pass you by at a later date.

7
Early Tests

At this time, it seems important to digress somewhat from the flow of information which I am sharing. After I returned from the West Coast following my first experiences with remote viewing, much of what I believed to be true about the world and how it operated began falling apart. It didn't happen all at once, nor did the change come roaring in like a south-bound freight train. In fact it was nothing major—not like a full-fledged spontaneous hallucination or a macro-materialization of something larger than a bread-box—it was the little things.

I had begun to really wonder about the fallout from the successes in remote viewing. If remote viewing was possible, then there must be a storehouse of information somewhere into which the remote viewing was tapping. Not only that, but there also would have to be some form of a communications link connecting the brain/mind to the storehouse. I was too new and naive to understand there might be a possible difference between *brain* and *mind.* Was I going inside my head to collect the information which I was reporting during the remote viewing experiments? I didn't have the foggiest idea. But wondering *where* certainly left a great question mark in my mind.

Immediately following my return to the East Coast, we put together some target packages comprised of targets from the Washington, D.C., and Baltimore area. My first twenty-four attempts to replicate the experiments I had experienced at SRI-International were dismal failures. By the time we had gone through the entire string, I had come to a conclusion that there must be something else to it, something I missed seeing in the original set. What was different between the West Coast experience and the twenty-four trials back home? Certainly there were technical rules regarding how remote viewing worked, although, at the time, I had no idea what they might be. My only sense of it at the time was that there was a missing element. Maybe I had lost faith, had somehow stopped believing remote viewing would work. If it dealt with a leap in faith, there was someone who I could talk with who might understand. I knew that Robert Monroe, the man who wrote *Journeys Out of the Body*, lived only hours away in the Blue Ridge Mountains. Thus began the new experience **B2**.

It took some months to arrange a meeting with Mr. Monroe. I did so by driving down to the Charlottesville area of Virginia. I remember that it was a weekend in October 1979. He was living in what has since become known as the Gatehouse, a rustic two-story building perched at the entry road to a private valley. The valley was in its natural state then, with no roads except for an old logging trail, negotiable by four-wheeled vehicles. Comprised of over eight hundred acres of rolling pasture and woodland, the valley faced west into the Blue Ridge Mountains. Back then, standing on one of the higher hills, I remember you could see the ski resort of Wintergreen.

I was nervous about meeting Bob. I knew him only from his book. I knew he had what amounted to a lifetime of experience with out-of-body experiences. There was no way to be sure that my spontaneous OBEs were even the same as what he might call an OBE. My worry was for nothing. Bob turned out to be every bit as gracious as his book and reputation represented him to be. As an added benefit, I was introduced to his charming wife Nancy, every bit the Southern Lady.

Our initial discussion dealt primarily with my explaining my own experiences and asking a multitude of questions. I don't recall many of the specifics of our first conversation, just that his responses appeared to be so natural and straightforward that I found myself comfortable with my own experiences for the first time. Here was a man who, having been a senior executive for a major New York conglomerate, was talking about the paranormal as if it were a normal daily occurrence in his life. If he could do it, then I could too.

There are two things which occurred during our first conversation together, which I will never forget. The first was his suggestion that I come stay for a week and take his Gateway Voyage seminar. He had recently completed the new Monroe Institute Center, the first of what would eventually become a cluster of three buildings. The second suggestion was a warning that I was stroking his female black cat, Blackie, too hard. He told me she had a tendency to become excited when someone stroked her too hard or too long.

I left with a promise to attend the seminar the following year, as well as a fang hole completely through my left thumbnail, compliments of Blackie, whom I stroked too long and too hard.

Returning to my home in Reston, Virginia, I continued working with the remote viewing. I found that I was no longer focused on the result as much as I was on the method. Tearing the protocol apart, it wasn't long until I made my first discovery. It wasn't a large revelation, but it seemed so at the time. I noticed there were three things which seemed important to the remote viewing effort. These were *time* or *date*, *location*, and *event*.

It appeared that successful remote viewing occurred when at least two of the three were known. Not known to the viewer specifically, but known by whomever put the targeting package together. It appeared as if two of the three known elements acted as an address for the third portion, or the unknown part of the target. It worked exceptionally well when the *time/date* and *location* were known, and the target was the *event*. Why? I didn't know. More importantly, it was the first original thought about the subject which I had made alone.

As I mentioned in the earlier chapters, one has to be ready for change. What I thought was a simple discovery turned out being the first step in the right direction. By observing the three elements or requirements for remote viewing, I had begun the development of my own reasoning for the existence of paranormal functioning. I wasn't reading it from a book or gleaning it from someone else's philosophy. This first step I drew in my notebook as follows:

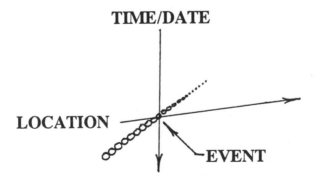

Under it, I drew *a rudimentary example of a single event reality in time space.* My thought was that maybe what we experience as life is nothing more than a string of these events. It almost seemed too simple. Of course, I hadn't yet burdened myself with abstract thoughts like who's in charge of getting us from event to event, what about shared realities, or how about multiple universes? Those would all come later. The most interesting effect from drawing the chart in my notes was the immediate improvement of the remote viewing. When I asked my friend, who was developing targets for me, to pay particular attention to fixing *location* and *time/date*, there was an immediate and dramatic jump in the amount of correct data that I was associating with a target.

In later notes I wrote ". . .in order for someone to see reality as it is occurring there must be mental processing. Mental processing requires time; small amount that it might be, it is still sufficient to make an observation history. In other words, everything we humans believe we are seeing is in the *past*." This notation triggered my next adventure, which was to seek out other people, other psychics whom I might be able to study and observe. I knew I would discover additional information that would add to my overly simplistic view of reality. I was right.

What can one learn from a professional psychic, one who earns a living providing information relevant to a person's past or present? Aside from human nature and degrees of gullibility, believe it or not, one can learn a lot. Once again, the trick is not to look at the ash and flash, but to study the little things.

Many of the people I met over the course of almost two years were not psychic, at least not in the conventional use of the term. For me, psychic means *someone who is sensitive to information not otherwise available through normal means*; or, in the case of remote viewing, *non-sensory transfer of information from "somewhere" to the mind*. In turn-of-the-century terms, the latter is sometimes referred to as clairvoyance. However, there were some who were obviously gifted, and you could see that—but only after you got past the ash and flash.

What do I mean by "ash and flash"? The staged set, the drama, the accoutrements of the trade; crystal balls, tea leaves in a cup, the burning incense stick, lots of candles, the darkened room, over-the-head shawl, cards, and yes, the Ouija Board. Initially, I, like a large proportion of the population, was turned off by these accoutrements. This was most regrettable, since indirectly it has a lot to do with valid psychic functioning.

As an example, let's suppose a young girl is born with a cognitive talent (CT), and she is sensitive to future events that may affect her family, friends, or even strangers. She knows from contact with the society and culture around her that her CT is not regarded as normal. She can't turn it off, but neither can she practice it openly. *Unless. . .*she can show her CT to be from a mystical source, usually something over which she has no control. She may resort to using a crystal ball or Tarot Cards. They then become the medium through which she can express her CT without fear of condemnation.

These media may hold even more value when you come to understand that they allow her to perform her talent without changing any of her *normal* realities, which perhaps include her religion. So it would appear that using a crystal ball does have additional benefits not normally observed or visible to us on the outside looking in.

How do you tell the valid psychics from charlatans? The only way I know is by the information they provide. If the information is valid, then their CT is valid. The only way I know to guarantee the information comes from psychic sources is to keep the information exchange going one way. The psychic must be totally blind to the individual. This is hard to do while sitting in front of someone. A simple course in Neural Linguistics will establish how much information is passed through body language alone, the positioning of the eyes, etc., never mind the clothes you wear, the jewelry, even the way you comb your hair.

Some of the best psychics I have ever met said it all with their eyes. One woman in particular comes to mind. She would talk for hours, staring into a bowl of water. I would sit and watch her eyes. Most of what she had to say was gibberish, but every now and then her eyes would give her away. For a fraction of a second she would lose focus, and it would appear that she was no longer focused on the room, the water, or anything else. In that fraction of a second she would hesitate. It was almost not perceivable. The next statement from her mouth I would write on my pad. Of the statements I collected, 95 percent were accurate to the smallest detail. I suspect the bowl of water and the gibberish were nothing more than a vehicle to her CT.

Consider the following quote from Frank Herbert's book, *Heretics of Dune* (Ace Books, G. P. Putnam's Sons, 1987):

We are not looking at a new state of matter but at a newly recognized relationship between consciousness and matter, which provides a more penetrating insight into the working of prescience. The oracle shapes a projected inner universe to produce new external probabilities of forces that are not understood. There is no need to understand these forces before using them to shape the physical universe. Ancient metal workers had no need to understand the molecular and submolecular complexities of their steel, bronze, copper, gold, and tin. They invented mystical powers to describe the unknown while they continued to operate their forges and wield their hammers.

Fiction? Perhaps, but this truly sums up how a remote viewer feels a couple of years into the process. In admitting that we don't know how or why it works, that it just does, we find ourselves inadvertently establishing well-rounded rituals or systematic methods for exercising the talent, at the same time slipping into a natural re-mystification process.

The scientists want to measure it from stem to stern and lay it all out with agonizingly detailed studies. But we, the remote viewers, want to cut to the quick. Let's just call it mystical and get better at it.

Maybe there are tests that can be performed to establish the more sensitive human from another. I don't know. A lot of interest has centered around remote viewers, simply because they perform within scientific parameters. During the past decade, I have experienced almost every test that can be run. I've been subjected to most of them a minimum of three times. A very small sample follows.

The *Sixteen Personality Factor Questionnaire (16 PF)*, developed by R.B. Cattell, Ph.D., University of Illinois; Herbert W. Eber, Ph.D., Psychological Resources Associates; and Maurice M. Tatsuoka, Ph.D., University of Illinois. It is an objectively scored test devised by basic research in psychology to give the most complete coverage of personality possible in a brief time. In addition to sixteen primary factors, the test is used as a measure of at least four secondary dimensions which are broader traits, scored from the component primary factors. The secondary dimensions are Extraversion, Anxiety, Tough Poise, and Independence. I tested low in Extraversion and Anxiety and high in Tough Poise and Independence.

Another test is the *Edwards Personal Preference Schedule (EPPS)*, developed by Allen L. Edwards, University of Washington. The EEPS was designed primarily as an instrument for research and counseling purposes, to provide quick and convenient measures of a number of relatively independent normal personality variables. The EPPS differs from many other inventories since it doesn't purport to measure such traits as emotional stability, anxiety, adjustment, neuroticism, schizophrenia, paranoia, or hysteria. It does, however, measure achievement, deference, order, exhibition, autonomy, affiliations, intraception, succorance, dominance, abasement, nurturance, change, endurance, heterosexuality, and aggression. I scored high in achievement, exhibition, autonomy, intraception, change, and endurance; low in affiliations, succorance, abasement, and aggression; and split the difference in need for order, nurturance, and heterosexuality. There was a considerable spread between the scores of other remote viewers and my scores.

In addition, there are other tests: the *California Psychological Inventory (CPI)*, developed by Harrison G. Gough, Ph.D., Consulting Psychologists Press, Inc.; the *FIRO-B*, developed by Will Schutz, Ph.D., Consulting Psychologists Press, Inc.; the *Gordon Personal Profile-Inventory (GPPI)*, developed by L.V. Gordon, The Psychological Corporation; *The Minnesota Multiphasic Personality Inventory (MMPI)*, developed by S.R. Hathaway, Ph.D., and J.C. McKinley, M.D., The Psychological Corporation; and the *Myers-Briggs Type Indicator (MBTI)*, as developed by Isabel Briggs Myers, Consulting Psychologists Press, Inc.

I've been tested five times with the Myers-Briggs, which resulted in a consistent classification of INTP or INTJ. This translates generally to introvert, intuitive, thinking, and perceptive person. The last value (P or J) has frequently jumped back and forth across the line from perceptive to judgmental (INTJ-INTP). Testing of other remote viewers has shown a tendency toward INTJ or INTP, but this has never been a hard and fast rule. If anything can be said about testing remote viewers over the years, it would be that testing has shown that we are as normal as anyone else with regard to thinking and rationalization. We are also as different from one another as one human being can be from another.

Other, more experimental testing classifications have shown that, as an introvert, I was found to be intimate, quiet, reserved, contained, reflective, but with extrovert tendencies toward leadership. The Army would probably agree with the latter.

My intuitive portion scored high in the abstract, imaginative, intellectual, theoretical and unconventional side of the scale—not a complete surprise.

While showing feelings of trust and thinking in a carefree, logical and reasonable way, I walked the middle ground on being critical versus accepting, firm versus warm, and defiant versus compliant.

Finally, I'm a poly-active but systematic, spontaneous but planned, and otherwise organized, decisive and pro-active person.

None of the above would surprise my wife, since she is an astrologer and uses astrological tools to obtain similar information. For those of you out there who are also astrologers, I was born in

Miami, Florida, at 12:12 A.M., January 10, 1946. I also have a twin sister who came into the world trailing me by eighteen minutes. The most interesting test done, at least from my point of view, was a test developed by MARS Measurement Associates of Lawrenceville, New Jersey, one of the principal architects of a performance measure of personality known as the *Personality Assessment System* (PAS). The PAS is a unique psychological instrument because it is based on performance rather than self-report. It primarily deals with fourth dimension, coping behavior, problem-solving style, time-orientation, and stress, especially preferred levels of stress and stress tolerance.

In addition to the psychological, there are other tests and measurements that can and are sometimes taken during a remote viewing session. These are physiological. Some can be quite invasive; most are non-invasive, requiring only tape or a strap to the body or body extremities. Some of them are listed here as a small excerpt only to show the reader to what extremes science will sometimes drift. When you think about these, remember the remote viewer must be able to do the remote viewing as these measurements are being taken as well. A strong reminder—if you are going to learn how to do remote viewing, it must be with the attitude that you can do it anywhere and under any condition.

Possible measurements may include but are not limited to: heart, blood pressure, body temperature, electromyograph, galvanic skin response, electrical skin resistance, the electroencephalograph (which measures surface brain activity), breath rate, eye movement, inside environmental temperature, external environmental temperature, inside and outside humidity differences, barometric differences, bio-rhythm statistics, high- and low-tide correlations or moon effects, electromagnetic environmental effects, internal and external ion ambience, sunspot activity levels with timing marks, subject, facilitator or monitor voice print stress analysis, external ambient noise or frequency interference, subjective and objective analysis of moods and feelings, magnetoencephalography (MEG) using a cryogenic super-conducting quantum interference device (SQUID), multiple cameras, lights, ad infinitum.

I could go on, but suffice it to say that science and the remote viewer differ radically on what each might have an interest in. In spite of this, the viewer must be prepared to perform under all the above conditions and more and must go the distance in the validation of his/her CT.

To what areas should attention be paid? This is hard to determine.

My own experience has shown that psychological measurements are of no value in determining the future or current ability of a psychic person. Most physical attributes or measurements seem flawed as well, with the exception of the MEG. The MEG alone holds promise for providing information at this point in time, simply because it is capable of studying the electrical fields deep within the brain (deeper than the first quarter-inch of the outer skull).

Aside from these and other experiments currently being done at the Cognitive Science Laboratory at Science Applications International Corporation in Menlo Park, the nature of which are still proprietary, there has been very little correlation of psychological or physiological testing of remote viewers and evaluation of skill.

So, what are we left with, if the tests don't tell us much about what goes on inside a remote viewer's head? We are left with the remote viewer's perceptions of what is going on inside. We are left with discussing the experiences that the remote viewers are having and the observed effects of those observations on their minds. In the early years I was able to seek out help in this area by attending a Gateway Voyage seminar at The Monroe Institute, in Faber, Virginia.

8
Exercises

I am more than my physical body. Because I am more than physical matter, I can perceive that which is greater than the physical world. Therefore, in these exercises, I deeply desire to Expand, to Experience; to Know, to Understand; to Control, to Use such greater energies and energy systems as may be beneficial and constructive to me and to those who follow me. Also during these exercises, I deeply desire the help and cooperation, the assistance, the understanding of those individuals whose wisdom, development and experience are equal or greater than my own. I ask their guidance and protection from any influence or any source that might provide me with less than my stated desires.

This is the Gateway Affirmation, which hangs on the wall of The Monroe Institute in Virginia. It is the first of many meaningful and informative tools that one receives when attending one of the Institute's seminars. My purpose for being there was to attend the Gateway program, which Bob had encouraged me to do.

What is a Gateway Program? In the beginning, 1973, the Institute, specifically Robert Monroe, was invited to the Esalen Center in Big Sur, California, to conduct a weekend workshop which would incorporate some of the methods and techniques it had developed. In that weekend, and one that followed in San Francisco, the Institute opened a new aspect of its exploration of consciousness. As additional requests for similar sessions began coming in, a decision was made to present other weekend programs in a semi-public manner. Thus was born the M-5000 Program, which ultimately became known as the Gateway Seminar.

By the time I decided to attend a Gateway, Bob had finished the construction of a new facility on his property in Nelson County, Virginia. What had originally begun as a weekend program had been stretched to six days, Saturday through Friday.

The Gateway Program is dedicated to the development and exploration of human consciousness through a system of exercises using Hemi-Sync. Designed so that you may learn and experience profound areas of expanded awareness, these exercises assist the individual to know and better understand the total self. It is the goal of the Institute to provide an array of experiences in mental states of deep relaxation at the very threshold of consciousness. The various levels of consciousness are defined as: Focus 10, a level at which the physical body is asleep but the mind is awake and alert; Focus 12, expanded awareness, where perception is expanded beyond the physical body; Focus 15, a state of no-time, where the time factor is no longer of any importance; and Focus 16-21, the doorway to other realities and energy systems beyond time-space-physical matter.

These levels are achieved in the Gateway Voyage through the use of the Frequency Following Response (FFR), a process developed and patented by Robert Monroe, wherein certain sound patterns create a Frequency Following Response in the electrical activity of the brain.

The Institute states in their brochures:

These blended and sequenced sound patterns can gently lead the brain into various states, such as deep relaxation or sleep. A generic patent in this field was issued to Robert Monroe in 1975. Drawing upon this discovery and the work of others, Mr. Monroe employed a system of *Binaural Beats*, by feeding a separate sound pulse into each ear with stereo headphones. The two hemispheres of the brain act in unison to hear a third signal. The difference between the sound pulses is a third signal which is not an actual sound, but an electrical signal that can only be created by both brain hemispheres acting and working together, simultaneously. This unique coherent brain state results in what is known as hemispheric synchronization, or *Hemi-Sync*.

While hemispheric synchronization occurs naturally in day-to-day life, it typically exists only for random, brief periods of time. The Hemi-Sync audio technologies developed by The Monroe Institute assist the seminar student in achieving and sustaining this highly productive, coherent brain state.

I should report at this point that the Hemi-Sync applications are used in other areas besides the Gateway Voyage. They can be found in education, specifically elementary through college and advanced individual training areas; health, psychotherapy, sleep-restorative training, and music. As of this writing, the Gateway Voyage has now been conducted for more than nineteen years, with thousands of participants from all over the world attending, many of whom have reported significant, meaningful, and life-changing experiences.

In 1980, when I considered attending the Voyage Program, I felt that it was possible that it could provide new insight and additional mental tools which would enhance remote viewing learning. I wasn't wrong. At a minimum, it provided new insight into sleep and dreaming, learning and memory, my physical and mental health, creativity and problem solving, stress management, and—most of all—meditative states of consciousness. I have now been a professional member of the Institute for all the years since my first Gateway experience.

What specifically attracted me to the Institute was their methods and techniques for establishing control of mental functioning at the sleep threshold, the hypnogogic state. I felt that that point in consciousness is where my unconscious mind was passing information I was seeking through remote viewing. As Bob would later say, "The right-brain territory, without limitation, is a rich and fertile ground for mining operations by the left brain. It is in this coherent or *whole brain* region of consciousness that produces the precious nuggets of information."

Figure 3 on page 80 illustrates how the different states developed at the Institute fall within the natural phases of the human cycle.

Prior to attending the Institute program, I was spending a great deal of time preparing for each remote viewing experiment. As mentioned earlier, there is a portion of the remote viewing experiment which is called the *cool down* period. It is that epoch of time the remote viewer experiences just prior to when s/he is required to collect information on a target. In the beginning, this cool down period was relatively short, perhaps thirty to thirty-five minutes, mainly because, as a new remote viewer, I didn't know what I was doing anyway. The half-hour was usually spent discussing paranormal functioning with the interviewer. What I didn't realize at the time, but do now, is that I was using this half-hour to create a proper mind set for paranormal functioning. In other words, I was preparing myself subconsciously to accept the experience. I was *temporarily suspending my disbelief*, to allow an unusual experience to happen.

Later, after being exposed to many remote viewing exercises, the cool down period becomes elongated. It stretches out. Why? My own perception is that, as you gain more and more experience with the remote viewing act, you begin to doubt what you are observing. This

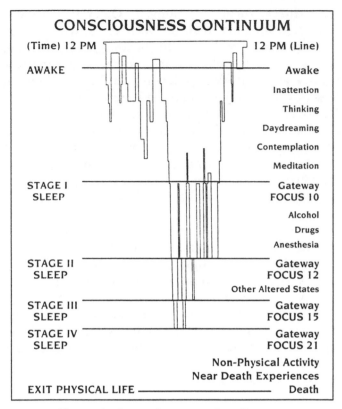

Figure 3. Consciousness Continuum.
(Copied with the permission of The Monroe Institute.)

occurs because you haven't really crossed the line from the *I believe* to the *I know*. Even though I might have already experienced seventy or eighty remote viewing experiments, I had never really changed my belief structure sufficiently to affect my personal concepts of reality. In other words, I'd never yet been threatened by the act of remote viewing; I'd only been playing in it.

Jumping the boundary philosophically at this point is terribly difficult, because you are asking your rational mind to ignore all that it has been taught regarding information-gathering since birth. The concept with which you are dealing flies in the face of all that you have been imprinted with, by parents, siblings, friends, peer group, school, religion, etc. Not an easy change to make, never mind *accept*. So you deal with it by elongating the time you spend before a remote viewing session in order to convince yourself that what you are about to do is ok. Consciously, on the surface, what you appear to be doing is getting your mind-set right. At least this is how I translated the cool down period. The major problem this causes is aggravation. In my own case, my cool down period was being extended from the original thirty or so minutes to hours.

If I were scheduled to perform a remote viewing session in the laboratory at 9:00 A.M., then I was having to show up at 7:00 in order to get my mind-set right. Of course I blamed it on everything else that was going on in my life: the early morning traffic made me hyper; I had an argument with my wife; the dog was sick and I was worried; I stubbed my toe on the lab threshold, etc. You get the picture.

The effect the Monroe exercise tapes had on this cool down period was phenomenal, probably for two reasons. First, my exposure to the tapes in a seminar format allowed me to see that there were at least twenty other people who were beginning to feel and think as I did. It allowed for the paranormal experience to become more natural and less threatening. It helped to integrate the unusual experiences I was having into a normal framework. Second, it provided me with tools for efficient meditation, without having to move to India or having to study for ten years or more. I learned to release stress and induce a meditative state very rapidly. It actually cut my cool down period to less than five minutes.

There are a few skills which add to the remote viewing experience. These are: learning to achieve relaxation; meditation, or learning to become centered; opening your awareness and sensitivity; and communicating your intuitive perceptions.

All of these can be garnered from a visit to The Monroe Institute. These skills enable and enhance one's ability to perform adequately in the psychic collection of data against remote targets, but they also contribute a great deal to the mastering of one's environment, regardless of occupation. Many of these skills can be learned informally, simply by practicing them. Others may require a more formal atmosphere of learning. All of them will enhance your abilities. In addition to that which you might obtain from the Institute are the following thoughts about these skills:

Skill One
Learning to achieve relaxation. This can be accomplished by training in progressive relaxation techniques and through the use of biofeedback. Yoga, self-control exercises, and autogenic training techniques are other methods by which such a skill can be acquired.

Peace of mind and body-strengthening will support relaxation.

There are numerous Oriental fitness exercises to improve mind, body, and spirit. I find the use of the bow and arrow a special blend of all three. There are numerous books on the market which can guide you to learning how to really relax.

Even if you have no intention of pursuing remote viewing, learning to relax and spending time with yourself can be of remarkable benefit to your overall health.

Skill Two
Meditation, or learning to become centered. Meditation or learning to become centered in a comfortable position or place of no thought can be learned through isolation, concentration, and mnemonic/mental exercises.

What do I mean by the term *centered*? Essentially, meditating to a point of bringing one's thoughts to a minimum. Quieting the mental chatter, feeling a complete sense of peace and quiet within. It's very much like balancing on a fence, only doing so mentally.

Through exercises of inward concentration, one learns to close out external sensory input. Sometimes devices are used to achieve this state. Concentration on mandalas, candles, incense smoke trails, or any other simple object sometimes helps.

My own technique involves closing my eyes and thinking of an image that can support input. The image I most consistently use is a slowly spinning Taiji diagram of yin/yang *(Figure 4)*.

Figure 4.

Skill Three
Opening your awareness and becoming sensitive to the outside world. Doing so allows the outer-world messages to filter in. The minimum beginning requirement is the keeping of notes (all of the time). Keeping records about dreams and what you think they mean, taking notes from visual imagery exercises and from your meditation exercises, and constantly paying attention to subtle nonverbal messages from individuals or groups. The Monroe Institute strongly encouraged note taking.

Any exercises that address communications with the world around you (other than verbal) will help. Observe what is going on around you and try to do so with a sharper awareness, a more conscious acknowledgement that life is constantly moving, changing, and communicating.

Such contemplation exercises will assist in your creation of an altered view of reality. It will be a view that is more sensitive and connective to how things really are. There is a helpful hint which I can present here. As you observe, *do not judge*. Retain the clarity of the observations without clouding them with judgments or sets of contrived values. *Try not to reach conclusions.*

I watch my cats very carefully. I study how they communicate with subtle body movements and attitudes. Then I try to communicate with them using some of their own language. The result is that I become more sensitive and aware of their world, especially when I am around them. They have become more gentle and relaxed around me.

Skill Four

Communicating or presenting intuitive perceptions. This skill is most easily acquired through brain-hemispheric and brain-dominance training. Drawing classes, sketching techniques, practice at non-analytic reporting, and simple exercises in perception/reinforcement will aid in improving how you report or present your intuitive perceptions.

Have someone put an object in a box and seal it with tape. Leave it on a table or place where you know it won't be disturbed. Pick at it mentally every day for three or four days and write down a list of one-word descriptions which you sense about the object. To the right of these, write how you feel about each of the words that you've written. Open the box, underline the words on your list that are associated with the object, and study the feelings that you've written to the right or the symbols you may have sketched. Observe where descriptive words might have been too general, or inadequately complex, and try to eliminate them from your vocabulary.

I usually pick a table or shelf in someone else's house, someone I will be seeing on a Saturday, for example. I then go through this exercise and try to define in as simple terms as possible what I might see in the box or on the table or shelf when I go to visit. A warning here. Don't be surprised by some of the input you get during such targeting, and don't forget to target the approximate time of when you will be looking at the table. Otherwise, you will list a lot of things that might be placed in the box and/or removed from it prior to your arrival. Remember that every box has a history. You're interested only in the history you've decided to target. In other words, you will be seeing bits and pieces of all possible targets that will ever be placed within the box, or the contents of the box before it is used for targeting.

How do you know when you have adequately achieved a particular skill? Well, you don't. I do know, however, that your skills will improve with time and the improvement will begin to show in remote viewing achievements. You will be observing your own advancement relative to past performance.

There are a number of additional things which anyone can do to improve concentration, sensitivity, and remote perception. Following are some of these exercises.

Exercise One: When you are planning a trip to the shopping center, select the parking space in which you want to park before you leave the house. Drive to it with the intention of parking there. You will be surprised at the result. Don't be put off if it doesn't work all the time. Timing is everything.

When I first did this exercise I would arrive at the shopping center and there wouldn't be an open slot. I'd search out another space to put my car and then, as I would walk into the building, I would see the person backing out of the original slot I had planned on taking. Is it a mere slip in time? Or is the open-space message I received back at the house my later observation of the person backing out of the slot while I was walking into the center? I could write a second book on the hypothetical reasons for appearing and disappearing parking slots. The idea here is to reach a point of precision that coordinates your psychic observations with real-time action.

Exercise Two: Before you have company coming over for coffee or just to chat, get a piece of paper and write out a list of non-connective words. Not a long list, but one with at least ten words. The list should have such non-connective expressions as: *Boat, Green, Bird-man, Apparent, Apples, Negative,* etc. Leave it where you will be sitting. When your friend arrives and you are comfortably chatting, tick off each of the words as s/he says them within the conversation. I think you will be surprised at how many get a check next to them.

Are they being psychic and giving you the words you wrote down? Are you being psychic and just listing what they might be going to say? Who knows? Remember, the idea here is to generate an experience which gets you from the *I believe* to the *I know*.

Exercise Three: Have a friend draw a picture or symbol and seal it inside an envelope, preferably an opaque envelope that you can't see through. Spend some time clearly focusing on the envelope and then try to replicate the symbol or drawing contained within.

You'll notice in the earlier stages that parts and pieces will be drawn correctly, but they won't be connected together properly. That's ok. It's a normal effect in the initial efforts at remote viewing. You get the ABC's right, but they just aren't in alphabetical order. The order comes later. Practice makes perfect.

Try to pay attention to what you haven't connected together correctly and make notes in your notebook about what you think happened. You'll find your notes will begin to make sense to you just about the time you start putting the ABC's in proper order. The following three drawings are examples of targets sealed in an envelope. These are followed by typical drawings, usually sketches of pieces or portions of the targets, of the targets as they are perceived in early phases of remote viewing *(Figure 5)*.

TARGET SYMBOL ONE	TARGET SYMBOL TWO	TARGET SYMBOL THREE

RESULT ONE	RESULT TWO	RESULT THREE

Figure 5.

Exercise Four: Always write out-of-the-blue perceptions into your notebook. No matter how crazy or mixed-up they might appear to be. At first, they will never seem to connect with anything. They will sometimes connect to events weeks or even months later. You'll witness an event that is similar, but which you might have written about differently in the notebook. There are a number of oddities that will occur. But, over time, things will begin to smooth out. The more you pay attention, the longer you keep the notes, the more sensitive you become, the more open your attitude develops, the more accurate and descriptive your out-of-the-blue perceptions will become.

As you begin to have more and more success, with more and more correct detail, such success in turn improves the ability; confidence is born out of conviction. In other words, your concepts of reality, or knowledge of how things work, is changing. It's a slow process, a long, drawn out procedure. But when you are finally well along the road, things will suddenly begin to accelerate. Remarkable changes will begin to occur. Don't fight them. It took many years to bury the talent, so it will take a lot of time to uncover it.

There are numerous other exercises which can be designed for your own use. Note the exact time (to the minute) you will arrive somewhere, before you leave; decide what the final total will be on the grocery bill before you shop; determine how much gasoline your car will take before you put the gas in; pick the date and time for the next rainfall; get someone else to participate and make bets on who will be closer— bet a picnic, a dinner, a movie, or who will pay for the groceries.

I could continue to present ideas here, but if you proceed with these few, you will be able to invent some of your own with which to practice. There are some basic rules to informal practice exercises, however, and I would be remiss if I didn't share them. They are necessary because they deal with the all-important idea of maintaining a proper structure.

Rules
a. Don't cheat. The less you know, the better.
b. Pay very careful attention to specific times and dates.
c. Don't throw anything (information) away.
d. Write everything down.
e. Take the exercises seriously.
f. Never stop practicing.

Whether or not it was due to integration, a change in personal belief about reality, or meditation, much of what I've said in this chapter has made a significant difference in my performance in the lab.

Whether you intend to pursue remote viewing or are only interested in becoming more centered, the listed exercises will always be a help. Regarding The Monroe Institute, it is a place, an experience, where anyone can take home something of value. Those who are interested can contact The Monroe Institute, 62 Roberts Mountain Road, Faber, Virginia 22938-2317 (ATTN: Director of Programs), or call: 804-361-1500/1501.

9
Early Examples

One of the best measures of progress can be found in comparisons of earlier targets to targets occurring in later years. At this particular point in the book, it would be appropriate to show examples of what remote viewing looks like in the beginning.

I should also say that the examples I present in this chapter are selected based on their success. It would be of little or no value to show total failures, other than as feedback for myself. However, you should be aware that there are just as many, if not more, fully documented *fall-flat-on-your-face* failures as there excellent examples. Failures in the view of scientist or observers do exist; there are many of them. The scientists keep track of the percentages and statistics, and these are in constant flux or change.

After my experiences with the first series of six targets at the SRI-International, and after I got through the rough and rugged beginning of my own initial efforts, my practice sessions quickly settled down into a routine, not unlike any other mode of learning.

In my opinion, learning to remote view is more a combination of *unlearning* and *learning*. On the unlearning side, we find ourselves trying to forget all of the rules and directions we've inherited from our peer groups, schools, teachers, and yes, even our parents. Many of the things we were taught about reality have no basis in fact. So, I look at one half of the problem as getting rid of the clutter in our minds about how things are supposed to be and replacing it with the things we eventually come to know. Part two is very similar to learning a language or learning to play a musical instrument. Except that, instead of French or German, it is the language of the mind. Instead of musical notes, it is the dance of mental perception.

Therefore, if it appears that I am skipping the earliest parts, the rote memorizing of grammatical rules, the constant playing of scales, etc., I probably am. You should know that common rote memorization is there. I had hundreds of my own symbols and thoughts logged and categorized before I could say I was in a learning mode. So the stage of viewing I am in now could probably be called the post-memorization stage, or post-beginning. In jumping to these earliest pieces I hope to show the thought process which was happening at the time. Don't mistake these examples as simple stuff, or beginner's material, as the required effort to produce it is as complicated as any effort in psychic functioning could be. Just understand that you will spend a long time, many months, climbing the long ladder to the remote viewing which someone might consider exceptional.

As I present each case, I will describe the circumstances surrounding the targeting and how it was accomplished. Then I will discuss the result and talk about it somewhat, so you can understand some of the problems, beginning expectations, and places where improvement can later be expected to occur. In all of the examples I present, you will have additional questions that will pop into your minds which may not be answered, at least not immediately. Please bear with me, and most of your questions will be addressed before you've reached the end of the book. (*Note*: I am deliberately avoiding the use of military related targets in this book, since the vast majority of military-related targets (99.9%) are still classified—application-type targets for obvious reasons. But since many of the practice targets were also geared along intelligence lines they too would be of high interest to the enemies of our nation.)

Example One

Target: A lighthouse on the central coast of Oregon.

Method of targeting utilized: A friend put a photograph (*Figure 6*) into a double-wrapped and sealed opaque envelope. The word *target* was written on the outside of the envelope and it was edge-sealed with scotch tape.

Remote Viewer: The author.

Result: Sketch with labels and single-word descriptions (*Figure 7*).

Discussion: First, note that the target stands out well from its surroundings. There is no competition here. It is obvious that the gestalt for mountains or mounds came booming through in a very clear way. They usually do, in the beginning. It is also obvious that there was a feeling for buildings. The light and dark squiggly line might be the defining line between the water and land, water and shore.

There are no red roofs. Where that might have come from is anyone's guess, but there a number of possibilities. I would suggest, based on my knowledge of remote viewing, that when I was targeted against this particular site, the image of buildings was one of squares in an open field, and perhaps my mind created an imaginary overlay,

Figure 6.

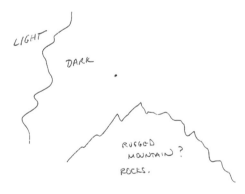

> Buildings — Square — White
> Fat Buildings
> Red Roofs.
> Feet — Font — Ford of
> Mounds.

Figure 7.

turning them into barns or farm buildings, which sometimes have red roofs. Farms and farm buildings usually have an overall gestalt that is read as "buildings in the open—buildings surrounded with open country, etc." This was a *forced* and therefore *unnecessary* conclusion. A major rule of remote viewing is *not to jump to conclusions*. It takes a while for all of the bits and pieces of data coming in to be sorted and collated. Jumping to a conclusion will almost inevitably be wrong.

The terms "feet-foot-foot of" is an interesting perception which defines an otherwise indescribable image of the water being at the "foot of" the mountains. Had I had more experience at this point in time, I might have eventually figured out the gestalt meaning for the images I was seeing mentally. There are many things that become apparent *after* you see what the target was. Keep notes on these items regarding perceptions.

Note the general lack of detail about the target. There is no mention at all of the light or lighthouse. The obvious ruggedness and isolation of the target should have come through as a gestalt as well, but for some reason was missed. The violence of the ocean water is also evident but never mentioned. Otherwise, it was a good target with a better-than-average outcome. At least it didn't turn into a shopping mall, a waterfall, or a burger joint!

Example Two

Target: Mount Rainier from Steven's Canyon Road lookout (*Figure 8*). An extinct volcano in western Washington near Puget Sound. Covered with snow and glaciers year-round.

Method of targeting: A post card picture placed within a double-wrapped and opaque envelope with the word *target* written on the outside.

Remote Viewer: The Author.

Result: Figure 9.

Discussion: Again, notice the major, overwhelming gestalt about the target came booming in. The "perspective," the "view," was outward, obviously toward a "horizon."

At first there was some confusion. I drew mountains as a horizon then changed it to a flat horizon. It could be that I was sensing the flat surface of the lake and mixing it with the overall view. It's sometimes hard in the beginning to differentiate between parts or portions of the whole in the overall gestalt. That's what a gestalt is—the overall or whole of the parts. So, it is difficult, if not impossible, for the beginning remote viewer to separate one element from another. It takes lots of time and persistence.

Figure 8.

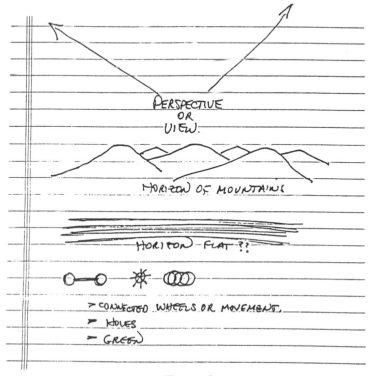

Figure 9.

Green is an overwhelming color pertinent to the target. But then, so are blue and white. Why weren't they mentioned? The beginning remote viewer will usually reject white as a color in the beginning, because white mentally signifies nothing or a lack of color.

The "connected wheels, holes, or movement" may be a perception of the automobile in the right-hand edge of the picture. It might have to do with the rounded or oval headlights, or perhaps the wheels.

Again, this target exemplifies overall gestalt images being picked up, but lacks the detail of the parts and pieces. There was no central mountain mentioned, no central feature presented during the course of viewing.

Example Three

Target: Stanford Shopping Center.

Method of targeting: An out-bounder team was dispatched to the Stanford Shopping Center (*Figure 10*), after generating a random set of numbers and obtaining a sealed opaque envelope with instructions from the lab director's safe. They drove around for fifteen minutes before opening the envelope. Every effort was made to insure there could be no contamination between the out-bounder team and the viewer. A pre-selected and agreed-upon time-window of fifteen minutes put the out-bounder team at the target when targeted by the viewer.

Remote Viewer: Referred to as Viewer #372 (the author).

Result: Figure 11.

Discussion: Notice the statement of "Under arch!? ...or arch form!?" Clearly, at the time, the overwhelming feeling or gestalt was that there was a prevalence of both arches and the forms of arches.

The drawing of the "dark & light yellow" and "disk shimmers" is possibly created by the preponderance of circular, globe-like lights or fixtures around each of the support poles. The "spoke type object" is how they are affixed to the support poles.

There is both overall gestalt as well as detail presented in this targeting effort. But, as with most beginning remote viewers, there is an inability to put things together in their appropriate formats or constructs.

The overall gestalt overwhelms the new viewer and punches through the mind like a waterfall, drowning out the detailed perspectives. Any details that do come through are usually disjointed or out of context, unrelated to each other.

Figure 10. (Provided by Dr. Edwin C. May.)

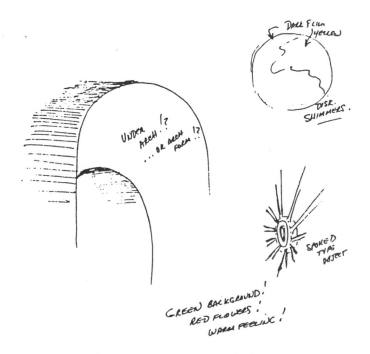

Figure 11. (Sketch completed by Author;
provided by Dr. Edwin C. May.)

Example Four

Target: A statue (See *Figure 12*).

Method of targeting: A remote viewing monitor opened an envelope containing the following coordinates and read them to the remote viewer: 37° 31' 21" North, 122° 21' 11" West. These coordinates were repeated twice. Neither the remote viewer nor the remote viewing monitor knew what was located at the coordinates prior to targeting.

Remote Viewer: The Author.

Result: Figure 13.

Discussion: General description of the surroundings is accurate. Not shown in the picture of the target is the fact that it actually does stand in a place overlooking a multi-lane road, a modern highway. It isn't as close to the water as depicted in the drawing; however, the positioning of water relative to the road is correct. The scale is what is not correct. Scale is not part of a general overwhelming gestalt.

There are multiple references to the word "view" or words essentially having like meaning, such as "lookout," "picture," "to see." It is a place where people stop to see. The drawing would indicate that it is a singular view and not a multiple view.

There is absolutely no mention of the statue. The primary target is not talked about. Why? Again, it would seem as if the overall gestalt here has blown out the details of the target. It is so overwhelming that it doesn't permit the beginning remote viewer to even process them.

37° 31' 21" North
122° 21' 11" West

Figure 12. (Provided by Ms. Martha Thompson.)

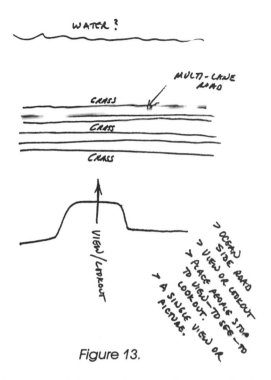

Figure 13.

These are only a few of the good examples from the beginning. What is clearly being shown in these examples is that, when remote viewing works, the gestalt or overwhelming message will always pierce through to consciousness. The focus of the beginning viewer's mind appears to be opened to its widest point. Like the lens of a camera in near-darkness, it is opened to gather in as much light as possible. This is probably a mental over-correction, a reaction to a new sensual input. We've never tried to deliberately use it before, so we open it up all the way and hope that it captures something. It does. The overwhelming gestalt comes blasting through.

This is good. It means we are on the right trail. It gives us some good supportive feedback that is positive in nature and drives us to a better or more refined information-collection process. Our beliefs are drastically changed by these early results. Suddenly we find that what we never knew was true in the past is proven true. We have a psychic ability, we really can see things with our minds. A whole new world of perceptive input is opened. Thoughts are suddenly kindled that we never knew we had within us. Bitten by the bug, we continue to practice and to try to better refine the result. And, it does get better.

10
Early Stages

In the first few years of practice, it became apparent that there were more than a few levels of remote viewing competency. In fact, it was almost as difficult determining the differences between levels of learning as it was trying to stay within them.

Discussions with other remote viewers, interviewers, scientists, and observers resulted in a determination that there were probably, at a minimum, four levels of perception. Some participants put this number at six. Whether there are four or six levels is not as material as determining which degree of detail or data falls within which category. The idea is to organize the different levels of complexity in order to understand how and when they are achieved.

From my own viewpoint, the number of levels eventually jumped to six from four and then quickly changed again to eight, then to nine as I gained more experience in defining the lines of demarcation.

However, at this point in the information I am presenting, I really don't want to confine the remote viewing to any levels. There will be plenty of time later, in which I will be able to notate the different levels as well as explain them in detail. It is my intention only to provide a very basic understanding of what occurs first and why.

In the simplest of terms, the original four stages can be loosely identified as follows:

Overall Gestalts

More than likely, all beginning perceptions are based on simple overall *gestalts*. Single-word descriptions are generally the rule at the entry level of remote viewing. The new remote viewer will say things in a general way and will usually shy away from specifics.

"The target is tall. It's wider at the bottom than at the top. The target is large, it's dark, it's mostly rounded. It has a specific pattern to it; it has stripes, it has interconnected circles, it consists of many block shapes, etc."

The new viewer will be unable to identify specifics about the target beyond these generalizations because of an inability to separate out the differences in detail. The discriminating circuits are opened to their widest setting. The overall *sense* of the target will be the major proponent reported. Whatever overwhelms the individual's mind is what s/he will report. The following, for example, are responses from entry-level remote viewers when the Eiffel Tower was a target:

"The target is high up." (No sketch)
"It's a waterfall." (*Figure 14*)
"I get uneven vertical lines." (*Figure 15*)

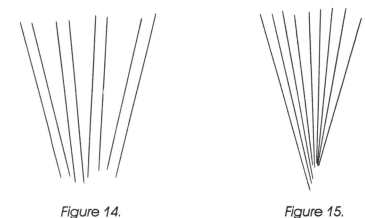

Figure 14.   Figure 15.

Feelings & Proportions

The remote viewer begins to perceive differences in proportions of the target's parts. In other words, a perception that there are dimensional differences within the target will begin to appear here.

"I feel like there are two ends of different sizes. There are black shapes overlaying lighter shapes. The target is heavier at one end than at the other."

The viewer will introduce *feelings* about the target at this point as well, becoming more personal in the descriptions. S/he will begin to interact with the target.

"It feels hard to the touch. It's colder than the ambient temperature. It's a rough surface. *Feels* more like metal than wood."

Since the things reported by the remote viewer will tend to be sensual inputs, s/he will have difficulty in connecting them to drawings or will attempt to draw the feelings. Such an example, using the Eiffel Tower, would be "There's a bumpy feeling to it." But the sketch usually drawn will have no immediate direct or apparent connection to the target. (See *Figure 16*.)

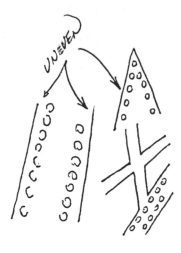

Figure 16.

Abstract Values

This is where things really begin to cook for the remote viewer. By this time the viewer is probably twelve months into the experience. The target will begin to take form and shape. It will become a dimensional object or place that fits into a picture in the remote viewer's mind. Portions of the target that were previously drawn in parts and pieces will begin to come together.

The remote viewer will begin to make abstract inferences about the target. "It feels like a park setting. I want to draw an organized garden around it. It's a form of sculpture. It's delicate and artful."

The drawings the remote viewer make will contain much more detail, and this detail will be innovative and connective; in other words, it will begin to make sense. Figure 17, still with the Eiffel Tower as the target, illustrates this stage.

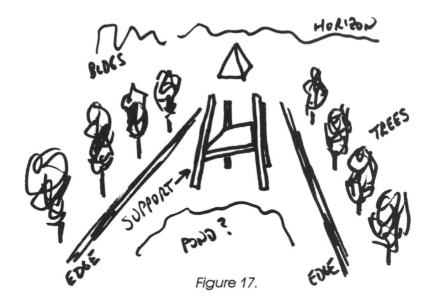

Figure 17.

Notice there is still insufficient information to name the target, but concepts about the target can be inferred from what is presented.

At this point in learning, some remote viewers will become highly agitated and frustrated with their inability to depict what they are sensing as input. Other modalities for displaying information about the target should be taken into consideration at this point in time, such as the use of clay to present a three-dimensional view of the target.

Dimension & Detail

This isn't the most difficult level of viewing to achieve, but it is one of the most valuable from a scientific or information-collection point of view. This is where the information derived can be identified, assessed, and evaluated. Replication at this point can be achieved, and records can be kept, in support of carefully established studies.

Full dimensional and spatial appreciation of the target is achieved. The size of the target in relationship to its surroundings is fully recognized. The details regarding the target become rational with regard to where and how they are integrated. *Details* are accurate and there is an overwhelming number of them associated to the target.

Concepts regarding the target become identifiable and are integral to the picture the remote viewer presents. With regard to the Eiffel Tower target I've been using as a representation, the viewer will begin to provide statements of fact that will have depth. "It's a tall structure that tourists visit. It provides an overlook or view of a foreign city. Its superstructure is constructed as an open grid-work of steel. It's old, but in good repair."

The advanced remote viewer may or may not specifically name the target in any given experiment. Only on the rarest of occasions can the viewer do so, especially if s/he is doing everything else right. Remember, the viewer is trying not to come to a conclusion. In most cases where a conclusion is reached, it will more than likely be wrong.

I have given a general overall or generic description of the beginning levels of remote viewing. Some say there is considerable cause and argument for breaking these down into sub-groups and then further into sub-groups of sub-sub-groups. However, there will always be difficulty in doing so. The reason is quite simple. No one ever responds within only one specific learning level.

Think of remote viewing as operating as a cyclic power system. At any given time the mind is cycling in or out of a different level of power. Only it's not operating power that we are talking about. We are talking about how long and how deep we have dipped into the information stream. This could be represented by Figure 18.

Physical Reality

Quantum Information Storage?

Figure 18.

Now, complicate this simple dipping in and out by applying additional rules.

Rule One
You will probably *sense* at different strengths with each dip. In other words, you gather different and varying amounts of data at the individual learning levels with each dip.

Rule Two
You are generating additional information that has no relevancy to the target information you're attempting to collect. In other words, your brain is generating chatter which has nothing to do with the target.

Rule Three
You are also dealing with natural human instincts and habits that inhibit you from doing the right thing, at least with regard to good remote viewing. These instincts or habits corrupt the information you're trying to process. Some of these are:

1. You feel you must absolutely reach a *conclusion*. That, however, is the last thing you should be trying to do.
2. You may be setting yourself up by *thinking* things must work the way you envision them as working, when they may actually work in an entirely different fashion.
3. Everything you are thinking must make *sense*. But in remote viewing, each part or piece of information is nothing more than just that, a piece of a larger puzzle. As in a jigsaw puzzle, different parts do not necessarily have to go together.
4. You feel you *must* be right the first time around; you must succeed or you will be a failure. This generates a fear of failure or an unnecessary requirement to perform. I believe the psychological need for success and recognition is probably one of the most instinctive drives we have. Don't be fooled by it. Control of the ego is essential to a balanced approach. It's the ego that gets more psychics in trouble than anything else.

Rule Four
There are major philosophic questions cropping up and they directly affect your belief and concepts of reality. Not addressing them, or rejecting a change in a belief or concept, will impact on the results of your remote viewing effort. There will be negative as well as positive effects based on the degree to which you are willing to be open, the extent to which you will be willing to change.

All of these considerations having been presented, the question that is foremost in most readers' minds at this point is "Can remote viewing really be taught?" The answer, surprisingly, is a resounding *yes and no.*

There have been numerous attempts at teaching remote viewing, by me as well as others. I cannot speak with authority about others or the effectiveness of their methods of instruction, but I can speak with authority about my own.

I have attempted to teach remote viewing to individuals as well as to groups. The group sizes have ranged in numbers from three to fourteen. The techniques I've used to teach remote viewing have varied. Some of these techniques were well-structured and intense, and some of them were less so, some of them worked and some of them didn't. The bottom-line result is that I no longer try to teach it, at least not within the last nine years.

After some years of effort, I have come to the conclusion that teaching remote viewing is possible, but only within an intense, well-designed, and well-structured methodology. If teaching is attempted, then the number of individuals should probably never exceed three. Out of those three perhaps only one, 33 percent, will finish the training schedule, and, even then, there is an even chance that one might not become a competent remote viewer. Competent, in this case, meaning able to replicate with a high degree of success and/or accuracy. More often than not, the student loses interest at the mid-way mark.

There are many difficulties and there are reasons for each of them. Most of them are minor, some of them are major. Some of the minor reasons might be:

Lack of endurance. I would not entertain the idea of teaching remote viewing to someone over a period of less than eighteen months. A more realistic period would actually be two years or possibly longer.

Frustration. There are long periods of frustration, where it seems like you are sitting on a plateau and can't go up or down. The student is unable to advance or improve. This is common to the learning process, but it becomes even more accentuated while learning to remote view. Figure 19 is a simplistic illustration of how the learning curve operates.

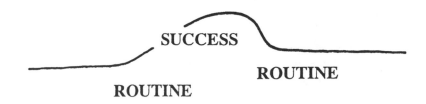

SUCCESS

ROUTINE

ROUTINE

Figure 19.

Ego. Almost without exception, the inevitable teacher-pupil conflicts will arise. There is nothing wrong with them, but they do have an impact. If they occur too frequently, the learning process breaks down.

Fear of the solo flight. The inability of a student to sever the dependence on the teacher and to step out and wing it alone. This is one of the most common reasons for failure. Why? Well, it's very much like learning to fly a plane. A large percentage of new pilots prove fully capable behind the stick—that is, up until the solo flight. When the instructor on whom they have come to rely says, "It's all yours," and then climbs out and walks away from the flight line, the student isn't long to follow.

Inability to change. The major reason for failure while trying to learn remote viewing is failure to meet *change* head-on. This includes change in philosophy as well as reality concepts. If you are not prepared to step through the doorway of change, you can't grow with the learning process. You can't smell and taste the fauna if you won't go into the jungle.

I've had numerous individuals tell me that change was the least likely problem with which they would have to deal. They assured me of this. But it proves to be the single greatest hang-up. There are many people I've met who consider themselves to be very close to the doorways of change. Most are metaphysically inclined. They are interested in the pursuit of knowledge and well-versed in the study of the philosophic cause or underlying nature of things. However, that doesn't mean they are willing to give up or alter their extant perception of how or why things work.

For example, I knew an individual who wanted more than anything else in the world to learn how to remote view. I've taken the liberty at this point to alter the personal description and delete specific dates or times, in order to prevent embarrassment. She was willing to expend a significant amount of time and energy in study, improvement, and learning all that she could about perceiving remote targets. Nearly two years into her training, somewhere between her second and third level, she began to develop physical manifestations of her philosophic realities. She began to actually get sick physically whenever it came time for a remote viewing lesson.

First, it was a chronic cold. This was then followed by a severe bout of the flu, followed by development of chest pains. The chest pains turned out to be stress-related. All of these problems directly interfered with her remote viewing lessons.

Prior to this period, there had been no evidence of any problem in the learning or any of the material being covered.

After the chronic nature of her physical sicknesses had reached a level where it was totally disruptive to learning, I met with her to discuss what the problem might be. The conversation quickly found its way to the source. It had to do with her religious belief. She was Roman Catholic. Some of the experiences she had begun having in her dreams—a direct result of changes to her philosophic beliefs, a direct result of seeing remote viewing work—were affecting the basic premise of her fundamental beliefs in God. From birth, she had been taught about God one way. There was no flexibility within her mind with regard toward who and what God might be as a concept of reality.

It became obvious to me that she was not addressing the philosophic challenge. In fact, to protect herself from further challenge, her mind created ways to keep her from receiving further input. I am almost convinced that she was making herself sick. Unconsciously perhaps, but nevertheless doing so.

So, while we may think we are totally open, we may not be. Each and every one of us may reach a time or place one day, where our minds would prefer to protect rather than expand. The only sure way of finding out, of course, is to meet the challenge head-on.

There is one additional problem which can develop during the teaching phase. It is one to which some teachers of the metaphysical don't pay much attention, whether they are teaching remote viewing, Qigong, T'ai-Chi-Ch'uan, Kung-Fu, or any other concept-altering reality. The problem can arise from the teacher-to-student responsibility that is sometimes totally ignored. The problem directly relates to philosophy, philosophic concepts, and belief constructs. If you provide to a student an experience which causes the destruction of a belief or concept, no matter how small, then as a teacher you must be prepared to provide a concept or reality to replace it. It must be reasonable, moral, and valid.

The effect which will occur if this is not done is what I refer to as the *Robe, Beads, and Sandals Effect*. In other words, a hole or vacant area is left in the person's concept of reality; and, without proper constructive guidance, he might fill it with almost anything.

I believe this is one of the primary reasons for the birth of so many cults in the '60s and early '70s. Many individuals wound up as lost souls, locked in the *Robe, Beads, and Sandals*, because they were unscrupulously taken advantage of at the most critical phase of their learning. It is grossly unethical for a teacher of truth to use the student's vulnerability for monetary, emotional, or social gain.

My current concept regarding the teaching of remote viewing is summed up with just a few words:

If you want to become a remote viewer, memorize a protocol and go for it. Practice, practice, practice, and then go out and practice some more. When you have unlearned enough of your old habits, false beliefs, erroneous concepts, and borrowed realities—when you've established your own concepts and developed a concrete foundation of self-generated beliefs—when you understand how and why things are real to you, and you've become accustomed to and welcome immediate or spontaneous change—then your remote viewing will be exceptional.

The art of remote viewing is like any other art or skill. Using music as an example, the protocol is the sheet of notes, and the practice makes the pianist. You've got to love the effort, the endurance that's required for the learning, in the same way the concert pianist loves his music. If you want to make a hobby of it, your remote viewing will be a hobby. If you want to do concert-level remote viewing, then you have to devote a lot of effort to getting there.

Contrary to current or popular belief, over the course of the Army project (17 years), there were probably a minimum of six or seven training methodologies which were designed, attempted, experimented with, and then either discarded totally, or discarded in part. No one method worked better than the others, and none were endorsed by SRI-International or the Cognitive Science Laboratory at Science Applications International Corporation.

There were various teaching methods that addressed how one thinks, that tried to help one recognize what was going on functionally within the mind, or which even attempted to address the philosophic changes in attitude or belief one might carry—but there is no evidence to date which establishes that it was possible to "make or change" someone into a expert psychic or a remote viewer.

Evidence collected within the research side of the project seems to indicate that whatever psychic talent you might have—what you have coming in the door—is what you are stuck with. But, like other talents—music or athletics—you can only take what you have and polish it, try to learn to control it. Some do very well at this and some never get any better. The range of psychic ability displayed by the Army participants over the 17-year history of the project supports this.

11
Getting To I Know

By the time I was into my third year of the remote-viewing experience, I realized that somewhere or some place in the beginning I had taken a high dive from the edge of a cliff and as a result was now stumbling around in a rather featureless canyon wondering where the path out might be. I was stuck somewhere between the *I believe* and the *I know*. I had simply *suspended my own disbelief* enough times that I no longer was sure what I believed. I certainly didn't feel as though I could say *I knew* anything. One can see in Figure 20 how it might relate to other experiences in life, especially those which might be considered religious in nature. It may not be the same, but the process may be similar.

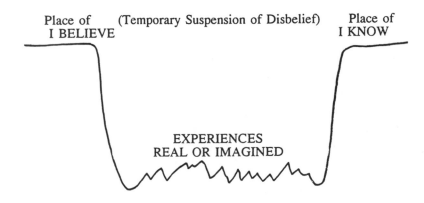

Place of   (Temporary Suspension of Disbelief)   Place of
I BELIEVE   I KNOW

EXPERIENCES
REAL OR IMAGINED

Figure 20.

What had actually happened was quite simple. Through no deliberate effort, I modified a sufficient number of personal realities or concepts, to unhinge my understanding of time/space, or at least the way I had been originally taught and understood it to work.

From the time of my NDE, I had been having spontaneous out-of-body experiences (OBEs). As I began experimenting with remote viewing and having some success, the OBEs increased in number as well as in significance. At the same time, other experiences began to occur which were a little more difficult to define but had just as great an impact. Why?

Think of your mind as a neatly fenced-in backyard. The limits or the reach of your imagination is dependent upon how far out you allow those fences to stretch. A scientist will argue those fences should never exceed that which can be proven through appropriately applied tests and protocols. However, if that were true, the Wright Brothers would never have left the ground. Remember the quote from Frank Herbert's *Heretics of Dune*; we don't need to know the molecular makeup of steel in order to make and use it. We only have to create a temporary mysticism that allows it to go together in the right proportions. Perhaps, with the right mysticism, we could have had a "pump" laser by the turn of the century, instead of waiting until the 1960s. In any event, if the word *mysticism* bothers you, just replace it with the word *creativity* or *imagination*.

As I said a few paragraphs earlier, I was also beginning to have *other* experiences. These are a little difficult to define in their early stages because they don't occur with regularity. There isn't any specific pattern to them; and if you aren't paying attention, you can miss them.

The only reason I was able to identify some of them myself was that I had developed the habit of keeping very detailed notebooks, in which I would keep all kinds of data that might seem relevant. Of course some of it wasn't, but I didn't know it at the time. I wish now that someone had directed me to do the note-keeping throughout the years. Unfortunately, no one did, so much of what I have experienced and learned is over the horizon forever. So. . .

Keep a notebook all the time. Write down anything that seems remotely important. You'll regret it if you don't.

An *other* experience which began somewhere in the beginning was what I call *flashes of spontaneous knowledge*. What does that mean? Small bits of data would jump into my mind when I wasn't expecting it. Perhaps when I would touch objects or people. It wasn't something that I wanted to happen; it just did. At first I would just write it down in my notebook and then forget about it, but then after a while I would begin to notice that I was getting feedback. The term *feedback* is important here because it probably has a great deal to do with the transmittal of psychic information. How or why it works I don't know, but it does.

I also recognized in the beginning that some of the information I was keeping in my notes turned out to be fallacious—it was wrong. Over time, I was able to determine that the wrong information was that which was more a conclusion than a statement of fact. As an example, I will relate something that happened long before I realized I was even capable of psychic functioning.

Very early on in my military career, I had a recurring dream (at the time it was a nightmare) in which I would always awake after being engulfed in a brilliant flash of white Light. It was so real that I was sure that it was an ominous warning about how I would die. For obvious reasons, the 1960s and early '70s were not the best of times to be in the military. With the recurring dream I was soon convinced beyond a doubt that I was going to die in a blast of fire; I was going out with a bang, probably a plane crash, or perhaps a direct hit with a rocket or mortar round. It was so real that I told people about it. I wanted it to be a matter of record. Of course it really unhinged my parents at the time, but in my ignorance I didn't realize that. This recurring dream began in 1964 and continued until my NDE in 1970, when I was engulfed in the white light I believed to be God. It was like coming full circle. My dream experience was absolutely accurate, but my conclusion wasn't.

This taught me a valuable lesson. I understood early on that the information is usually accurate; what we do with it, how we interpret it, usually isn't.

So, early into the first years of my remote viewing experiences, I began getting bits and pieces of data that I would write down in my notebook—data which at first had no relationship to what I was experiencing. As I improved in my observations of that data, however, coming to fewer conclusions and recording it as clearly and as cleanly as it actually came to me, I began to see interesting connections to later happenings. It was as if I were beginning to grasp how to control the input.

We have all had the *deja vu* experience. You are traveling up the East Coast for the first time and you stop in a roadside restaurant you have never been in before; on entering, you know all about the place.

You know where the bathrooms are located, you already remember what you are going to order, and even bits and pieces of conversation go through your head just prior to them happening. It's spooky. It's like you are getting the feedback before it actually happens.

Perhaps that is what psychic functioning is—a closed loop. We are simply sending ourselves the information which we will know at some future date anyway. If we produce a bit of information which has no connection to anything in the now, and then later observe the occurrence to which it connects, it gives us the appearance that we knew something we shouldn't have known, earlier than we should have known it. This makes sense if we ascribe to the reality that everything must occur in a linear fashion. But maybe it doesn't.

Another interesting experience began to occur with astounding regularity. I began having spontaneous lucid dreams. I would suddenly realize in the middle of a dream that I was sleeping, with the result that I would become mentally fully awake and alert, while remaining physically in the dream state. Being mentally alert and aware created the perfect scenario in which I would then seek out remote viewing targets which I might be working on and try to sneak a peek.

Initially, this turned out to be a particularly fertile area for collecting accurate information pertinent to a specific target. However, there were a number of times that the information I had collected wasn't right. I had to ask myself why would the remote viewing improve sometimes but not all the time? My conclusion was that it again had something to do with the interpretation. After a lengthy period of subjective observation, I noted that the lucid dream state was an exceptionally good place in which the imagination could operate. Therefore, it is also an exceptional area for the subconscious to communicate with the conscious mind. It was the ultimate theater or playhouse.

Understanding this, I was able to create scenarios of clarity, where my subconscious could communicate what it needed to, without conscious mental overlay or interference. The information improved, but the translation or interpretation didn't. I was still subject to human necessity. I still required conclusions, interpretations, and a linear reality construct. Since the old realities weren't allowing improvement, I began to search for new concepts.

Those of you out there who are open to having your concepts of time and space challenged without going through the long and exhaustive remote viewing, or *unlearning*, process, might have an easy way out. I say "might" only because I believe that most learning accomplished without an experiential input goes straight into the *I believe* column, instead of the *I know*. So there is no real change to the basic belief structure.

Nevertheless, I offer information for those who would like to try a short cut. There are two very good books which I heartily recommend for reading that discuss the topics of time/space as concepts. They are both written so that they will make sense, even to a layman with little or no physics background. They are:

Time Warps, by John Gribbin (Delacorte Press, 1979) and
Parallel Universes, by Fred Alan Wolf (Simon and Schuster, 1988).

Both of these books address reality from the standpoint of what it might be and how it might be constructed. Just as I have spent a number of years gleaning from the experience of remote viewing, these writers quickly conclude that reality certainly isn't what we are predisposed to believe it to be.

Concepts of how reality works are important to remote viewing because they have a direct bearing on where the information comes from and how it might be getting to a remote viewer. They also affect the allowances that might be made within the viewer's mind, the degree of temporary belief suspension, or how far a viewer is willing to go in order to accomplish psychic functioning.

Within the initial stages of psychic investigation, the functioning is viewed as fairly simple. It's based on a simple proposal for function and/or expectancy. However, these simple or initially expected rules quickly begin to fall apart under study and through experience.

One of the first exceptions to the established rule that goes out the window is that there is a difference between past, present, and future information. In the beginning, the remote viewer believes all three types are different and not quite equally accessible.

In the earliest part of the study of psychic functioning, an individual will assume that information is fixed in time, specifically the present, and that one is merely observing what is happening in real time.

It isn't difficult to understand that such an assumption is quite necessary at the outset in order to collect information on a real-time target. Real-time targets are the easiest to understand and to use in beginning a psychic study or learning program.

So persons newly introduced to psychic functioning focus on the here-and-now. As a result, they assume the information to be fixed in time/space in order to target it. This happened with me, as I am sure it will happen with others. Looking back, I can now see that the preponderance of my targets were real-time, or out-bounder types of targets. The targets were places that real people went to and these were targeted at specific times and dates in real time. The fact that remote viewing works and works well against real-time targets seems to support the assumption that information is fixed. But that is probably not how it actually works.

After the beginning remote viewer becomes comfortable with accessing real-time targets, things quickly begin to fall apart, at least conceptually. In other words, once you accept real-time psychic functioning as possible, you automatically begin to violate the assumption of fixed information. There are a number of examples that I can give to show this to be the case.

During the early '80s, I met with friends in California to run a series of out-bounder supported, real-time targets. In these, as previously explained, a specific person or team is targeted in real-time, as they go to a target location. My friends had agreed to help me develop my skills, a long and arduous process.

In this series there was a target that consisted of a brick yard. I had by this time, of course, become comfortable with the idea that you could collect information on real-time targets.

During the information-collection portion of the experiment, I drew a picture of the target which essentially consisted of a series of cubes, squares, and rectangles, with blocks or sections of horizontal and vertical crossed lines. I called them "cubes within cubes" and "blocks within blocks." And literally, that was all that I could perceive.

My friend, acting as the experiment monitor at the time, pressed me to expand on my perceptions. I guess he felt that it was too simple a representation of the target. I pressed on for some time trying to collect additional information but could perceive only squares within squares.

Finally, toward the end of the session, after I was pressed very hard for additional information, a picture of a metal girder-like tower with pennant flags popped into my mind and I drew this in the middle of the block figures on the paper. I remember being angry about it. "There. . .are you satisfied? That is all there is to the target."

After recording the information collected in the experiment, the out-bounder returned and we all then traveled back to the target to provide me with my feedback. I remember feeling very good about finding out that it was indeed a brick yard. While there, my friends suggested that I walk among the stacks of cement building blocks and cubes of bricks in order to get a better feel for the target as a whole. Of course I was somewhat disappointed that there was no girder-tower with pennant flags and felt that I had allowed my friends to press me to the point of invention.

I suppose we must have looked a little strange to the owner/manager, meandering through his yard, fondling his bricks. He slowly approached us, nervously asking what we were doing. This of course resulted in introductions all around and a full explanation of the experimental process. He was quite interested. I showed him a copy of the drawing which I had done back at my friend's house and his eyes lit up with delight. He quickly went into his office and, rummaging through a drawer, produced a black and white photograph of the brick yard on its opening day three years earlier. There, in the middle of the photo, was a crane with pennant flags. I remember one of my friends smiling and saying, "It looks as if you slipped in time."

In my own mind, time suddenly became something different from what I had always thought it to be. My mind flooded with *what if* questions. Did I slip in time? If so, why? Did I draw the tower with flags as a self-fulfilling prophecy, simply because the owner/manager had showed me the picture? If that were true, then didn't that mean we could see our own future? Or, did we simply send the information backward in time to ourselves after the event happened?

I know that I temporarily went a little crazy, trying to put it all into an acceptable perspective. I unfortunately blew the majority of the remaining targets in our planned series.

It has taken many years, but I believe that I now know why it happened.

As Fred Alan Wolf states throughout his book, *Parallel Universes*, reality and existence are not mutually identifiable. Like the atom in quantum physics, in order to study one you have to eliminate the other. He also states, "Information passes from the past to the present and from the future to the present." Over the years, through the remote viewing experience, I have come to know this as truth.

Quantum waves do travel in both directions through time. Therefore, in the fullest sense of the word, existence becomes a sum of *all* information. Like a great sea with far-reaching shores. It's a place where *all* possibilities exist simultaneously. There is no past, no present, and no future—there just *is*. To define our place within it, we require a tool some call cognitive perception.

Perception is a process that allows us to place ourselves within a specific point of time and space by observation; cognition allows us to understand its dimensions. In simpler terms, we collect information from the past and the future, combine it with what we have in a temporary historical reference (or what we call memory), and our minds then tells us where and when we are. Being psychic is simply being more sensitive to the sea around us. It's simply a method that allows for additional sense of being.

When I first began dealing with these issues in my own mind, it made me quite nervous. Such concepts seemed to seriously modify, or in some cases even attack and destroy, basic beliefs regarding such subjects as predestination, free will, and God's influence. These concepts implied fixed futures, parallel universes, and an overall or grand design, doing away with innovative or changing possibilities. But, over time, I've come to understand that the effect is actually quite the opposite. These concepts have reinforced my understanding of what free will really means and has expanded my concepts of the great engineer we call God. In shorter terms, I now have an even greater miracle to ponder.

In our desire to seek time travel, we have failed to understand that *we* are the ultimate time machine. Our consciousness is one with and a part of the sea, and through the process called life we pick the space and place in time in which we desire to participate, to exist. Through the tools of perception and cognition, we mold and shape our concept of reality and make reality what it is.

This is a scary concept for some people because it implies that we must hold a great deal more responsibility for our acts while traveling (living) than we might have previously been willing to accept. It also implies that we are totally in control of our trip, the good, the bad and the ugly. What ultimately happens to us is of our own making, our own fault, not God's.

An even better example of how time and space become liquid within the bounds of remote viewing happened a couple of years later. Hartley and Ken, two very close friends of mine, participated with me in a psychometry experiment in a lab in Maryland. In psychometry, a target object is held or touched, and the resulting information is then produced relative to the targeted object.

In this case, the object was put inside a box, approximately half the size of a shoe box, and was subsequently wrapped with tin foil and edge-sealed with tape. The object was selected and wrapped by someone who did not participate in the rest of the experiment, thus creating a blind target for Hartley, Ken, and me.

The target box was placed in the center of a table in a room, and each of us (isolated one from the other) was allowed to enter the room and touch it. We were not allowed to move it or to pick it up. I don't know how it was touched by my two friends, as we were only allowed to approach it separately, but in my turn I simply placed my hand flat on the top surface and concentrated on what came into my mind.

We then separately produced written statements about what we thought the object was within the box or what it might represent. We were also encouraged to do drawings if we felt they might be appropriate or important to the production of information.

My friend Hartley produced a beautifully detailed page of information that described a Native American scene from the 1700s. It centered on dancing around a fire, the celebration of a successful hunt, and was rich in detail regarding the shape and size of the stone-circled fire and the ceremony.

Ken, on the other hand, while also describing a Native American scene, focused on the grinding of grain and preparation of food with stone-shaped tools. His descriptions were apparently from a time period much earlier than Hartley's.

My own input was one of a small stone structure on an open plain. I described a frigid place, quite open and harsh in the winter, but warm with a sea of grass in the summer. I had an overwhelming feeling of a tiny farm somewhere in the Midwest. A stone, single-room building, with a sod roof.

What is interesting here is that there was some similarity to all three of our perceptions—we all three said something about *stone*, a stone-circled fire, a stone-grinding implement, and a small stone structure. All three descriptions were of different time periods.

When we opened the box, we were not so surprised to find the target to be a blackened and smooth-shaped stone. The stone came from a collection of early implements that had been found in a field in Kansas.

What was learned from this experiment?

I learned that objects have histories. That throughout their existence, they contribute to reality. I learned that this connection to reality and time/space cannot be destroyed, even when the object is altered or changed. I learned that time, while incredibly important as regards focus, in no way restricts us with regard to collecting information. But, most importantly, I learned that the only limits to time and space as regards remote viewing were going to be those which I might create in my own mind.

There was one other, perhaps less obvious, lesson from this single experiment in psychometry, but I didn't realize it at the time. It actually took some years for it to sink in. For some unknown reason, each of us had chosen a different time period for which to target the blackened stone. Why? How could we have known which time period the others might have chosen? Were we interacting on some non-cognitive level?

Back then, there was no way I could know it, but because of that and other experiences, I had already begun to understand that all humans, perhaps all living things, share at least a non-cognitive inner-connection. Beginning as a small pin-prick of light at the end of a long dark tunnel, I began to focus on the possibility that all living matter might be in some way strung together, with many tangent points, one after the other. That on some other level, perhaps through some form of quantum bridging, we were interacting and reacting to a dance called life. I began to think that maybe we were all partners in the formation of reality, that we all have an equal share in its formation. Suddenly the levels of responsibility were jumping higher with leaps and bounds.

Finally, one other significant change became apparent. Somewhere in the experiences that were going on in my reality, I stopped caring about proving anything to anyone. I suddenly acknowledged that I *knew* remote viewing worked, psi-functioning worked. In fact, I expected it to. So, many of my older concepts of time and space simply withered on the vine and died. The path of my adventure had changed direction, and there was a new horizon to face.

12
Remote Viewing at TMI

God's definitely *the* Master Engineer to have created this, I thought, as I gazed out at the foothills of the Blue Ridge Mountains. It was just a few minutes past 6:00 A.M.., on a cool morning in October 1983. I remember the sky as being crystal clear and baby blue, except where the slight pink of early morning still lingered on the eastern horizon.

I had a truly advantageous view, too—point blank, into the base of the nearest mountain where it rose out of a multi-colored forest less than half a mile away. Standing framed and centered in a large open window, I was still awakening from a deep sleep. I remember stretching in that early morning light, my hands up over my head, and taking in deep breaths of fresh air, feeling the cool morning breeze on my skin. There were even song birds in the limbs of a tulip poplar standing nearby, birds not yet gone for the winter, now just around the corner.

Now why would I remember that morning so much more vividly than all the others in so many other places? The events centered around a short string of those mornings helped to anchor my mind to that time in my life. It was one of those unique moments in one's life where you can say something really spectacular happened.

I've selected this time period deliberately in order to share what kind of experiences I was having after five years of playing at remote viewing. The events that occurred those days in 1983 bring together and coalesce all of my experience gathered over the five years prior.

In the beginning, in 1979, there were paranormal events which I had previously experienced and which I had already buried away. Buried so effectively that they no longer existed. I had no room within my consciousness for them. They were events that didn't fit within the well-ordered and structured belief concepts that had been carefully and methodically constructed for me over most of my life time.

I know that it might sound as though I am trying to shirk responsibility for how I might have been thinking prior to 1979, but I'm not. I am only trying to establish that prior to that time I most assuredly had been lazy enough to have allowed others to formulate, teach, and orchestrate how and what I might have accepted as truth or reality. In fact, until 1979 my mind had remained a fenced-in stockade, a place controlled by other elements in my life. It was like an egg, hard-boiled against outside influence as if encased in steel and reinforced concrete, defending against almost any opening form of experience exterior to it—especially any kind requiring change.

Now that I look back, I can say with honesty that even the NDE that occurred in 1970, an event which severely cracked the hardened crust of my reality, had only caused the stiffening of my resolve and a short but hectic few months of damage control. Perhaps I was unsuccessful in completely burying the experience, but there were sufficient Band-Aids that I no longer had to deal with it. I ignored the implications. It was easy. Culture, peer-group belief, church, and even state provided me with ample ammunition to ignore the outside effect. At least it made me feel as though I was successful in dealing with it. My surrounding support system assisted in the defense, providing the necessary reasons to reject anything that might threaten its continued existence.

Unknown to me, of course, the crack had never healed. In fact, it was stretched and widened by time. By 1979, I was nearing the process of forced hatching. My mind was preparing to pop open, quite suddenly and without warning. I was about to be shoved feetfirst through doorways of change. I would enter a region from which I would never again look back. I've already talked about 1979 and its profound effects in a previous chapter—now it's 1983 and a lot had happened since then.

As I previously said, this was one of a string of days all pretty much the same. After a hot shower and leisurely breakfast at a local bed and breakfast, I would drive the four miles of curving back roads to The Monroe Institute Laboratory. Located in the picturesque hills near Nellysford, Virginia, it is a building approximately fifty-by-thirty feet, which is half-buried in the ground. It was there that I and the Institute's founder, Robert A. Monroe, and others had begun a series of experiments some months earlier. These experiments would prove to be some of the most interesting remote viewing that I had yet done.

Back in those days, inside the Institute lab, there was a small control room adjacent to a ready room, with a wall separating them from a larger room or more general experimental area. In addition to two doors into the area, there was a fixed glass window through which an observer could see into the larger open area from the control room. During 1983, the remote viewing experiments in which I participated were all held inside the control room and the ready room. The monitors, or people controlling the experiments, were located in the control area and were able to carry on conversations with me by way of headsets and microphones. All microphones could be switched on or off only in the control room area. If they were switched on, then they would automatically record on a cassette tape deck. If they were switched off, they were essentially dead and would not record any conversation at all. During any experiment, they would tape all that I might say, but I was never privy to their discussions unless they enabled a microphone to ask a specific question.

While in the ready room I could either sit up in an easy chair or lie down on a waterbed which was warmed with temperature controls. I liked the old ready room that we used in those days. It was small, with room sufficient to hold only the chair, bed, and a small table with a lamp. It was also warm and comfortable, being heavily insulated by earth on one side and having heavily sound-proofed walls on the other three sides. When the light was switched off there was absolutely no light visible inside, so it was easy to fall into a relaxed state. When they constructed the room, they had installed seals along the edges of the door, so that even the little light around the door frame could not enter. This made it easy to imagine or conjure up almost any scene that might come into one's mind.

During much of the remote viewing we did over those months of time, I was hooked up to two of the many machines within the lab, or monitoring area. One was designed to monitor galvanic skin response, and the other provided a measurement of overall body voltage with accompanying plus or minus polarity shifts. I don't recall at this point which of my fingers or toes, legs or arms had been wired, only that they did have wires coming from them. I do have a memory from earlier on of being concerned about having them tangle, or of one shorting the other out. This, of course, was not possible the way they were taped, although at the time I didn't know that.

Prior to my being made comfortable in the ready room, Robert Monroe and his assistant always showed me a double-wrapped and opaque envelope which had been edge-sealed with tape. Each time they did this, they informed me that my target for that specific session was contained within the envelope and that the envelope would be in Robert Monroe's left shirt pocket until the beginning of the experiment. The targeting methodology would not be presented until just prior to actual remote viewing.

I had no idea at the time who had selected the target or how it had been selected, nor was it particularly important to me. We had been experimenting in the lab for over six months, and I had become both comfortable with and very much used to the numerous mechanisms for targeting.

After I was hooked up to the monitoring equipment and sealed inside the room, they would switch off all the lights in my area and allow me to relax for a period of approximately ten to fifteen minutes. This relaxation period allowed the after-images on the inside of my eye lids to disappear and also provided me with a period of time in which my mind was able to slow down and become more at ease.

I must digress at this point and talk about what kind of experiments we were interested in performing at the lab. Six months earlier, I had suggested to Bob that, if we were to work together, we might be able to develop an individualized tape using his hemispheric-synchronization techniques which might improve my remote viewing capability. I wasn't sure that it would, but there was no way to know unless we tried. After discussing it on a number of occasions, we decided to begin a series of experiments that would produce such a tape. Not only that, but we would attempt to also harness what I had previously been experiencing as spontaneous OBEs, bringing them under control, and then attempt a series of targets using remote viewing as well as OBE techniques to collect information. A formidable task which eventually led to a concentrated thirteen-month effort before we were through.

Once we had agreed to attempt such a test, we developed a priority list of goals, with one hopefully supporting the other. These were:

Goal One: Develop a special Monroe Hemi-Sync tape solely for my own use, which would be specifically designed to encourage the appropriate mental state to support remote viewing.

Goal Two: Target a series of places, objects, or things using remote viewing technology while under the influence of the tape to determine if there would be improvement in the degree of information collected.

Goal Three: Use the Monroe Hemi-Sync tape techniques in an attempt to harness my spontaneous OBE states, permitting control-led out-of-body targeting of the same or like targets.

Although it appeared the simplest of the three goals, Goal One took approximately four months of effort; but we eventually suc-ceeded in developing a series of Hemi-Sync frequencies on a tape that would enable me to enter or re-capture what appeared to be the same window or mental state that allowed for successful remote viewing.

How do you know when you've been successful in achieving this window? Aside from the obvious (good remote viewing with con-sistency), there are a number of ways. In the case of the window as produced by the Monroe tape, the following applies:

1. The state of mind always *feels* the same. I've tried explaining this *feeling* to a number of people and it is difficult at best. The closest I've ever been able to come is to say that it is like trying to balance on a fence. Only in this case, once you have achieved the balance, to recognize it is to destroy it. The tape experience is to *feel* in balance without having to recognize it. It's a place of being.

2. The tape produced some noticeable side-effects. One was the opening of my sinuses. I would then sound as if I had a bad cold whenever I was doing a remote viewing using the Hemi-Sync tape. Why? I haven't the foggiest notion. It was a harmless side-effect.

3. The bio-measuring devices would show total relaxation similar to the hypnogogic state. There was always a physical sensation of partial paralysis.

4. While brain-wave state wasn't monitored in those days, my sense of it was that I was producing a predominantly alpha wave state, with some delta. This has proven to be the case in later years, where brain monitoring was performed.

Another noticeable effect from the use of the tape was an imme-diate and significant reduction in the *cool down* period, the period of time necessary to get one's mind-set ready for a remote viewing experiment. Remember, the cool down period was pretty much of a problem in earlier experiments. I found that as we progressed through the months using the Hemi-Sync tape, I was able to reduce the cool down period from well over an hour, sometimes two, to just a few minutes. This was probably the most significant result from use of the tape which Bob had developed for me, one for which I am the most appreciative.

In fact, as we progressed through the thirteen months of remote viewing and OBE exercises, the tape became less and less a requirement. I had simply to remember what it sounded like to replicate the mental state necessary. So it is my opinion that, through constant and repetitive use of the Monroe Tape, I had trained my mind to recapture the remote viewing window whenever necessary.

The success of Goal Two can be measured by the remote viewing that developed during the remaining months. Of the scores of targets we attempted in the lab, approximately 50 percent could be termed successful and 50 percent failures. Of those we concluded successful, a number were truly outstanding. These two are presented here for comparison.

Target One

After I took my place in the ready-room and went through a ten-minute cool down period under the Hemi-Sync tape, the interviewer who was sitting with Bob in the control area opened the envelope and read the following coordinates:

38 degrees, 37 minutes, 28 seconds North
90 degrees, 11 minutes, 14 seconds West

The following conversation is taken directly from the verbal transcripts during targeting. (**Int** represents the interviewer, and **Joe** represents the Author.)

Joe: The surface, seems it would be an edge of a V or an edge of an angle.

Int: OK. Back up from it a little bit so you can see it better.

Joe: Smooth flowing arc.

Int: Describe your position, your perspective, as you look at this smooth flowing arc.

Joe: Sitting about 300 feet off the ground. Looking directly at it. It goes—arcs across left to right. Feels like I'm getting hit right in the face with bright reflected sunlight. See some kind of metallic bolts—not bolts—more like dimples in metal.

Int: All right. Move to the top of this thing that you see and give me the compass from standing on top of this thing that you see.

Joe: Ok. Runs north to south. Looking north I see old buildings, looking northeast I see a railroad bridge, a trestle bridge across a river, east there is some industry, I see some smokestacks of industry type building; southeast, a heavily industrialized area with overpasses and bridges. They are further down the river. South, main roads, thoroughfares, some buildings, small; southwest, a stadium or something. I see an enclosed field, large round building. Tall buildings around it, some exposed—girders, like they are under construction. Due west, major city, tall buildings, roads running east and west. In the west there is also a church in the foreground, an old church. Northwest, tall buildings.

Int: All right. Describe the surface that you are standing on.

Joe: Concrete. A big pad of concrete. White, hard. I don't think it's marble, but it's very smooth finished concrete. Sense walls, off to my left, I can't tell if they're walls or if they're in the ground.

Figure 21. St. Louis Arch.

Int: OK. I need to know your position, your relative perspective, position again.

Joe: I can't tell. Every time I get close to the target, I just get this overwhelming sweep of reflected metal. I feel like I'm on it and under it at the same time.

Int: That's typical. Let's back away from it so that you can describe it to me.

Joe: It just arches overhead.

Int: Move further away from it.

Joe: I feel like I'm in St. Louis, at the St. Louis Arch.

Target Two

Again, after I relaxed in the dark ready-room for approximately ten minutes, listening to the Hemi-Sync tape, the interviewer began the session.

Int: Relax now. Focus your attention—focus solely and completely on

**44 degrees, 35 minutes, 26 seconds North,
104 degrees, 42 minutes, 54 seconds West.**

and describe your perceptions to me.

Joe: I'm at a very huge pile of rocks. Broad up-and-down vertical lines.

Int: All right. As you look at these up-and-down vertical lines, describe your perspective, your position relative to this.

Joe: Standing at the base of something. I'm looking up at vertical lines. Grays and blacks. Mixed color.

Int: OK. Let's back up away from it so that you can describe it to me.

Joe: A little bit wider at the base than at the top, thick heavy stone. Black-gray, and vertical lines.

Figure 22. Devil's Tower.

Int: Now back up some more now, so that you can get some change in aperture to your perspective.

Joe: Park-like setting. It's that Devil's thing, the Devil's Tower.

As you can see from the pictures provided, the accuracy of the descriptions was phenomenal. There were many others which were not quite so phenomenal. So even though remote viewing is somewhat unpredictable, these examples were selected to show how detailed it can become when everything clicks.

Why would someone spend so much time trying to expand on a talent that was so undependable or so unpredictable? Well, it's unfortunate that we are unable to climb inside each other's head. It would provide a quick and simple solution for the problem of having to try to explain everything that was going through mine, especially during these two example sessions.

The dialogue shown above implies that I was "seeing," in every sense of the word, the St. Louis Arch and its complete environment, or at least out to about ten city blocks, and the Devil's tower. In actuality, I wasn't *seeing* anything. Instead, my mind was filled with an assortment of inputs, everything from scenes of old movies to make-believe, all twisted together and run like a quick-moving film clip, end to end.

The decision to report with a statement that ". . .it feels like I'm getting hit in the face with bright reflective sun light. . ." didn't come from it actually happening. Instead, it was an amalgamation. A gluing together of many bits of information all rushing through my mind at the same time. A *feeling* of heat, warmth to my front, a sense of something bright, a *mental* flashing off and on, an encrypted mental vision of large and small squares changing places.

Never seeing a full picture, the remote viewer pieces together the finished product from a splatter of input that comes rapid-fire, over and over again. Bits and pieces scattered through the mind like residue from an exploded planet. Almost an impossible function of learning, yet it still works in a big way sometimes. At least enough to keep this viewer interested.

There are readers out there who are already saying "Coordinates! Heck. Why not just give him a picture of the target?" There are a number of reasons for using coordinates for targets, reasons which are addressed in the next chapter—Targeting—but it would be only fair to address the question here, at least in part.

Using the St. Louis Arch as an example, the area described in the session is roughly a five-by-five-city-block area. This is also roughly about the same amount of area on the ground which is represented by coordinates to the second. It's actually a much larger area. In the case of the target pool, from which the St. Louis Arch was chosen, the same set of coordinates are used for the old church, the St. Louis stadium, the old trestle bridge, the river boats along the shore, a statue in the plaza across from the Arch, etc. In other words, the coordinates to the second are not that precise. Especially in a crowded city target environment. There are nine separate targets in the pool which are all targeted through means of the same set of coordinates. Interestingly, however, the wrong target is never described. Only the *intended* target is the center of focus. Of course you have to hit the target in the first place.

At one point, while using coordinates, I was accused of having memorized all the major coordinate intersections in the world. A ridiculous notion. Especially when you then add the time and date factor. As an example, someone might know the coordinate for Lakehurst, New Jersey. But given the date May 6, 1937, they may still not know that was when the great airship *Hindenburg* crashed and burned. It may be especially difficult when the date specified is placed within a double-wrapped and sealed envelope.

What are the coordinates for your house, the place you work, the center of your home town? Most of us don't know. The coordinate system was used for a brief period in remote viewing for entirely different reasons. This is further explained in the next chapter, which deals with different targeting methodologies. For now, please accept coordinates as a reasonable targeting method.

Goal Three—going to a target in the out-of-body state—proved to be the most elusive of all. But, even so, we were eventually able to accomplish it. There was a lot of difficulty with this phase of the effort while at The Monroe Institute, but not for any of the reasons which may first jump into one's mind. It had mostly to do with me.

The out-of-body state is even more elusive than the remote viewing window. In trial after trial, we worked our way closer and closer to it. Near the end of the effort, approximately the tenth month, I was able to capture the same feeling that I had encountered numerous times before, but which had occurred only in a spontaneous way.

The first out-of-body experience actually began with a tingling sensation throughout my body. Recognizing it as similar to previous experiences, I allowed myself to relax into it. This encouraged the tingling sensation to rise in amplitude, and it soon became an electrical charge that began to pass up and down my body. I felt as though I was beginning to sway back and forth, side to side. As the swaying motion increased, I began to feel as though I could roll over without physically moving. Instead of a sensing that I was rolling over, there was a separating sensation, like peeling a label from a jar. This sensation continued until it finally culminated in what felt like a distinct *pop*, and I suddenly found myself floating in the air.

Through the effort, when I had finally felt success, I become so excited that I was immediately slammed back downward and into my body. The excitement itself had grounded me. As it turned out, it took a number of preliminary attempts and many more weeks before I could control the excitement sufficiently to stay out. Once out, it took additional weeks and quite a few more trials before I was able to stray from the ready-room itself. Throughout this period, I was spending an average of six or seven days trying to integrate each of the experiences I was having.

Toward the end of the thirteen-month period, I was successful in leaving the ready-room only twice to reach a target. In neither case was I able to recapture the target in the remote viewing mode.

While there was a partial failure in achieving Goal Three, there can be some information shared concerning the differences of information perceived via the out-of-body state versus remote viewing.

In the out-of-body state:

1. You arrive at the target just as if you had gone there physically.

2. You know that your consciousness is totally at the target location and where you left your physical body is somewhere else.

3. You see objects and people at the target location, just as if you were seeing them with physical eyes. Both animate as well as inanimate elements are seen with such pristine clarity that you can actually discriminate molecular movement within them. For example, looking at a table is like looking at an energy field in the shape of a table, with billions of component parts or elements contained within the energy field moving or interacting with each other.

4. Seeing into the next room requires having to pass through a wall, which feels something akin to pushing your body through a veil of Jell-o.

In the remote viewing state:

1. You access the target location with your mind only.

2. Consciousness is still very much located with the physical body and you are always aware of this.

3. Collection of data in the remote viewing state is in bits and pieces, over a considerably longer time. Translation of the data is necessary, which in most cases is far more difficult than just seeing something. However, the amount of data available seems to be far greater. It's hard to see if someone is East European versus West European in the out-of-body state. In remote viewing, the information seems to be more readily available.

As it turns out, the out-of-body state is far more difficult to achieve with any regularity. At least that was the case with me. At the time I assumed that there was a severe departure of pathways at this point, with remote viewing leading off in one direction and out-of-body in the other. I felt I needed to make a choice of which to follow. I chose remote viewing for the following reasons:

1. Even with the data coming *in pieces*, I felt it was easier to achieve the necessary mind window in remote viewing.

2. At the time, I felt that remote viewing was less esoteric, therefore less threatening.

3. There seemed to be more in the way of applications with remote viewing, especially with regard to science and the establishment of protocols of study.

Of course in the end, none of the above reasoning mattered. As it turned out, I just chose a different path to the same ballpark.

13
Targeting

In the earlier years, the targeting methodology was simple. An *out-bounder*, one of the participants of the experiment, was usually targeted at a specific place and time. There was no rule initially about how many out-bounders were necessary or how many could be at the target site together. However, there were other requirements which had to be met. Some of these were:

1. The viewer wasn't allowed to have any contact with the out-bounder or out-bounder team until they returned from the target site.

2. The out-bounder team had to be at the target location at the time specified. For example, if the remote viewer was looking at a time window of 9:30 to 10:00 A.M., then the out-bounder team had to be at the location for that thirty minutes of time.

3. The out-bounder team was required to give their impressions of the target site while there, to provide comparative information later, usually during the judging, after the termination of the remote viewing.

4. The out-bounder team was asked not to discuss the target with the remote viewer until the remote viewer had a chance to physically see the target.

5. The out-bounder team was not allowed to discuss the target(s) with anyone other than the viewer and interviewer during the debriefing at the target.

As you can see, the rules were pretty basic, as they probably should have been at the time. The actual out-bounder scenario would usually go as follows:

The out-bounder person or team would leave the remote viewing area thirty to forty-five minutes prior to the actual scheduled start of the remote viewing session. The out-bounder team would then go to the person holding the target packages. This person wasn't part of the overall project, but was usually someone who was providing safekeeping for the envelopes which contained the pre-selected targets. The out-bounder team would present a random number sequence, usually three, five or seven digits, and the keeper of the targets would pull that specific packet from the target pool. Once the out-bounder team had the packet they would go to their car and proceed to drive around within the target area. In those days the target area was the San Francisco Bay area, a large area when you consider the many possible targets between San Francisco Airport and Mountain View. Twenty minutes prior to the beginning of the designated remote viewing period, the out-bounder team would open the target packet which would provide them with driving directions to the target and the target's name. The packet also contained suggestions on how the team might want to interact with the target, such as: target is a bowling alley—bowl a game; target is a graveyard—put hands on tombstones; target is a toxic waste storage area—walk around the area; etc. After spending the allotted time at the target, the out-bounder team would return to the remote viewing area to pick up the remote viewer and interviewer. The remote viewing team as well as the out-bounder team would then return to the target, driving down the same roads and making the same turns the out-bounder team made. Once they arrived, the out-bounder team would describe what they did while at the target.

The process sounds more complicated than it really is. Most people ask, why not take a picture and just return with that and show it to the remote viewer? Well, in the beginning that might have sounded quite reasonable, but, since no one could really be sure where the information was coming from, it wasn't used.

The first assumption might be that the information the remote viewer produced came from the target, but there was no way of knowing how. Did it come from the minds of the out-bounder team? Perhaps it came from the target itself. Or, maybe it came from the mind of the remote viewer when he was later taken back to the target for feedback. Early efforts suggested all three and then some. The remote viewer would report data the out-bounder team reported they were feeling, seeing, or acting out. The viewer would also report items about the target which were not apparent to the out-bounder team on the first or second trip, but discovered later during judging.

Additionally, there would always be some form of abstract data which took considerable study of the target to dig out.

After a few hundred local out-bounder targets had been attempted, a question was raised as to how distance might affect the result. So out-bounder teams were sent to targets out of state. I participated in a number of experiments where the targets were located in different states or outside of the United States' borders. Maryland to Virginia, central Virginia to Washington, D.C., Virginia to Italy, Virginia to Germany, Virginia to California, California to Virginia, Virginia to Panama, and many other combinations. Of course, while attempting the long-distance viewing, the feedback was provided by photographs of the target location with which the out-bounder teams returned. I'm not sure whether it was the great expense of sending the out-bounder teams to those vacation paradises or the grumpy mumbling of remote viewing subjects who weren't getting to go for their feedback that forced a change in the targeting mechanism. Perhaps both, as well as a desire to change the targeting methodology in order to determine what the carrier might be. In any event, a cheaper and more expedient way of targeting needed to be found.

Coordinate Remote Viewing or CRV seemed to fit the requirement. This technique was pioneered by SRI-International and one of their exceptional remote viewers, a psychic by the name of Ingo Swann (author of *Natural ESP*, a Bantam Book, July 1987).

At the time, it was hypothesized that all that was needed was a common addressing method for any target location. Since map coordinates were something the entire world agreed upon regarding location, it was felt that it would be appropriate to use them for targeting purposes. The coordinates were always given to the degree, minute, and second when used as a targeting mechanism. It wasn't necessary for the remote viewer to be able to read a map by coordinates. In fact, it was usually better if the remote viewer didn't know how coordinates worked, in that it would reduce the wasted time spent trying to guess approximately where a set of coordinates might be on the face of the earth.

Initially there was a fairly large response from the critics with regard to the use of coordinates. They felt someone with exceptional memory could recognize the specific targets by a coordinate, especially if they had been previously exposed to maps and knew how the coordinate system worked. I have always held this to be a ridiculous notion.

Pick up a world atlas sometime and let it flop open to some place in the middle. Perhaps you've opened it to eastern Pakistan. Look at any of the cities and you can see that they are represented by small black dots or squares. If you can find a major feature adjacent to a city or perhaps one from a city map insert, measure out the coordinates to the second and then ask everyone you meet what they represent. They could represent a hydro-electric dam, but only one in seven million people might be able to tell you that. Even then, they'll know only because they were one of 300 engineers to work on it fifteen years ago.

Also, there is a problem with multiple targets within a few hundred meters of each other. You'll find that unless you have the capacity for measuring the coordinates to the thousandth of a second, one set will pretty much cover a number of targets in close proximity. And yet remote viewers seem able to discriminate among the separate targets. It's almost as if they are guided to the target through instinct—or perhaps it is only through *intent*.

In any event, if you desire to use coordinates for a targeting methodology, the way it works is as follows:

Have someone who is not going to be involved in the experiment select a target somewhere in the world. Write the name of the target or what it is on a card and slip this into a double-wrapped opaque envelope. On the exterior of the envelope write the coordinates by degree, minutes, and seconds. Have the interviewer read the coordinates to the remote viewer at the beginning of the session. After the session is over, open the envelope and show the remote viewer what was targeted.

Some of the drawbacks to using coordinates are that it's easy to make a mistake while lifting them from the map; usually only the larger or more significant targets are used; and it is somewhat difficult to capture abstract targets using this methodology. Specific events and detail are lost.

Another method of targeting is the use of pictures. All you need is a good supply. Cutting targets from *National Geographic*, *Travel*, and other magazines is a preferred method. You simply find a picture which appears to offer a good target and cut it from the magazine.

There are some rules, however. Have someone who isn't going to participate in the remote viewing experiment make the targets. Again, the target packets should be numbered and chosen randomly. The pictures should always be pasted down onto a clean white sheet of bond paper. This is to prevent the pictures or paragraphs (ideas) on the opposite side from becoming targets as well. If the interviewer and remote viewer never see the reverse they may never comment on it. You probably noticed that I used the word *may*. Before this chapter is over, I will explain why it is still possible to remote view information on the pasted down side of the picture.

One of the great things about using pictures from magazines is that it gives you almost instant feedback on how well you might or might not have done. It's easy to search through a magazine which covers the planet to find possible targeting material. Or is it?

Some of the drawbacks to using magazine photo-targets are the possibility of inappropriate target selection; the likelihood of remote viewers becoming easily bored with the targeting methodology; and the difficulty of judging the results.

Targeting things by picture doesn't imply that the target must be a place. Pictures of objects and people also make exceptional targets. Don't be disappointed at the failure rate with pictures; it's normal. It may be that a picture just doesn't convey the same degree of action or energy which real-world targets provide.

The next form of targeting is targeting in the abstract. An abstract target might be a combination of the above. A name and picture of someone in an envelope, with coordinates written on the outside. In such a case, the coordinates might represent the place of a specific event. Or maybe a question written on a sheet of paper: "How was the Great Pyramid built?" Or "What happened to Uncle Ralph, when he disappeared June 5, 1958?"

The double-wrapped and sealed envelope has since become one of the most valuable targeting methodologies. Having a target inside an opaque envelope and insuring that neither the remote viewer nor the interviewer has any contact with the target prior to the specific targeting time goes a long way toward establishing the reality of psi-functioning.

Even so, there are critics who would have you believe that somehow the information concerning the target which is in a double-wrapped and opaque envelope was passed to the viewer other than psychically. Can anyone go any further to convince these critics that the targeting methodologies are valid and that psi-functioning exists? The answer is yes. The current or preferred method of targeting is to locate the remote viewer as far as possible from the targeting material. A vast majority of my own targeting is now done in the following way:

Someone unknown to me selects a group of targets and these are placed in opaque envelopes and randomly shuffled and numbered, thus creating a target pool. I have no idea where the pool is kept or who has access to the envelopes. An agreement is reached to target these envelopes within specific time periods on a specific day of the week, let's say Wednesdays from 11:00 A.M. to 12:00 noon.

On Wednesday at 11:00 a.m., I sit down at my desk in central Virginia with paper and pen and produce what I believe to be a picture of the target contained within the sealed envelope. The sealed envelope is on a desk in Menlo Park, California. I then FAX my drawings to the office in California and they, in turn, then open the envelope and FAX a picture of the target to me.

The following constitutes an example of just such a targeting methodology. A picture was sealed inside an envelope by someone I have never met in Maryland. This envelope was then put on a table in an office with which I am familiar in Washington, D.C. I then produced a drawing of what I believed to be the picture and FAXed my drawings to the office in Washington, D.C., after which the envelope was then mailed to me as feedback. I believe the picture (*Figure 23*) and drawings (*Figure 24*) speak for themselves, as to the effectiveness of remote viewing.

Figure 23. Target Picture in Washington, D.C., Office.

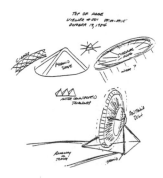

Figure 24. Drawing from Central Virginia Office of Author.

There are additional elements which affect targeting, regardless of which method is being utilized. These are time, intent, and the remote viewer. The first two appear to be of equal importance as to the degree of interference or support which they might produce. The third, on the other hand, can be either the most supportive or the most destructive.

Time, left to our own devices, we remote viewers can wreak havoc with a target that hasn't been pinned down with regard to time. In early 1984 I worked a string of six targets in the lab at SRI-International, two of which were judged as dismal failures. They were rife with exquisite detail, but the details had nothing in common with the actual targeted sites. One was a lumber yard attached to a small hardware store, and the other was an old BART train station and platform. I described the first as a multi-story high-tech building with off-set balconies and hanging gardens, the second as a parking lot. Where (or when) I was certainly didn't pertain to the actual targets. They were filed as total misses. This disturbed me somewhat, in that I felt the information I was interpreting was of good value. They both felt like targets that were booming in.

Almost a year later, after flying out to the West Coast to participate in a series of new experiments, I was driving to my hotel from the airport the evening I arrived and was somewhat surprised to find the first of my two misses had been bulldozed away and replaced with a new building of concrete and glass. The balconies of the building were offset and had lots of green plants hanging from their ledges. I noticed this simply because it looked exactly like the image that I had in my mind the previous year. After checking into my hotel, I drove my rental car to the second target site and was even more pleased when greeted by a brand-new parking lot.

How did this happen? When I pulled the series from the file at the lab, it became quickly apparent that nowhere in the series was there any time or date mentioned in the targeting material. We had all assumed the targeting was real-time, the date and time in which the targeting took place. Unfortunately, such an assumption didn't appear to have been much of a support to my remote viewing efforts at the time. In hindsight, it appeared that I had gone to a different time. Why? Perhaps it was because the target held greater interest for me at a later time, or, as I like to believe, I needed a lesson to understand that time was of greater importance to the remote viewing effort than I had previously believed.

The real kick in the pants is how such news is received by science. It is impossible to go back and re-judge a series after the initial judging without suffering the critic's wrath. Yet, in my own mind, it speaks of how modern scientific methods may fall short of properly investigating true psychic functioning.

So, time is critically important to the proper framework of targeting, regardless of the method selected and/or used.

Intent. By now, everyone has read at least one article on how intent impacts on scientific study. Within the experimental remote viewing effort, it is considered the glue which holds RV together. In my own mind, it is more than that. It is a glue which holds *everything* together. All of reality, as we know it, exists because we intend it to. I suspect that if we didn't intend it to be, then it wouldn't.

In the experimental design for remote viewing, all participants— the remote viewer, the interviewer, the target selector, the analyst, and the judge—all agree on the intent. The experiment is intended to be successful.

This is another reason why good scientific protocol is of extreme importance while investigating remote viewing. The strength and clarity of the protocol, the expectations it projects, produce a solid support base for everyone's intentions. It gets everyone on a single track, all going in the same direction. When the intentions of the participants are not unified, there will be a higher degree of failure, or the experiment will not produce the results expected. The results will be of lesser quality.

There are hundreds of examples from fifteen years of remote viewing that point to this truth. Coordinates have been incorrectly read, but the right target described; the spelling of a target's name is wrong, but the information is correct about the targeted individual; the system breaks down at the last minute and a target envelope isn't put where it is expected to be, but the description of the target is accurate anyway; and there are many other examples. Intent appears to be a sort of magical cord which strings all the elements together; it's what makes the remote viewing effort work.

So, if you are thinking of trying your hand at remote viewing, be sure to pay close attention to your and everyone else's intent. Select only those people who you know will be supportive, who will have the same intentions toward targeting and success as you have. Intend to be successful and you will be.

This doesn't preclude the presence of critics or skeptics during an experiment. Some of my best work has been done with strong skeptics in the room. What they probably don't know is that they are actually assisting in the direction or focus of the remote viewing effort.

I remember once when I met a young man who "...didn't believe in any of this hocus-pocus." I bet him that in a first attempt he would do better than chance expectancy on a simple test—flipping a coin forty times and calling out whether or not it would be heads or tails. Chance dictates twenty flips will be heads and twenty will be tails. So in effect I was betting that he would flip more he called right than wrong. He took the bet and began flipping. He was right only ten out of the forty flips. He smiled a large told-you-so smile, as he handed the coin back to me. His smile faded when I pointed out that he may not have called them, but he had missed greater than chance in his calls. He had accomplished what we all accomplish at some time in our life. It's called *psi-missing*. Missing more than chance expectation. If you are into stocks, bonds, and commodities, you probably want to make a note of this. It is possible to fail (exceeding chance) as easily as to win (exceeding chance).

This brings me to the **remote viewer**. It is impossible to climb into the mind of a remote viewer and read or watch what is going on in there. However, you can take my word for it—there is usually a lot going on. One of the primary filters in the mind of a viewer is how he might feel about the targeting methodology. No matter how smooth the protocol, or how much the focus of intent, if the viewer isn't convinced it is possible then it isn't going to happen.

If you remember, in an earlier chapter I spoke of getting from one side of a canyon to another, going from the *I believe* to the *I know*. This is done through a multitude of experiences over a long course of time. Opening the mind is a prerequisite to making such a journey. If you close your mind to the challenge, you will almost surely fail.

So, if a remote viewer is presented with a new challenge, let's say the first time going against a photograph of a target that has been placed within a sealed envelope, it must be understood that the viewer's belief constructs have to first open, before he can succeed. For if he believes it is impossible, it will always remain so.

For a long time I believed that targeting the now as well as the past was ok, but targeting the future wouldn't work. I believed this because I was heavily invested in the idea of a God-given free will. If I could target the future and be right, then free will must be an inaccurate concept. Unable to deal with letting go of old beliefs, and unable to deal with changes in concept, I set the circumstances for failure whenever I was targeted toward the future. I didn't fail most of the time; I failed all the time, when the target was someplace and/or sometime in the future.

The same holds true if a viewer decides he can't target a human without permission, or the inside of a restricted area, or over distances greater than a light-year, or through lead, under two miles of water, or the back side of the moon. Whatever he believes he can't do, I am here to tell you he won't do. The most restrictive element in the study of remote viewing are the *remote viewers* themselves.

Cut the ribbons of reality. Stretch beyond that which is currently known. Believe that anything is possible and it will be. It is not only the key to good remote viewing, or psi-functioning, it is the key to tomorrow.

14
Retirement & Death

By the year 1984, I had made the decision to retire from the Army and to pursue my investigations into remote viewing. It was a difficult decision for a number of reasons. First and foremost, I had been in the Army twenty years and didn't have any idea what I might do after leaving the service. I certainly didn't know anyone who had been able to earn a living doing remote viewing. There was some consulting which could be done, but aside from that it certainly wouldn't constitute a major source of income.

Secondly, I was separated from my second wife and going through the processes of a divorce. As many can attest to, a life in the Army can be disastrous to many a relationship. In my case it was disastrous to two. How much the effects of my interest in the paranormal had on my marriage, I don't know. At the time I'm sure it had a great deal more to do with the destruction of the relationship than I was willing to acknowledge. Now that I am able to look back on it, there were a number of processes going on that would have inevitably led to the same result.

Finally coming to grips with the effects of the near-death experience, and all the experiences which followed, had a severe impact on how I addressed life. I no longer accepted what I had been taught and had been raised to believe. Life and death meant something entirely different from that which I had understood to be true since my childhood. I felt that I had become an outsider to the circle of friends and peers to which I had previously been attached. My new-found sensitivity had irrevocably changed my view of God and organized religion. My understanding of what constituted the basics of good and evil, life and death, the concepts of man and his relationship to his environment, and many other beliefs had been profoundly altered. I could no longer communicate my feelings about these and other philosophic ideas to those around me. For the most part, they didn't want to hear about them. It was with great difficulty that I had begun to seriously look at my life and what I was doing with it. I realized there was a much greater challenge, one in which I would have to take more responsibility regarding my own actions, my own beliefs. I had begun to see where I had been content for years to let others invent my philosophy for me, and in such a way compromise my own values. I no longer wanted to hide how I felt about things; I wanted to express myself, to talk about what I was thinking and why. In a sense, I must have appeared to be very much like a born-again evangelist.

There is no doubt that the changes in my core beliefs dealt the final blow to most of my relationships. In retrospect, the failing of my marriage was something that would have eventually occurred in spite of all that was going on. I had lived the last few years in that relationship, burying my discontent, always making just one more sacrifice, issuing forth with one last effort, always toward keeping everything normal. Now I am glad that I endured, that I was able to break free from those restrictive and destructive processes. I look back and now see that I was slowly dying on the inside. The decisions I made then reversed my course in history.

I made the decision about retirement from the Army in late 1983, the same time my second wife and I separated. My actual date of retirement wouldn't be until September 1984. After the decision was made, I began moving my belongings to central Virginia, to a small town called Nellysford. There were a number of reasons I had chosen that specific area. First, it was a location which was close to the Monroe Institute. After working for nearly a year with Robert Monroe in his lab, I wanted to be close to the Institute, where I could go to be with others of like thoughts. There were people there who didn't look on remote viewing or psychic functioning as being out of the norm, and they were supportive of my desire to continue my investigations into the paranormal.

Secondly, Nellysford was close to Afton Mountain, a place to which I had already traveled twice in my life to rest and recuperate from two tours in Southeast Asia. The foothills of central Virginia, near Skyline Drive, look very much like the Central Highlands area of Vietnam. The climate is better and the forests and rugged mountains made me feel comfortable and secure. Why, I don't know. Maybe it was only because that was the first place I came to on my return to the United States.

Finally, it was within commuting distance to my work in the Washington, D.C., area. I still had at least seven months until my retirement date. I spent those months with weekends in the mountains and weekdays on the job, not something I would recommend to the average commuter. I found out something about myself in the experience, however. I found that even though I wasn't aware of it, I had become increasingly more stressed by the crowded conditions of city life. I suspect that the increased sensitivity, a result of working at the remote viewing, had opened me up to all sorts of congested mental noise. My weekends in the country were becoming more and more necessary for not only my comfort, but my mental health. Since those early days of my move, I have noticed, particularly at lectures and seminars, that there really is a congestion or clutter that occurs around large groups of people. After a number of years I even noticed degrees of difference between general public lectures and seminars with paranormal orientation. The noise is less enervating at the latter.

The decision to spend my weekends in the country and commute during the week to work turned out to be one of the best decisions of my life. As a result, I began spending time with a wonderful woman by the name of Nancy Honeycutt. I had met her previously during a trip to the Institute. She was one of Robert Monroe's step-daughters. What I found most likeable was her ability to understand the paranormal without succumbing to the *beads and sandals* attitude.

I had learned early on that a large percentage of people who begin to play and dwell within the paranormal field lose track of reality. This usually happens as a direct result of what I call a macro-experience. The macro-experience is usually brought on by the *temporary suspension of disbelief* that I spoke of in an earlier chapter. The experience can happen singularly or in a group. Most macro-experiences appear to happen in a group, especially where the group dynamic has an identity of its own. An example would be almost any New Age seminar. New Age seminars usually create an atmosphere conducive to dealing with issues that are not normally addressed. Why? Well, primarily because they create a time and place which is safe for having an emotionally moving experience. Not only is it safe, but the other participants become intimately associated with the experience. This produces a warm and comfortable feeling of togetherness. It makes the experience, whatever it might be, not only safe but enjoyable and usually very moving.

What kind of an experience am I talking about? It might be as complicated as achieving closure with a long-dead relative, by finally dealing with the loss. Or it might be as simple as understanding why we have been so focused on a singular issue in life, perhaps years of anger with an old friend. Whatever the issue, it usually comes up within the framework of the workshop. It is emotional, and the group always provides support in terms of love and compassion.

In almost all of the times I have witnessed a macro-experience I have seen it produce a major change in the individual who is experiencing it. It is that major change, that sudden *awakening* which, if left uncontrolled or unguided, produces the inevitable jump to *beads and sandals*.

A good trainer or seminar conductor will recognize when this is happening and will help to guide a person through the experience, will help the person understand what he is experiencing and why. If that guidance isn't there, if the person is left to his own devices, he will sometimes change radically in an unguided way. This results in a break from reality.

Of course this unique form of experiencing can be misdirected. This is probably where the cult master derives his power over fellow human beings. Misdirected, the individual usually ends up in *bead and sandals*, giving away his personal wealth and belongings to another, who has no intention of caring for him or anyone else. The person who can enjoy the new-found freedoms resulting from the macro-experience without giving his life away to another has found the secret to personal happiness.

Nancy was someone who clearly understood the inherent dangers as well as the responsibility toward others. As a result, we began to work closely together in an attempt to improve my remote viewing. We spent a great deal of time together in the seven months until my retirement. Much of our time together dealt with remote viewing, but a lot of it was social. As a result, we were married two months after I left the Army.

Following my retirement I was able to pursue remote viewing full-time. This was possible only because Nancy continued to work. Her support in those days and since has enabled me to learn far more than I could otherwise. I continued to do consultation to the laboratory at SRI-International and began a business which we called Intuitive Intelligence Applications, Inc.

Essentially, the business was split into two parts. The first was designed to provide both subjects and experience to any lab investigating psychic functioning. The second was designed to proffer support to any private institution or business interested in applying remote viewing for commercial purposes. The only guarantees which my business made were *to try hard* and *to guarantee total anonymity* to the customer. Fee schedules were to be worked out through negotiations. We opened business early in 1985. I had no idea what was looming on the horizon.

In June 1985, Nancy and I had decided to take a well-earned vacation. Instead of spending huge sums of money traveling half the way around the world for relaxation, we decided to spend the time at home. This was a fortunate decision. I had begun to write my first book and thought the time spent focusing on this would be relaxing. Nancy, on the other hand, had quit her job in publishing to take over management of The Monroe Institute. A vacation at that point seemed in our best interests.

The first day of our vacation we planned on spending at the lake near the Institute. It's a fourteen-acre lake which Robert Monroe had recently completed building for use by the local community. In the center of the lake, there was a community-constructed raft which was the ideal place to relax and sunbathe. That is where we were in the early afternoon of June 17, 1985. I didn't know it at the time, but I was about to test all that I had learned from my near-death experience fifteen years earlier.

I took a long sip of iced tea from the jug that we had brought along and rolled over on the towel to take a nap, when I felt as if someone had suddenly kicked me hard in the sternum. It caused me to catch my breath. The sudden pain began to rapidly grow in intensity. I knew without a doubt that, at thirty-nine years of age, I was having a heart attack.

A number of interesting things went rapidly through my mind, not the least of which was an acknowledgement that I could be dying. Nancy knew there was something wrong when I rolled over because I couldn't hide the grimace. She asked me what was wrong and I lied. I told her that I had probably slipped a disk in my back and it hurt sufficiently that I thought it would be a good idea to go and check it out.

We loaded our equipment into the small aluminum boat and I rowed us ashore, all the while trying to hide the pain in my chest which was growing much worse and was beginning to come in waves. We walked from the dam of the lake to the car and drove home where we changed from our bathing suits to street clothes. Nancy asked a number of times about the pain and I assured her that it was nothing to worry about. After showering and changing, we left the house, she driving, and began the long drive to the hospital. There were two of approximately equal distances, one in Waynesboro twenty-three miles away, and one in Charlottesville, at twenty-eight miles.

By the time we began the ride to the hospital, the pain was to the point that I was trying not to pass out. It was at that point that I knew

I was dying. I remembered my near-death experience in 1970 and made a conscious decision to go with it, to pay attention to every detail, to fully participate in the experience of dying. I remember feeling that it was ok, it was all right if I died. The only question I couldn't answer was when to tell Nancy what was actually happening. Throughout the drive I faded in and out of reality. One minute the pain was excruciating, the next it seem to fade away into the background and I could feel a sense of relaxation, of release. Then I would fade back in and the pain would begin again.

When we reached the crossroad, where we had to make a decision on which hospital, I said Waynesboro simply because I knew the traffic would be less. At this point I knew I didn't have much time left. My whole world was pain and it was coming in cyclic waves. I concentrated on staying conscious. I wanted to experience it all. I felt as if I were falling backward into the sea of pain. As I relaxed into it, as I let go, the pain would again fade and each time I sensed that if I let go of that last thread of consciousness, then I wouldn't be coming back. I needed to tell Nancy what was happening, but I didn't know how. The time didn't feel right.

We finally arrived at the emergency room door at the Waynesboro Hospital and that is when I told her. I remember saying very clearly, "Go inside and tell them your husband is in the car having a heart attack." That was the last I remembered because I had finally let go, and my body was sliding sideways onto the seat. I remember being somewhat upset with my self because, as I pulled away from the physical, I had failed to say the most important thing that I had wanted to say. I hadn't told her how much I loved her.

I regained consciousness in the emergency room. There were a number of people all around me, sticking something in or pulling something out. A doctor was looking into my eyes with a pen light. He smiled and said, "Welcome back."

The next six days were spent in the twilight of drugs. I didn't know it at the time, but they were having a great deal of difficulty in stabilizing me. I was constantly going to the edge of death and balancing there, unable to move one way or the other. I remember having dreams which were almost as exotic as the drugs that were inducing them. Finally, in the very early morning of the seventh day, they moved me by ambulance to the hospital in Charlottesville. There they did an angiogram and quickly wheeled me into emergency surgery for a triple by-pass. I was conscious long enough, lying on the gurney in the hallway, to finally say to my wife, "Everything is going to be ok. I love you."

What does this all have to do with remote viewing, the study of the paranormal? I believe that it was the growth and understanding which developed, beginning with the near-death experience in 1970, up and through the beginning of my business in early 1985, that set the stage for surviving the heart attack and open-heart surgery.

I've discussed it with a number of doctors, and they have all said the same thing It was probably the ability to relax into it, the lack of fear, the control of anxiety that kept me alive long enough to reach the hospital. I welcomed death as *ok*, as something that was *all right*, and as a result survived when I otherwise might not have. Also, going into the experience with core changes in my philosophy, I was able to open the door to whole new realms of reality. I had experiences in those two weeks, while balancing at the door to eternity, that others might have had but don't want to talk about. Experiences that I was able to test, rationalize, and integrate into my life. Experiences that I can now share with others who have not yet been there. The paranormal world is but the tip of an iceberg.

15
Opening the Heart

For a long time general anesthesia has been thought of as the threshold to death. In the early years it probably was. From about 1850 through the turn of the century, nitrous oxide gas and ether, or possibly a combination of the two, were used to anesthetize a patient for surgery. By the year 1900 most had switched to chloroform. Just about anyone could use it for surgery, because all that it required was a butler or general hospital orderly administering it by holding a rag over the patient's mouth and dripping it from a bottle. A patient taken too deeply with the chloroform would sometimes die because it would stop the heart. Modern medicine, of course, uses a much more complex mixture of gases for anesthetic purposes. However, even with their complexity, how deep the patient must go is determined by the type of operation. Only the deepest levels of anesthesia will relax the various muscle groups of the body. The more invasive the operation, the deeper the anesthesia and, therefore, the closer the patient is taken to the doorway to eternity. Open-heart surgery is definitely a trip to the outer edge.

After signing a handful of papers, I was wheeled into the operating room. Knowing that I was soon to be going under anesthesia, I began repeating over and over in my mind that I wanted to get out, I wanted to leave my body. I imagined being back in the Monroe Institute lab and listening to the tapes that we had used during our experiments. As the drugs took hold, it was easy to peel away from my body and drift up and outward. I found myself in a black void and there was a Light on a far horizon. I knew that was where I wanted to go.

Somewhere between the decision to go to the Light and the getting there, I felt myself consciously fade out and then in again. When I regained my consciousness, I knew that I was still out of body but didn't know where I was. It was a place of rose and pale-orange hues; it was a place that at least felt safe. The original

Light that I had seen was very close, but I instinctively knew that I wasn't allowed to go there. The feeling made me angry because I could remember the feeling I had in my first encounter with the Light and I wanted to feel it again. That is when I noticed the entities.

There were four in close proximity to me. Three looked alike, and the fourth appeared to be much larger and more aloof. The three closest to me were much smaller in stature. I wanted to ask them who they were and the thought of asking seemed to throw the question outward. I received a response, but it was delivered directly to my mind, as if I myself had thought it. They said; *You are in a place of waiting, a place where you can relax and re-energize.*

As I listened to their response I made a careful study of how they looked. All three were exactly alike. Humanoid in form, but with no visible fingers or toes. They looked as if they were wearing soft boots and mittens. They appeared to be constructed of millions of tiny points of light all held together with a black outline or silhouette of shape. I asked them where they came from and I sensed a feeling of laughter and amusement.

By that point I wasn't sure if what I was seeing was really what they looked like. Or was I being shown something I could deal with? It was almost as if they had changed form in order to make me comfortable. So I asked them why they were with me. The response was very clear. *We are here to insure that you don't wander off.* I then asked if I could go to the Light, and they responded, *No, you are not allowed to do that this time.*

Turning my attention to the fourth entity, I asked the other three who the fourth entity was and why it wasn't with the other three, why it didn't look the same. The response was *It has its own job to do and therefore it is not the same.* I thought, well that makes sense, they are probably divided up according to function.

Intrigued, I willed myself over to the fourth entity and thought, who are you? It responded with a feeling of great compassion. So I thought, what are you? Again I got a feeling of great compassion. I studied the fourth entity. It was constructed the same way as the other three, but it had a different color. Whereas the three were predominantly a pastel rose and light orange, the fourth seemed to be made up of flecks of grey to silver, with a slight rainbow of shimmer rippling across its form now and again, much like the skin of a fish removed from water. The fourth entity was also at least twice the size of the others.

Feeling very inadequate next to it, I asked, are you God? The response was instantaneous: *Of course I am.* My sense of it, however, was that the entity had limits. So I was either being played with or lied to. I quickly asked, are you what Bob Monroe calls an *Inspect*? An *Inspect* was an entity that Robert Monroe had addressed in his book, *Far Journeys* (Dolphin, 1985). I had been fortunate enough to have read the then-unpublished manuscript prior to my heart attack. The tall being of light responded, *Of course I am.*

This confused me. How could it be both? I think it interpreted my *thought question* because I got a *feeling* answer. This entity would respond to whatever I asked with an answer that I would always be able to handle. It would never exceed the limits of my reality. If I had asked it, are you my mother? It would have answered with *of course I am.* Again, I got a *feeling* of being correct. My first assumption at that point was to think these entities might be a self-constructed hallucination. How could I test them to see if they were real?

I turned to the smaller three entities and thought my next question: am I going to be all right? *Yes.* Then I need proof that you are real. You must give me something that I can check in my own reality that will prove that you are real.

First came a sense of humor, followed by an affirmative. In my mind I heard them say, *You can have these things to take with you. You will be allowed to return early and watch the closing of your wound. You will heal quickly with no complications. We will tell you about an interaction that Robert Monroe will have with us at a future date, but you are absolutely forbidden to tell him or anyone else about it.* There was not to be any dickering over the issue. I quickly agreed to the terms.

At that point, they passed me the information about Robert Monroe. It was delivered as an entire memory. That was the first time that I had any information passed that way and it was a very unusual feeling. Sort of like having a plug or block removed from an information channel. Then I felt as if I was being turned sideways and rolled in light-orange fuzz. I felt sleepy but safe. I drifted off into the black void.

I awoke, hovering over my body, looking straight down into the chest cavity which was being held open by a stainless steel (for lack of a better word) crank-type jack. I was overwhelmed by sudden excruciating pain. I blacked out. In the void I heard a voice say, *It's ok. You are having emotional pain; it isn't physical. Let go of it, enjoy the ride.* I let go and then faded through the black, back into the operating room.

I again found myself hovering directly over my open chest. This time there was no immediate pain, so I watched carefully as they finished what they were doing (inserting clips and small metal rings) and then closed up my body. I tried to memorize as much as I could of the procedure. Two or three items stuck in my mind. They were how the chromed jack looked (*Figure 25*); a sudden drop in blood pressure, perhaps sixty points; and how they twisted the ends of the wire holding my rib cage together.

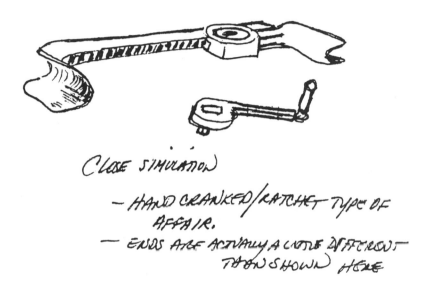

Figure 25. Implement drawn by Author.

After being with the entities of light, I thought the process I witnessed in the operating room was primitive by comparison. Somehow this thought saddened me a great deal. As they were putting the stitches in, I faded to black and then woke up in the Surgical Intensive Care Unit (SICU).

I thoroughly surprised the nursing staff with my awakening. Any doctors who may be reading this will understand why. Upon awakening, I was fully coherent; I snatched a pen from the pocket of a nurse who walked up to my gurney and made scribbling signs in the air indicating that I wanted something to write on. I also pointed to my wedding band indicating that I wanted to see my wife, Nancy. I still had the breathing tube inserted in my throat and couldn't talk. I indicated that I wanted it removed immediately. The nurse told me she couldn't do that, because it was breathing for me and it was too early to have it taken out. She asked me to relax and let the tube do the work it was meant to do. They went and got my wife while I began writing notes so that I wouldn't forget anything that had happened. When my wife entered the room, I began showing her the notes and continued writing other things in reference to my experience while under the anesthetic. I wanted her to know as much as I could share with her at that point. After ten or fifteen minutes the breathing tube became exceedingly uncomfortable and I began choking, eventually throwing the tube up. Freed of the encumbrance, I was finally able to talk about the experience with my wife. This also surprised the nurses, who later told me that it was very unusual for a patient to talk immediately after the tube's removal.

Later, my wife told me a number of other things that were interesting. Her first comment was how surprised the staff had been that I was making so much sense when I awoke. It was considered very unusual coming out of general anesthesia the way I did in the Surgical Intensive Care Unit. Secondly, she said that my eyes were very strange. They gave the impression that I had just seen something that was truly wonderful. She said it was the same look people have when they've just seen something so incredible that they can't find words. I wrote as much as I could remember of my experience on the pad. I even noted that I had seen something which had not yet happened but was careful not to mention what or whom it would involve. When I had finished writing down all that I could remember, I drifted off to sleep. Later I had an opportunity to write the information down in my weekly notes prior to leaving the hospital. A copy is presented here (*Figure 26*).

My recovery went very smoothly. I went through the step-down units very quickly and was up walking around on the third morning following surgery. I was sore and felt weak, but I wanted to leave the hospital. The doctor finally relented and I went home on the fifth day.

Who were these entities? I've given a great deal of thought to this. Certainly, they had provided me with three very specific items to check out. I had witnessed the closing of my body after surgery; my recovery, beginning with the SICU, had been rapid and without any problems; and I had the information which eventually I hoped would check out; but there was something that still. . .well, felt different about the whole experience. It was something that I spent many days

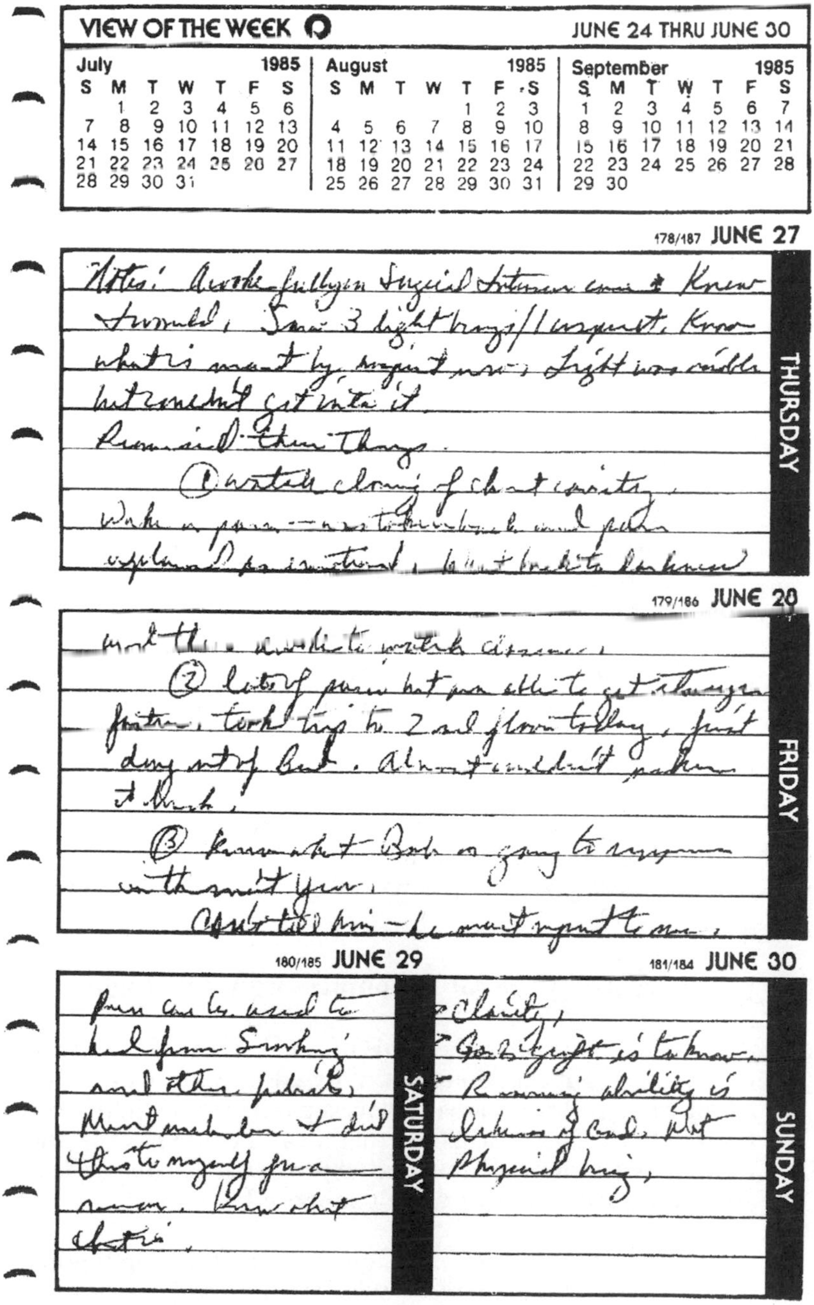
VIEW OF THE WEEK
JUNE 24 THRU JUNE 30
July 1985
S M T W T F S
1 2 3 4 5 6
7 8 9 10 11 12 13
14 15 16 17 18 19 20
21 22 23 24 25 26 27
28 29 30 31
August 1985
S M T W T F S
1 2 3
4 5 6 7 8 9 10
11 12 13 14 15 16 17
18 19 20 21 22 23 24
25 26 27 28 29 30 31
September 1985
S M T W T F S
1 2 3 4 5 6 7
8 9 10 11 12 13 14
15 16 17 18 19 20 21
22 23 24 25 26 27 28
29 30
178/187 JUNE 27
THURSDAY
179/186 JUNE 28
FRIDAY
180/185 JUNE 29
SATURDAY
181/184 JUNE 30
SUNDAY

Figure 26. Notes from weekly calendar.

and weeks going over and over again in my mind. By the time I was fully recovered from the surgery, I felt that I might have found a small thread with which I could unravel an answer.

My first conclusion was that the experience was real and what I had learned from it was:

Regarding the Entities

1. They always seemed to respond within the limits of what I could believe was true. They never made any claims. Only when I challenged them did they respond with an answer and then only gave me information that I could deal with. Why did they only respond within the limits of my belief? What was their value in what was happening to me?

2. They had no specific names or other identification that would make them separate, or uniquely different, one from the other. Within each specific function, regardless of number, they appeared to think, act, and respond together or in unison. Were the rose-colored entities interconnected, were they of a single origin?

3. There appeared to be a hierarchy, separating each group from the next. They were content with their own group, happy with the separation. Why weren't the rose-colored curious of the silver entity?

4. They provided me with information about which I had no previous knowledge. But then, so does remote viewing. Could I have gotten the same information through psychic functioning?

Regarding the All-Encompassing White Light

1. In comparison to the NDE of 1970, I was allowed only to see the Light this time, not allowed to meld with it. The Light was a restricted area. It was separate from where I was, limited to another area. Could that mean I could have learned more about it through a second experience? Or maybe learn something about it that I wasn't supposed to know?

2. What I knew about the Light was that being in it was to feel *at home, total, complete, whole, warm and comfortable*. Remembering this and not being allowed inside the Light this second time made me feel *torn apart, shattered, incomplete,*

lacking, and vulnerable. Was the Light a part of me?

3. I was kept outside of the Light during the second experience. In viewing it from the outside, I felt that it had limits or edges. Perhaps it didn't encompass all around it, perhaps it was finite. If the Light were God, then it should have encompassed everything anyway. Is God ever separate from that which is created from God? Therefore, it probably isn't God. Did I think it was God originally simply because, at the time, I didn't know what else to call it?

As a result of these thoughts, I finally arrived at a startling conclusion. One born out of a sudden realization that all of the information I received from the entities—the knowledge derived from the experience itself, to include the earlier NDE—was information I probably could have eventually obtained through psychic functioning anyway. I could have produced the information. Therefore, the entities could be of *my own creation*, and the Light could be. . .what? The *totality of self!*

Something about this conclusion felt right. My memory of being in the Light is one of complete satisfaction, complete comfort and wholeness. Could it represent the restructuring and coming together of my own energy? The overwhelming response now is—*Yes!*

Whenever I look into a mirror now, I think of the Light. I know that I am seeing only a small fragment of my own totality. The figure staring back at me is the barest representation of who and what I may actually be. I know that beyond this primitive place called physical reality, we perhaps exist in a fashion that only God could have conceived. If we believe in a maker and believe that we are created in the maker's own image, then our maker is probably an energy of awesome power.

These new thoughts impacted heavily upon me. I suddenly felt as if I had awakened to a new and enormously complex world. A place where my responsibility extends well beyond the best and most that I could have imagined. If the Light is the totality of self, then we have truly been asleep for a long long time. My previous concepts of God and the range of power that God represents were shattered. I suddenly found that I could no longer conceive of who or what God is.

New thoughts, modifications of my extant belief structure, erupted in my mind. I began throwing out old concepts by the bucket load. If what I now believed was true, and there was no reason that it shouldn't be, then whole new concepts of reality were possible.

Dozens of new perceptions entered my mind over the weeks that followed. I began to build my own cosmology, my own understanding of how the physical world might work and what our place might be in it. Even more astounding was the thought that the non-physical world could be just as real, and maybe God didn't reside there either. I eventually came to understand they are both God's creation.

Perhaps we humans are unique. We reside totally in neither one nor the other; we operate with one foot in the physical reality and one foot in the non-physical. If we resided totally in one or the other, then there would be no dichotomy, no confusion. In order to know or be aware that there is a creator, we require a dichotomy which makes us question who and where we come from and of what or how our reality is made up.

In order to understand this concept, one must first understand that what we are in the physical is not what we are in the non-physical. Logic, linear thinking, and mystical beliefs occur in the physical world but are not possible outside of it. On the other side of physical reality there is no logic because it isn't necessary for understanding. In the non-physical universe there is only knowing or truth. Also, on the non-physical side there are no linear patterns. The view of physical reality from the outside-in is that everything just *is*. Since everything simply *is* and is *truth*, there is no necessity for beginnings or ends and therefore no construct which can be mystical. What complicates our understanding of the non-physical reality is thinking that everything flows from here to there, or conversely, from there to here, when actually there is no flow at all. Humankind simply straddles the dividing line. There may be other creatures which do the same, so we may not be as unique as we think we are.

Through straddling both, the physical and non-physical sides of the dividing line, we are able to experience both; that is, we can come to see how one relates to the other. So out of this relationship, of one side to the other, there appear dichotomies which to our minds are unsolvable. We are forced to turn to a mystical source. By default, we force ourselves to see a God, a supreme being, where otherwise we might not ever find one.

For me, the most important point in all of this is the possibility of both the physical and the non-physical existing, neither having anything to do with that being we call God, except of course, that God has created the physical and non-physical realities as equal conditions.

16
Another World

How far can one go with remote viewing? Are there limits to what can be targeted?

Initially, back in the mid-1980s, I would have said yes, there are limits to remote viewing. You can go only so far with it. But now I'm not so sure. During the mid- to late 1980s I began getting involved with some targets that would stretch the realm of probability to its limits. These targets were certainly not of my choosing because, as usual, I was being kept totally blind to what they were throughout the targeting and information collection process. I would also add that the example which I am about to present came within the context of four or five other targets, all of which were fairly normal, e.g., the St. Louis Arch, Devil's Tower, Pompeii, and other notable places or locations.

Therefore, I present the example exactly as it occurred and ask that you make up your own mind. I will purposely wait until the end of the chapter to tell you what the target is.

It was the twenty-second of May, 1984, when I entered the lab at the Monroe Institute prepared to do an exercise in remote viewing. Many of the targets which I had previously done there were interesting for the most part but certainly not unusual. That particular morning was no different from the previous two or three.

I was met by Robert Monroe and the interviewer and prepared for the remote viewing session. They connected the Bio-monitoring devices to my body and escorted me to the remote viewing room, where I made myself comfortable by lying down on the bed on my back and arranging the wires so that they wouldn't interfere with my becoming relaxed. They extinguished the lights in the room and pulled the heavy sound-proofed door shut behind them, effectively sealing me into a totally black chamber where it was quiet enough to hear a pin drop. I listened to the special Hemi-Sync™ tape which Robert had made for me and drifted off into relaxation. After approximately ten minutes, when my bio-monitoring equipment established that I was totally relaxed and ready, they gave me the targeting cues. The following represents exactly what occurred that morning in May. The comments and who made them are indicated by the following: **RAM** = Robert A. Monroe; **Int** = Interviewer; and **Joe** = me. The actual target was in a double-wrapped and opaque envelope, in Robert Monroe's shirt pocket. I was told where it was but was not allowed to handle it.

RAM: RJ 522. . .time, 10:09 A.M.

Int: *Plus ten minutes and ready to start.* [Note made on the tape but not heard by me in the remote viewing room.]

Target Number One

Int: All right now, using the information in the envelope. . .exclusively focusing your attention now. . .using the information in the envelope. . .focus on forty point eight nine degrees north, nine point five five degrees west.

Joe: I want to say that it looks like a. . .what it looks like is a great view of a pyramid like. . .a pyramid form. . .it's very high. . .it's like sitting in a large depressed area.

Int: All right.

Joe: It's yellowish. . .ahhhh. . .okra-colored.

Int: Move in time to the time indicated in the envelope and describe what's happening.

Joe: An impression of severe. . .severe clouds. . .more like dust storm. . .aaah, feels like it's ahhh. . .seems to be like ah. . .I've got to iron this out, it's real weird.

Int: Just report your raw perceptions at this time.

Joe: I'm looking at the aftereffect of a major geological trauma.

Int: Ok, go back to the time before the major geologic problem.

(Long pause)

Joe: Hmmmm, total difference. Before there is no. . .no. . .oh hell. . .it's like mounds of dirt appear and then they disappear when you go before. See a. . .large flat surfaces. . .very smooth, angles and walls, really large stuff. . .megalithic

Int: All right, at this period in time now, before the geologic activity, look around, in and around this area, and see if you can find any activity.

(Long pause)

Joe: Keep seeing ah. . .looks like a perception of a shadow of people. . .very tall. But it's only a shadow. . .it's as if they were there but they are not. . .not there anymore.

Int: Go back to a period of time when they are there.

Joe: Ah. . .it's like a I get a lot of static on the line and everything. . .breaking up all the time. . .very fragmentary. . .in pieces.

Int: Just report the raw data, don't try to put things together, just report the raw data.

Joe: I keep seeing a very large people. . .they appear very thin and tall, but they are very large. . .ah. . .wearing some kind of strange clothes, very tight. . .skin tight. . .almost can't see them.

Target Number Two

Int: All right, holding in this time period, holding in this time period, I want you to move your physical location in this space to another physical location, but in this time period.

Joe: Uh huh.

Int: Move now to forty-six point four five, forty-six point four five north, three hundred fifty-three point two two east. Move in this time to forty-six point four five north, three hundred fifty-three point two two east.

Joe: Feel like I'm inside a cavern. . .no not a cavern, it's more like a canyon. I'm looking up, up the sides of very steep walls that seem to go on forever. And there's like ah. . .structure there. . .it's like the wall of the canyon itself has been carved. Yeah. . .I'm getting very large structures. No ah. . .intricacies seem to be. . .just huge sections of smooth stone.

Int: Do these structures have insides and outsides?

Joe: Yes, they are very. . .it's like a rabbit warren. . .corridors and rooms, but they are really huge. I feel like I'm standing in one and it's really huge. Perception is that the ceilings are very high and the walls very wide.

Int: *Real time, plus twenty-two minutes.* [Said and recorded on the tape but not heard by me in the remote viewing room.]

Target Number Three

Int: Yes, that would be correct. I would like to move now to another location nearby. All right, move now from this point in this time to forty-five point eight six north, three fifty-four point one east. Forty-five point eight six north, three fifty-four point one east.

Joe: It appears to be the end of a very large road. And there is a marker standing there. . .it's very large. Keep getting a Washington monument overlay. . .it's like an obelisk.

Target Number Four

Int: All right, from this point then, let us move to another point. Move now to thirty-five point two six north, thirty-five point two six north, two hundred thirteen point two four east. Move in this time to thirty-five point two six north, two hundred thirteen point two four east.

Joe: I feel like I'm in the middle of a huge circular basin. It's ringed with mountains almost all the way around. Very ragged. . .ragged mountains. There is a. . .basin's very very large. Scale seems to be off for some reason. . .everything seems really big. . .everything's big.

Int: I understand the problem, please continue.

Joe: I see the right corner angle to something, but that is all. I don't see anything else.

Target Number Five

Int: Ok, then let's move to a little different place, very close. Move from the point that you are now in this time to thirty four point six north, two hundred thirteen point zero nine east. Move now in this time to thirty-four point six north, two hundred and thirteen point zero nine east.

Joe: Something very white. . .very flat and white.

Int: What is your position of observation as you look at this thing that reflects white?

Joe: I'm at an oblique left angle. The sun is. . .the sun is weird.

Target Number Six

Int: All right, look back down at the ground now. We are going to move just a little bit from this place, just a little bit from this place. Thirty-four point five seven north, two hundred twelve point two two east, very close by. Move over now to thirty-four point five seven north, two hundred twelve point two two east.

Joe: Ah. . .ah. . .it's like I can just perceive ahhhh. . ..like a radiating pattern of some kind. It is like some real strange or kind of intersecting roads that are dug in the valleys. You know, when a road is just a slightly blurry edge.

Int: Tell me about the shapes of these things.

Joe: They are like real neat channels cut. They are very deep like the road is down.

Int: Ok, I have now. . .I notice electrically your null point has come out a little bit. I want you to stay deep and capture what you are focusing on.

Joe: That's really tough. . .it seems like it's just always very sporadic.

Target Number Seven

Int: Yes, I realize that, but it is very important that you maintain your focus. I have a movement exercise again for you, and this is some considerable distance away. So, holding the focus in time, remember the focus in time, that you had before and moving now to fifteen degrees north, one hundred ninety-eight degrees east. Get deeper and deeper and deeper like you were before. Fifteen degrees north, one hundred ninety-eight degrees east. Take some time, get back deep.

Joe: See ah. . .intersecting. . .whatever these things are. . .they are carved deeply. . .but are like road beds. See pointed tops of things on the horizon. Even the horizon looks funny. . .it's weird. . .like ah. . .different. You can see like very clearly but far away. . .and the vague.

Target Number Eight

Int: Ok, another movement now to eighty degrees south, eighty degrees south, sixty-four degrees east, sixty-four degrees east. Move now in this time to eighty degrees south, sixty-four degrees east.

Joe: Pyramids again. . .[Note: This is first actual mention of pyramids, but it is obvious that I must have had the thought in my mind for some time. The expertise of the interviewer is well displayed here, in that he didn't say or use the word pyramids until after I first used it. It is extremely important that the interviewer not lead the remote viewer. In most cases this is why the interviewer is kept as blind to the target as the viewer.] . . .but can't tell if it's overlay or not because they are different.

Int: Ok, do these pyramids have insides and outsides?

Joe: Yes, and they are very huge. It's really an interesting perception that I am getting.

Int: *I think he is losing his ability to move but he is still attracted to things that are interesting* [Joe is speaking in the background but cannot be understood] *so we are going to go ahead and explore what seems to be interesting him rather than move on the targets indicated.* [This is a note inserted on the tape, but which I didn't hear from the remote viewing room.]

Int: Could you please repeat that?

Joe: These are like shelters from storms.

Int: These structures you are seeing?

Joe: Yes. They are designed for that.

Int: All right, go inside one of these and find some activity to tell me about.

Int: *Plus thirty-seven minutes, real time.* [This is a note said on the tape, but not heard by me in the remote viewing room.]

Joe: Different chambers. . .but they're all stripped of any kind of furnishings or anything. . .it's like it is a strictly functional place. . .for sleeping. . .er. . .that's not a good word. . .hibernation. Some form. . .ah. . .I get real raw inputs. . .storms. . .savage storms. . .and sleeping through storms.

Int: Tell me about the ones who sleep through the storms.

Joe: Ahhhh. . .very tall again. . .very large people. But they are thin. They look thin because of their height. . .and they dress in. . .oh hell. . .looks like a real light silk, but it's not a flowing type of clothing, it looks like it's cut to fit.

Int: Move close to one of them and ask them to tell you about themselves.

(Very long pause)

Joe: An ancient people. But they are ahhhh. . .they're dying. It's past their time and age.

Int: Tell me about this.

Joe: They are responding in a very philosophic. . .they are looking for a way to survive. . .they can't see their way out. . .they can't seem to find the way out. So they are hanging on while they wait. . .for something to return. . .or something to. . .that's coming with the answer.

Int: What is it they are waiting for?

Joe: They are ahhhh. . .evidently there was a group or party of them that went to find a new place to live. It's like. . .I'm getting all kinds of overwhelming input of the corruption of their environment. It's failing very rapidly and that's why that group went somewhere, went a long way to find another place where. . .

Int: What was the cause of the atmospheric distur- bance. . .the environment disturbance?

Joe: I see a picture of a. . .a picture of like a. . .oh hell. . .it's almost a warp in the. . .it's like seeing. . .

Int: (Interrupting) Give me the raw data.

Joe: . . .a globe. . .that. . .it's like a globe that goes through a comet's tail. . .through a river of something. . .but it's all very cosmic. . .I keep getting like deep space pictures.

Int: All right, before you leave this individual. . .ask him if there's any way that you. . .ask him if he knows who you are. . .is there any way that you can help him in this present predicament?

Joe: All I get is that they must just wait. It doesn't know who I am. It thinks that it is seeing a hallucination or some- thing.

Int: Ok, when the others left. . .these people are wait- ing. . .when the others left, how did they go?

Joe: I get an impression of ahhhhh. . .I don't know what the hell it is. . .it looks like the inside of a large boat, very rounded walls. . .but shiny metal.

Int: Go along with them on their journey and find out where it is that they go.

(Long pause)

Joe: Impression of ah. . .of a really crazy place with vol- canoes and gas pockets. . .ah. . .strange plants. . .a very volatile place. It's very much like going from the frying pan into the fire. Difference is that there appears to be a lot of vegetation, where the other place didn't have any. A different kind of storm.

Int: All right, it's time to come back now to the sound of my voice, to the present time, to right now, the twenty-second of May, 1984, the sound of my voice. Move back now to the room, back to the sound of my voice, back further now to the sound of my voice. . .on the twenty-second of May, 1984. Ok, your voltages have come up now, , looking good Your polarity has reversed back, you've reversed back again.

Joe: I feel like I was a long way off.

Int: This will be an end of session then.

At this point, I moved from the remote viewing room to the experimental area of the lab and, while sitting with the others, I presented some views on what I had just experienced and responded to some questions.

Joe: My perception is that I was looking down a very long tunnel, and at the end is a cracked top to a series of filters. Only there aren't any real filters there and I don't know how to explain that. It's like very static-ridden. . .all blasted to hell and back. That's why I felt like I went a long way off the deep edge.

Int: Have you ever experienced this before?

Joe: I have in a sense, but not this bad. There are some very primal things about it that make the things true. But there are other things here that didn't have the mark of presence that would make them real enough. I feel like I went out there somewhere and touched the akashic records instead of the reality records. . .only that's not a good phrase.

Int: We've often talked about, in all states of time there is no distance difference, and that's a nice philosophical point to talk about. If I understand what you said, aside from that philosophical point you're telling me that you had to go a long ways to get this information?

Joe: Let me put it this way. And again this is a totally inappropriate way to say it, because we also refer to realities as different too. . .this is like a reality one step removed from a reality. That doesn't mean it is a different reality. . .but that it is one step removed for some reason. And ah. . .

Int: Are the people that you talked to a part of this reality then?

(A very long pause)

Joe: Gosh, I hope not.

(Lots of laughter)

Joe: These guys are really huge. Let me rephrase that, I think they are, but not now, that's why I think this is someplace in the future. These are really gargantuan people.

Int: Are they human?

Joe: Yes, they are very humanoid in form, but there are some basic differences. They looked very frail, but they weren't. They have this huge bone structure and everything, but they. . .and their musculature is ok for what they needed to do, but in appearance wise they don't look as strong as your usual stocky short. . .

Int: So, they were different in some ways?

Joe: Yes, they were different in a lot of ways. Philosophically. . .and there was some difference in their thinking. . .

Int: And this concept that you have that you went somewhere into the future, that these people exist somewhere in the future, how does that parallel with what you just said about this difficult concept that. . .

Joe: OK, if we mutated six times over the next 10,000 years, it's kind of like I was seeing the mutated effect, the mutated results.

Int: It's still part of this reality. . .

Joe: Yes, but it is still one reality removed, as we understand it. What I'm saying is. . .damn it. . .I can't apply our reality to it. It's different. . .it's. . .

Int: (Interrupting) Oh, I see, in an objective universe that you are thinking about. . .as opposed to a different energy system. It's the same energy system. . .

Joe: Yes, but it seems to be coming through a filter. And, I'm not sure if they are mutated, it's just that they are different.

Int: Ok, you said there was a marked difference. Apparently you said that some of these people left a place and went in a. . .ahhhh. . .

Joe: The concept that I get, and it's just a concept, is that they all got together and decided they were going to have to do something about the situation because geologically they were just barely hanging on. I had a feeling about these immense storms or something. . .

Int: Was there a singular event or something that caused this to happen?

Joe: Yes. And again, I keep getting the picture of a globe going through this huge mass of cosmic crapola, you know. It's like if you looked at a big comet. . .if you could get close to a comet's tail, and it's eight million light years across, or whatever. . .it's like this. . .it's large and you can see it, it's so vast in comparison to the emptiness of space.

Int: This catastrophic event, by your description, would be cosmic as opposed to being planetary?

Joe: No. . .

Int: What I'm really saying is they didn't explode a bunch of atomic bombs or anything?

Joe: No. It was cosmic, it wasn't of their choosing. Although their answer to it appears to be some form of hibernation. Vault-like. . .like lock yourself away in a vault and hibernate until help comes. The thought being that they sent this search party out to look for another place to live.

Int: And this place to which they went to live, is it different in some way from their original place?

Joe: Ah. . .it seemed to me to be just as wild and crazy and hairy, you know with volcanoes, pockets of gases, and violent storms, and electrical. . ..but it's a different kind of storm.

Int: You said there was vegetation at this. . .

Joe: Yes, and that's another thing, I felt like I was in Egypt the whole time, and maybe that's the pyramid overlay, a pyramid influence. I felt that it was dry, you know like there was water there, but they had to really process to get it. You just didn't go up to a pond and...

Int: Ok, so the next step from that was a place of vegetation?

Joe: Yes, there were like polar opposites. . .prime opposites. . .one place dying and one place coming about. . .I don't know if that's a good descript. . .

Int: That works. Anything else that you want to say?

Joe: No.

Int: Then we can go ahead and give you your feedback and shut this thing off now.

At this point, I was presented with my feedback on what the target actually was. Since I was moved around at the target so much, I have listed them in the order in which they were given as target numbers one through seven, along with their actual location and a short description of what they actually are believed to be.

Unusual Features on Mars

Target Number One: 40.89° North Latitude, 9.55° West Longitude
Face and Single Pyramid (*Figure 27*).

Figure 27 is a high-altitude photograph of the northern hemisphere of Mars taken by Viking I orbiter in 1976. At the upper center of the photograph is the unusual surface feature known as *The Face*, measuring approximately nine-tenths of a mile in diameter. At the bottom center of this feature is what appears to be a five-sided *pyramidal structure* which is approximately three times larger than the Great Pyramid in Egypt.

The information provided in the remote viewing for the first target is a large pyramid of the right color. It is intriguing that a complication is immediately noted which brings up information about a major geological activity that might have occurred at a much earlier time.

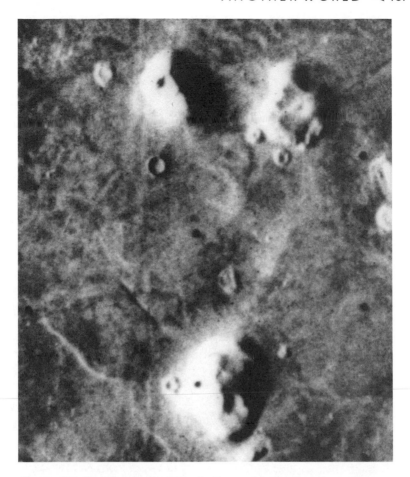

Figure 27. The Face and Single Pyramid, Blowup from Frame
70A13. Photograph provided courtesy of the National Space
Science Data Center, Greenbelt, Maryland, Dr. Michael H. Carr.

Target Number Two: 46.45° North Latitude, 353.22° East Longitude
A Crater With a Pyramid (*Figure 28*).

These features appear in the Cydonia region, approximately 190
miles northeast of the face. The wedge-shaped pyramid at the edge
of the crater gives rise to the question: how did the pyramid survive
the formation of the crater? Was it constructed after the crater was
formed? An interesting question considering the size of the pyramid.

Figure 28. The Crater With Pyramid, Blowup from Frame 43A04. Provided courtesy of the National Space Science Data Center, Greenbelt, Maryland, Dr. Michael H. Carr.

Note the long shadow cast from the pyramid toward the bottom of the page. Then compare it to the shadow on the inside rim of the crater. The pyramid is probably more like a Washington Monument in shape.

From the description I give in the transcript, my initial viewpoint is obviously from down inside the crater and looking up: *Feel like I'm inside a cavern. . .no not a cavern, it's more like a canyon. I'm looking up, up the sides of very steep walls that seem to go on forever.* The sides of the crater are quite steep and very high. Again, this accentuates the immense size of the pyramid formation beside it.

Target Number Three: 45.86° North Latitude, 354.1° East Longitude

Shaped Fields (*Figure 29*).

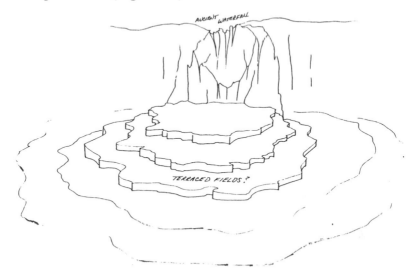

Figure 29. Drawing by Author. No photograph
is available of this feature.

Target Number Four: 35.26° North Latitude, 213.24° East Longitude

Rectangular Feature With Triangular Side (*Figure 30*).

Figure 30. Blowup of Frame 86A07. Photograph provided
courtesy of National Space Science Data Center,
Greenbelt, Maryland, Dr. Michael H. Carr.

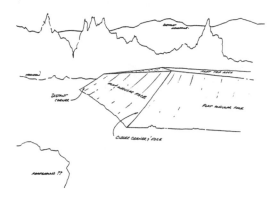

Figure 31. Sketch by Author, showing his view of the Rectangular Feature with Triangle, as perceived during the remote viewing session.

Target Number Five: 34.6° North Latitude, 213.09° East Longitude
Roadway (*Figure 32*).

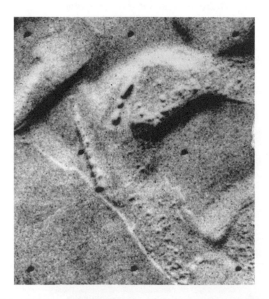

Figure 32. Frame 86A08 showing a Roadway. Photograph provided courtesy of the National Space Science Data Center, Greenbelt, Maryland, Dr. Michael H. Carr.

Additional blowup of Frame **86A08** shows other *Unique Features* and *In-ground* formations adjacent to the *Roadway* (*Figure 33*).

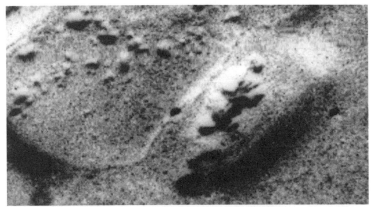

Figure 33. Blowup of Frame 86A08, showing other In-ground features. Provided courtesy of the National Space Science Data Center, Greenbelt, Maryland, Dr. Michael H. Carr.

Target Number Six: 34.57° North Latitude, 212.22° East Longitude
Structure With Triangular Wall (*Figure 34*).

Figure 34. Structure with Triangular Wall from Frame number 35A72. Photograph provided courtesy of the National Space Science Data Center, Greenbelt, Maryland, Dr. Michael H. Carr.

The information from the transcript doesn't appear to match with this particular feature. However, as noted within the transcript, I appeared to be losing my ability to concentrate on the target, as I was showing signs of this through the bio-monitoring equipment.

Target Number Seven: 15° North Latitude, 198° East Longitude
Pyramid Structures (*Figure 35*).

Figure 35. Pyramid Structures, Blowup of Frame 70A77.
Photograph provided courtesy of the National Space Science
Data Center, Greenbelt, Maryland, Dr. Michael H. Carr.

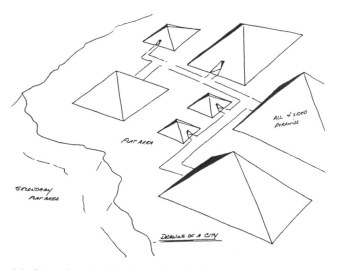

Figure 36. Drawing by Author depicting my own impression of
this area from the remote viewing session.

Pyramids (*Figure 37*).

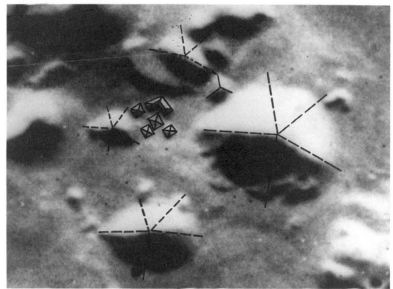

Figure 37. Pyramids. Blowup of Frame 70A77, showing the large group of Pyramids in more detail. Photograph provided Courtesy of The National Space Science Data Center, Greenbelt, Maryland, Dr. Michael H. Carr. Pyramids are outlined for clarity.

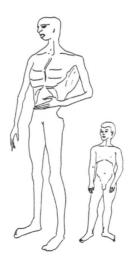

Figure 38. Drawing by Author showing THEY, the humanoids of Mars.

Is this for real? Has remote viewing produced irrefutable proof of the existence of aliens from Mars a million years ago? The answer is—I don't know. It is just as likely that the information produced was collected directly from previous information published in reference to the Face on Mars. There is a very good book titled *The Face on Mars*, by Randolfo Rafael Pozos (Chicago Review Press, 1986). If one reads the contents of this book, nearly all of the information found in the remote viewing transcript can be located— except for *THEY*, the people. The information collected at the terminus point of the session regarding the Martians themselves and the reason for their demise cannot be found anywhere, except of course in some science fiction.

I can believe there was a race of humanoids who fought for survival on neighboring Mars. I can believe they dispatched a lifeboat of some sort to seek out a place where they might flee. If they possessed the technology to build huge pyramids on the surface of Mars, even if it meant constructing them from existent mountains, then they most certainly might have had the ability to reach Earth. Unfortunately, I don't *know* this to be true.

The way to find out would be to target the *City of Pyramids*, or perhaps *The Monumental Pyramid* adjacent to the crater, or maybe the *Face* and *Great Pyramid*, or the structure with the *Triangular Wall* beside it, with a soft-landing exploratory vehicle. Given the probable cost and potential for discovery, I would think that people in our government wouldn't hesitate to investigate. It probably wouldn't cost more than a nuclear submarine!

Maybe it's fear that prevents us from doing so. Such a discovery would alter the course of history as we know it. We would have to acknowledge that we weren't the species supreme in our own universe. The impact on religions and philosophy alone would be incredible.

Martians aside, I will say that, in my own mind, I have become convinced there are other species of beings co-existing, probably living with and amongst us. They may occupy space-time in a harmonic away, but they are there, nevertheless. Perhaps just acknowledging the possibility would expand our sense of responsibility within our own world, our own place in time-space. What do you think?

17
A Snap in Reality

How close to the edge of reality can one venture and how much detail can be brought back? As can be seen in the last chapter, there is a lot of interesting information floating around out there, but how much of it can you trust? Where does the edge of reality cease and the land of make-believe begin? How much detail can be retrieved from that edge using remote viewing techniques? These are questions that hold a great deal of interest for all of us. Historically, this interest is especially true for the physicists as well as the historians. Their fixation with time-space and how it's all glued together has generated some very interesting targeting within the remote viewing area. In this chapter I will present a few examples of this targeting.

Reality. What constitutes the range of reality and where does it begin to break down? In the year 1492, Charles the VIII was taking control of the affairs of France; the son of Lorenzo de Medici, "The Magnificent," became the new ruler of Florence; and Columbus, at age forty-one, sailed from Palos, Spain, on the 235-ton *Santa Maria*, with seventy crewmen. He could not know that he would discover Watling Island in the Bahamas, Cuba, and Haiti and wreck his ship all in the same year. He was pushing the edge of reality in his time. In his year of triumph, most of the educated world believed that he would neither succeed nor return because he would most assuredly sail off the edge of the earth. So, for most, reality stopped at the illusive horizon somewhere west of Spain.

In order to completely understand the limits and range of remote viewing, one must push the envelope. Viewers must go as far out toward the edge as they can without falling off. This means that most people, the majority, are content to flounder somewhat closer to home—unchallenged but content. Even historians know not to ask questions they may not want answered. Physicists, on the other hand, break the mold. They are always looking for new ways of penetrating a little bit deeper into the void. This is certainly true with one of my friends. I'm unable to use her name here, since she holds a sensitive position in a government agency, so I will call her Anna.

We started with a question. How does one go about establishing the limits to physical reality? Where in space and time can you locate a fence, a line of demarcation, or a clearly defined stopping and starting point, where reality stops, at least as we assume to know it, and then begins again as something entirely different? Where is the edge of the world that Columbus sought and that others fear?

Perhaps one place might be where reality-matter takes a sharp turn or makes a complete and violent change within space-time as we know it. We might look inside a nuclear reactor, the atomic pile within a nuclear power plant at the precise time of ignition; or, perhaps we can look at ground zero of an atomic test site. Anywhere in which a rip in the fabric of time-space can be observed, not by using physical sensors, but through the use of psychic ones. In the latter part of 1982, this is what we did.

Target One

Anna selected the first target and included it with ten other *normal* targets. The method of targeting was by placing the name and date/time of the target inside a double-wrapped opaque envelope and mixing the envelope with ten others, prior to giving them a random-order numbering sequence of one through ten. These ten randomly numbered envelopes were then passed to an interviewer who had no knowledge of their contents, in order to create a double-blind environment for me, the remote viewer.

In the beginning of the series, the first four targets were what I would call run-of-the-mill experiments: a graveyard, a flower garden with brick pathways, a harbor with sailboat slips. But the fifth target was the ringer Anna had placed within the others.

The first impression was of an *old tower*. This was quickly described as constructed of wood, with inter-connecting support struts, built in three layers—the bottom or wider layer supporting two progressively narrow upper sections. There were some initial inaccuracies, as I attempted at first to make the tower into first a windmill and then an old-fashioned drilling platform. But eventually I settled on just an *old tower*.

The interviewer asked if there was anything else in the area of the tower and I told him that I perceived a very large flat and desolate area. That it felt very *scruffy*, very *arid*, and I felt that it was probably in a scrub desert area, not unlike our southwest. My perception was that the tower was sitting in a slight depression, irregular in shape but somewhat circular.

The interviewer suggested that I take a minute to explore the area and report on anything else that I might discover. This I did. I soon reported that I thought there were some metal rods sticking up out of the ground. They were peculiar, in that they were set in concrete, jutted upward perfectly vertical to the ground, but not very high. Neither were they connected to anything as far as I could tell. When asked what I thought they might be for, I suggested they were for *sensing*, or *measuring* an effect. What, I couldn't guess.

On further examination of the target, I perceived two box-like trailers or temporary shelters off to one side. Inside was electronic equipment, mostly relay equipment of some sort, with many wires running outward toward the tower. This time, however, I determined they weren't for sensing or monitoring, but had something to do with the tower—operation of the tower (*Figure 39*).

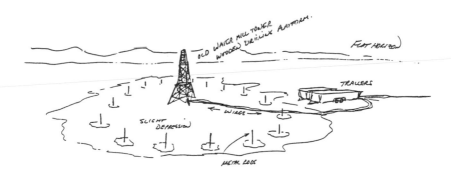

Figure 39.

At this point in time my mental image of the target shifted dramatically. One could equate it to a sensation not unlike snapping your fingers, only doing it with your mind. *Snap*—different scene. I even stated my surprise at the suddenness of the change. It was as if the entire target shifted and became something different.

I reported a very bright, white light on a flat horizon (*Figure 40*). The interviewer asked from what perspective I was seeing the light, and I told him that it was about two hundred miles away, on the flat horizon. There appeared to be low mountains in the background, but the light was sustained and very bright. It appeared to be spreading.

When pressed for more information, I commented that there was none. We spent a while longer trying to develop more information concerning the target location but were unable to do so.

VERY BRIGHT
WHITE LIGHT
A.7.

FLAT HORIZON

Figure 40.

Because the scene was radically different from the previous three targets, it was my assumption that something had gone wrong with the remote viewing session. Somehow, I had been motivated to leave the general area of the previous three targets and proceed to a new location. It was with the heavy feeling that we had somehow messed up the series that we passed on the information to Anna. She was ecstatic. The place and time that we had targeted was just before dawn, July 16, 1945—a place in the desert southwest called Trinity. The time and place of the first atom bomb test.

In the excited discussion that followed, I commented about what appeared to be a large spherical device that I kept associating with the tower. It was the circular form that made me first want to call it a windmill. My overwhelming impression of a large circle at the top reminded me of the circular blades of a windmill. Eventually I had discarded the notion, because no matter what I did with the impression of the circular object, I just couldn't turn it into the necessary windmill blades.

The aspiring remote viewer should circle the above paragraph. It represents one of the most difficult aspects of the remote viewing function—inappropriately discarding information simply because we can't figure out what to do with it or how it might fit within the overall scheme of things.

Always, always, *always* note the impression. That doesn't mean call it something, conclude what it might be, determine one way or another what function it performs. That means, simply write down or notate a basic description. In the above example, I should have said something like *There's a round shape at the top of the tower but I don't know what it is.* Or maybe *Associated with the tower is the image of a round object.*

I promise you—this will be one of the most difficult lessons that you will ever learn to apply. I've been doing this for fifteen years and I still leave out information simply because I can't figure out what to do with it.

Anna, on the other hand, knows exactly what to do with it. She told me to sit down and give her a detailed drawing and description of the interior of the device. She asked that I note what I felt was the most important elements to its construction and list them in order of importance (*Figure 41*).

Of primary concern is the construction of the *case*. It is particularly important with regard to its lack of flaws, its even thicknesses and hardness, the way the breakaway components are made in its core, and integral shielding.

Secondary are the specific shape of the charges, then the detonation timing, the triggers design, and finally the purity of U-239 (Plutonium).

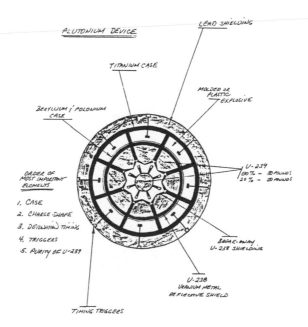

Figure 41. Drawing of nuclear device by Author.

The original plutonium bomb is very heavy, bulky, but not too difficult to create. It is messy and lacks any real power in comparison to today's more modern thermonuclear weapons. Of course, you would have trouble telling that to the large number of unfortunate human beings who were under it in Nagasaki when it went off.

Target Two

The same targeting methodology as above was used. The actual target name, a set of coordinates, and a specific date/time was selected and placed within a double-wrapped opaque envelope. The envelope was placed within a group of ten others during an entirely different series of targets. Again, the interviewer didn't know what the target was in order to provide for a double-blind scenario.

The initial information was a little strange. I described what I called a beehive or honeycomb-looking surface. I stated there were circular indentations in the top portion of each of the honeycomb areas. There was a sense of seals or rubber gaskets in connection with the center of each honeycomb channel. I had a feeling that there were black rods sticking downward through the whole affair.

The honeycomb sections turned into something very polished or shiny. My first guess was polished aluminum or steel of some sort.

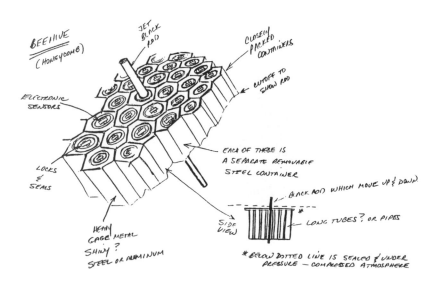

Figure 42. Drawing of Honeycomb/Beehive impression by Author.

Very hard casings or six-sided tubes. I decided on heavy-gauge metal, probably steel, due to a highly corrosive atmosphere or environment (*Figure 42*).

I had a strong feeling that this honeycomb was packed in something and said so. The interviewer asked me to describe what it was packed in, but I was unable to determine that. I remember at the time feeling very cramped and under great pressure—not unlike steam from a boiler. I even suggested that steam might be associated with the target.

I was in the process of describing how the black tubes interacted with the steel containers when I again felt as if I had been quickly and suddenly slapped in the face—*Snap*.

I told the interviewer that my entire perception of the target was changed. I had the feeling that I had begun at the right target but was now at the wrong one. I wanted to tear up my drawing and begin again with my description. The interviewer convinced me that I should probably wait and hold onto it and let Anna figure it all out.

I drew a second sheet (*Figure 43*). A basketball-shaped building sitting on a circular wall, with a very large building connected to the right and a mixture of many smaller building shapes connected to the left. I noted there was some kind of an exhaust system at one end as well, then suggested on the drawing that it might be associated with the steam perception earlier on in the session.

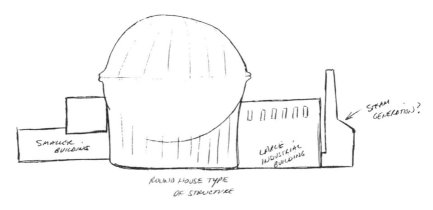

Figure 43. Author's impression of target after change.

An impression of the building jumped into my mind immediately following the *snap* feeling. Maybe five stories tall, with large buildings constructed to either side. My guess at the time was the target had something to do with production of power. My sense of it was that there were lots of details (50 KVA lines, power poles, steam, noise, and activity) which were there, but which I was only getting a partial feel for.

The target was a gas-cooled, graphite-moderated, uranium-oxide nuclear power plant, located in Windscale, England. As it turned out, the drawing of the honeycomb was a fairly good representation of the core area of the reactor. The dark rods (black rods) are the graphite rods used to control the fission process. While the second drawing isn't an exact replica of the reactor building, it is sufficient to enable recognition of the Windscale unit from other forms of gas-cooled power plants currently in existence.

One other target was done along the same lines during that year. It was a mini-nuclear-powered generator, not unlike the ones used to power the deep space probes and inaccessible mountain-top weather stations. Again, the unique *snap* occurred during the actual remote viewing and there was a significant change in perspective.

The *Snap*

What is the *snap*? What does it signify? I believe it occurs when a remote viewer (or psychic) is playing near the edges of reality. The detonation of a nuclear device, ignition of a nuclear pile, the start-up of a portable nuclear generator, all share one thing in common—they alter matter. It is a violent exchange of energy, the change of one physical format to another. The target dates for each of the targets coincided with the actual event date, the times with the actual event, only three minutes prior to its actually having happened. I was *there* (at least in a psychic sense) when the event occurred. So perhaps the *snap* is a safety mechanism to prevent some form of damage which might otherwise occur.

In the case of the Trinity Site Test, at what would have been the point of detonation in remote viewing time I was essentially describing ground zero. *Snap*—I am two hundred miles away describing the blast on the horizon. At point of ignition within the nuclear pile, *Snap*—I am outside the pile describing the building. A like occurrence with the portable nuclear-power generator also occurred.

Does nuclear power breach reality? Does it tear the fabric of our physical world? Perhaps. More interesting is what appears to be a safety mechanism which prevents us from being in the area of a reality-quake while or when it happens in a psychic sense. It's apparently ok if we are there physically; that would mean only our physical death. But we aren't allowed to be there non-physically. Is it too dangerous, or is it just impossible?

It's a shame, but we will probably never know the answer to that question. For the time being, however, my own belief dictates that it is probably just impossible for us to *not* exist—hence we just can't be where we can't exist. I'll hang on to this opinion until I experience something further on that changes it. That could be in the next five minutes.

18
How Does It Work?

In reviewing many of the questions that I have been asked over the years, I would have to say that the most frequently asked question is probably *How does remote viewing work?* How is the information transferred, where does it come from, and how is it processed? These are certainly essential elements of the same question.

Of course, if these were simple questions to answer, I would be comfortably wealthy and not quite as busy right now. But they aren't simple questions. They are tough ones, about which in some regard we are left only to hypothesize.

Over the years I have developed a few theories about how it might work. Portions of these theories have proven out and portions are still left to conjecture. In any event, I will share these theories with my readers in this chapter.

One of the ground rules learned early on is that since psi-functioning has been observed under both voluntary (controlled experiments) and involuntary (spontaneous events) conditions, then it must be *a talent which is naturally native to the human species. A talent which can be learned, recognized, or enhanced.*

This is not to say that it isn't native to other species; I'm just saying native to humans since that is what we are talking about here. I've had experiences with other species which would *seem* to indicate these other species might have a psychic ability, but since I've not been participant to more than a few such experiments, I don't feel qualified to make a statement. As far as I know, other species could just be more sensitive to frequencies, lights, or energies that exceed our own capacities. On the other hand, as I said earlier, I believe it is a naturally found experience or event which can occur almost anywhere, with anyone, at any time. Therefore, it is also no big deal. Tough to study, but no big deal.

We know, through observation of the phenomenon as it unfolds, that there are voluntary or planned paranormal events and there are the unplanned but observed events which we call spontaneous. Either can happen at any time and one can be as complete an event as the other. Such a mix of non-spontaneous and spontaneous paranormal activity would seem to imply that remote viewing has a wide range of occurrence, beginning with the accidental and running to the deliberate. . .controlled to uncontrolled.

This observation in itself implies that it is probably a natural human function or trait. It is a capability we may all possess, but not necessarily one in which we all excel. In other words, it is probably a natural talent but also a very rare one.

Being a natural talent, psi-functioning is automatically reliant on the mind and brain in order to function. *So the mind and brain are by necessity an interface to the event we call psi-functioning.*

You may notice that I am referring to *mind* and *brain* separately. An effective argument can be made that would establish the necessity for having a brain in order to have a mind, but this connection does not establish "like functions." I believe what the mind does is different from what the brain does, and vice versa. Both roles are supportive of each other, but distinctly different in scope.

The location of the brain is easily determined and common to all humans; it's in the skull. On the other hand, the location of mind is not established, only that the brain is required in order to communicate with it. We also know that the brain, the hard-wiring, must be relatively free of defect in order for the mind to communicate and think well. So the brain resides in the skull and has to be somewhat healthy, and the mind resides. . .where? A place I will call *Somewhere-else.*

How large the mind is in a physical sense is unknown, but we usually end up making a subjective judgment of its size by mixing brain and mind qualifiers, such as "what a head that person has on their shoulders; they're absolutely brilliant." Of course such qualifiers are meaningless, since size of head or brain has little to do with mind.

Some will argue that the mind resides in the brain because that is where some believe we store all the information we know. However, as a remote viewer, I will categorically state that is not necessarily true. I collect, analyze, and report information every day that I have never read, seen, or known prior to the experiment. It would seem that my mind is collecting it from somewhere. The mass of cerebral cells between my ears is the last place I think I would be looking for that information. No. . .there is a *Somewhere-else,* and our minds not only have access to it, but may in fact at least partially reside within it. How large that place is or what else is there is up for question. So there is at least one other place besides physical reality, and my mind has access to it. Through extrapolation, one could say that *there is at least a physical world as well as a non-physical world.*

Figure 44 illustrates how such a perspective might be viewed in a linear reality. It's probably far more complex than shown, but for illustrative purposes, the drawing is sufficient.

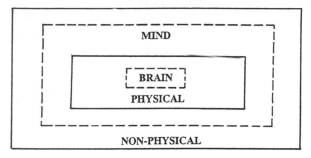

Figure 44.

Our brain, the hard wiring, is probably some form of *Central Interface Unit.* Through it, we receive all of the information we can collect using physical sensors within the physical reality. However, by itself, the brain cannot access the spiritual side, or non-physical reality. The mind is required in order to do this. So, now we have two tools out collecting information; the two collection arenas are as different as night and day from one another.

Which is the higher-functioning tool? The mind, obviously. On its own, the brain is very good at running the autonomic functions of the body. It regulates everything that is not chemically self-regulating. It generally does this very well, that is, unless it has been overridden by the mind.

Until recently, no one believed the mind could override the body. But the newest advances in bio-monitoring and feedback have established that our minds can control much more than we ever knew was possible. Our blood pressure, heart rate, temperature, and even the speed at which we heal can be controlled by the mind. The mind also controls all of the other inputs, both physical as well as spiritual, and integrates the information either to our betterment or our detriment. You shouldn't doubt this. In my experience I've watched men die in combat simply because they thought they were going to. The minor wounds that they had received certainly wouldn't have killed them otherwise. Likewise, I've seen men live who, in anyone's opinion, never stood a chance.

The mind also has a capacity for extracting additional knowledge from data that otherwise wouldn't make any sense to the brain. An example of this would be pleasure extracted from knowledge—watching a butterfly dance around a flower.

The mind is the higher function of the two collectors because it can straddle realities. It is comfortable in the physical reality, as well as the spiritual oblique, or non-physical reality. It can differentiate between the two and exercise conviction, based on the inputs from both. It is also fairly easy to establish the effects of input from both. They each have equal effect and importance in the molding or shaping of our lives. Anyone who has ever awakened from a gut-searing nightmare or discovered an answer to a particularly difficult engineering question while in a dream state can vouch for this.

Now we have a processing system. It's a system which gets its raw data from inside as well as outside physical reality. However, don't make the mistake of thinking it is a processor like we find inside the mother board of a computer. That comparison was made approximately thirty-five years ago, and look how long it has taken us to get rid of the notion. We don't operate like computers—never have and never will.

Then, what do we operate like? *We reside and operate in a constantly fluctuating past of our own creation.* Most people would rather hear this a little bit differently. It would be more palatable if we resided and operated by *reaction to* a constantly changing environment. In space-time, the actual processing sequence is probably closer to that which I've listed below. By the time our processing is of any use to us, we are already dealing with past events. Our reality is one we in fact invent or make up as we go.

Processing Sequence as a Function of Time

ZERO TIME 0:   We recognize incoming information about our current reality.

PLUS .00000:   We begin to make sense of the input from our five senses.

PLUS .00001:   We fish out additional information from our hard-wired brain memory modules.

PLUS .0001:   We reason a little about the information and decide we lack certain essentials to make any decisions.

PLUS .001:   We insert additional overlay, inaccurate as-

sumptions, and prejudice in order to make
it more palatable.

PLUS .01: We reach a conclusion regarding our surrounding physical reality.

PLUS .1: Assured of the accuracy of our reality understanding, we make corrections to our
hard-wired memory, file the conclusions
for quick reference in the next check to
make sure nothing changes too drastically,
and begin the process all over again.

Overlap these processing sequences and perform them at fifty times per second and you can see that not only is the accuracy somewhat questionable, but no matter how fast it operates, it will always be just a tad behind reality as it can be observed. We will always be subject to our own observations as well as our own belief concepts.

So what then is *consciousness*? Consciousness is a state of mind in the collection or the processing where we find ourselves awake. It is the mind awake. Consciousness can happen in either arena, physical reality or non-physical reality. So, consciousness is mobile. How bright or how dim depends upon how awake we might be at any given happening within the collection or processing modality. Consciousness is like a sliding glimmer or speck of light that slips and slides throughout both realities. Mind is required in order to have consciousness. The degree of wakefulness determines the degree of consciousness.

I like to think of consciousness, therefore, as the self-defining limits to the mind. How far I can go with my wakefulness determines the limits of my mind, thoughts, and reasoning power. The mind is probably nearly unlimited. It can be unwound to the farthest reaches of reality or non-reality. It is our consciousness that sets the boundary or fences of the mind. We can only be so attentive, so awake, at any given time.

The subconscious is that area of mind in which we are not normally awake. It's as real as the conscious part of our mind to us, but, because we are not awake within it, it appears to operate in an autonomic fashion. Or does it? I believe the subconscious is the gateway to the great unknown. That is the fertile ground from which the psychic information comes; it has access to all knowledge, all realities, and all possibilities. The exchange of information between the subconscious and conscious is the single filter which causes more problems than anything else with regard to understanding psychic information. Why? Because at that very threshold of knowing, communications seem to break down. There is no agreeable language between the consciousness and subconsciousness, no shared or common reference points.

How does a deaf mute describe the secrets of the universe over a twelve-foot fence? Or, to complicate matters even further, how is it done with a terrified self-developed dictator guarding or protecting us on this side? Our personal dictator is what we commonly refer to as our *ego*. It believes it is never wrong and it is *always* in charge.

A New Language

We can breach the wall by learning to communicate with our subconscious. We challenge our ego by mastering a new and totally different language, a language of the mind.

In the structured protocols of remote viewing, we set a stage where we can always return. It's a place where both the subconscious and conscious meet, time and time again, to attempt communications—first on a rudimentary level, using basic gestalts and overwhelming holistic projections, and then later in more refined ways, with details never thought possible. The study of this new language is difficult in the extreme, but nevertheless possible.

A proper study approach has to address three specific areas for three different reasons. These are:

1. **The Hard-wiring**. The physical brain itself requires detailed study in order to determine those areas in which psi-functioning might manifest itself. Recent innovations in both research techniques and equipment have now provided science with new inroads into the hard-wiring of the brain. Until recently, such research techniques were not available, unless of course they were piggybacked onto pathological studies of the brain during actual surgery. Methods available to study the hard-wiring of the human brain while actually psi-functioning include: nuclear magnetic resonance imaging (MRI), which exceeds computed tomography (CT) scans in their accuracy and detail; electroencephalogram (EEG) and brain electrical activity mapping (BEAM); positron emission tomography (PET) scans, wherein special radioactive isotopes are injected into the blood, after which they flow through the brain revealing metabolic processes and shifts in blood flow that accompany various types of mental activity; and magnetoencephalography (MEG) which can

determine the spatial distributions of specific groups of neurons participating in a given activity over time. Whereas original studies (by EEG and BEAM) were restricted to less than the first two centimeters of the brain, the MEG and PET open new windows to brain function at depths exceeding nine centimeters. That's like turning on the lights on the ocean floor!

2. **The Processing.** The mind and its power has unfolded before our eyes over centuries. But some would argue we know no more now than we did hundreds of years ago. When I speak of processing here, I am talking about the mind, not the brain. The mental processing I am talking about includes thinking, interpreting, and understanding. What makes us believe what we believe, why do no two people think alike, why is one person's understanding of a situation markedly different from another's? These questions have a direct bearing on how we function and how we process. Therefore, we need to study these areas in order to understand psi-functioning and the language of the mind.

3. **Integration.** Finally, we need to understand what effect the above two areas have on our reality. Since we are ultimately in charge of our reality, we decide what is real and not real in our universe. Therefore, we are also responsible for what happens to us while traveling through it. Some try to slip out from under this responsibility through the use of ritual. The invention of ritual assists in establishing a *quid pro quo* relationship between cause and effect. A proper study of how we assign responsibility and integrate it into our consciousness would go a long way toward understanding psi-functioning.

We can attempt a description of how psi-functioning or paranormal perception probably works. The psychic information comes through the wall between the conscious and sub-conscious. The information is probably retained by and stored in non-physical reality until required. Once it has passed through the consciousness wall, it must then be filtered, assessed, and made sensible by the mind (with the ego's help, of course). The information is then passed along to the hard-wire areas of the brain for further processing under physical-reality requirements, and then matched with old information, blocked into appropriate confining rules and accepted practices, and then sent to the conclusion station, where a decision is made as to whether or not it will be integrated. A long and arduous journey, after which the information arrives almost totally unrecognizable. However it arrives, we rarely accept responsibility for it, unless it will massage the ego.

Is there a common language? I believe there is. But it is common only to the subconscious. Our conscious minds are our own creation; we've hung every possible warning bell and whistle imaginable from them in order to warn ourselves of any approaching communication from the subconscious. Most of these warnings get in the way of psi-functioning and thoroughly stifle it.

To demonstrate what one needs to deal with, I've laid out the step-stone pattern of how psi-functioning probably works. It is a natural sequence of events, much of which happens in spite of the degree of our involvement. In a typical remote viewing event, the steps of cognition probably go something like this:

Cognition

1. The viewer attempts to re-create a meditative state free of as much interference as possible. It is a neutral state of mind wherein there is no on-going processing.

2. Once achieving the neutral state, the viewer will ask himself or herself a question which needs answering. It might be something like *Target now* or *Tell me what I need to know*.

3. A flicker of information will race across the brain. It won't last long, perhaps a quarter-second or less, but it will leave an impression.

4. The viewer will attempt to digest the small amount of information. Not in an analytic way, or the ego will slip in more information than was originally presented. Once digested, this small flicker of information is filed in temporary memory.

5. The viewer then attempts to recapture the neutral state and capture more flickers of information, as in steps 2-4 above.

6. Once sufficient flickers of information have been temporarily stored to develop a larger piece of the puzzle, an item, the viewer then tries to put it into perspective. This is done by going through long-term memory in the brain and looking for something that most closely resembles the overall perception.

7. Once sufficient larger puzzle pieces have been obtained and identified, the viewer attempts to produce a coherent picture. Again, every effort is made not to try and reach a final conclusion, as there are still not enough flickers of information, or larger puzzle pieces.

8. After some degree of effort, an overall picture becomes apparent. If every effort is made to do the above with the least amount of internally generated overlay possible, then more of the overall picture will be correct than not.

9. Once the target has been completed and the mental processing discontinued, every effort is then made to give the remote viewer a clear and precise feedback image of the actual target. This anchors the accurate and the inaccurate perceptions for learning purposes.

10. The viewer reviews the information and then decides what was accurate and why. This gets put into permanent (physical reality) memory regarding how the mental processing was done.

11. The viewer reviews the information and then decides what was inaccurate and why. This gets put into permanent memory regarding how the mental overlay might have occurred or was generated.

12. After review of past lessons learned, another remote viewing is then set up and attempted.

A simpler version would be that, in some way, a specific target—an event, place, person, or object—is identified to the viewer. This is done through standard targeting mechanisms: out-bounder teams, sealed envelopes, name, etc. The conscious mind then understands that it is to be on the lookout for incoming material. There is an expectation by the conscious mind that this material will be passed over from the subconscious. The subconscious, on the other hand, already knows what the target is and has begun a detailed search for the most effective means of transmission. Since the subconscious can't communicate using the logic of the conscious, it devises symbols, feelings, and insights (similar pictures), to convey the information. It has a choice about how to do this. First it can send an overall gestalt, that is, all the information possible in one huge package, or it can send bits of information a little at a time until an entire gestalt or overall picture has been delivered.

Meanwhile, the conscious mind, specifically the ego, decides that since it is "always in charge," it should be providing information as well. So, the areas of the conscious mind which generate creativity, imagination, conjecture, and so forth, are fired up as well. This pumps in useless information to the forefront of the mind, producing what has become known in remote viewing as overlay. Squeezed in between the overlay information bursts are the actual tidbits of accurate data being passed by the subconscious.

Since our conscious mind can't differentiate between the two, it begins to rapidly process all of the information in order to derive conclusions. These conclusions are further processed by comparing them to recorded (historical) knowledge, at which time anything that doesn't seem to fit is thrown out. If we are real lucky, we end up with about 5 percent usable data.

There are a number of reasons why this all works this way. The following are but a few of the major problems:

1. The ego doesn't "like" to be wrong.
2. It's part of our human nature to absolutely demand a conclusion.
3. Anything illogical will be pitched.
4. Anything we don't understand is either incomplete, inaccurate, or of no consequence.
5. Everything must have a basis in physical reality.
6. We have to be in control of everything on which we focus.
7. We are subject to reality.

In actuality, our ego is seldom right, we really don't need to come to a conclusion about anything, a possible action is inaction, logic isn't necessary to truth, we will probably never completely understand anything that isn't subject to immediate change or modification, we decide what constitutes reality, and observation isn't control.

Therefore, the valuable tools of a remote viewer or any psychic are being able to quiet the conscious (ego) mind, learning never to demand a conclusion, intensely focusing on nothing specific, being absolutely neutral towards a target, being able to establish a fertile ground for conscious/subconscious exchange, and developing a common language between the physical and non-physical realities.

19
Levels of RV

Now that remote viewing has been observed for a number of years, it has become apparent that there are discrete phases or levels of ability, dependent on how much experience the remote viewer might have. These levels or phases occur naturally in that each one is supported by the level previously experienced. One phase always follows the previous one and is dependent on it. A philosophic concept isn't necessary to learn and improve, provided a fixed process or ritual is present. In the case of remote viewing, the scientific study of psi-functioning, the protocol is the ritual.

Therefore, if one's psychic experience is derived from a "ritualistic practice," then performance will become dependent on whatever the original ritual was that was initially used. One might say: once a crystal ball reader, always a crystal ball reader.

This is one of the problems inherent in the study of psychic performance. It is nearly impossible to see the subtle shift in phase or level, or the change in psychic information production within different rituals.

I have found over the years that outright rejection of ritual can prove disastrous to individuals trying to develop their psychic abilities. This doesn't mean you must run out and purchase a crystal ball or a deck of Tarot Cards; it only means that some sort of ritual is necessary. In the case of remote viewing, the protocol becomes the most essential element of learning. Secondarily, the ritual of the approach comes next.

Before I get into what I perceive the levels of learning to be, or talk further about ritual, it is important that I mention some of the pitfalls which are found in the ritualization of psi-function. There are more than a few, and each can be disastrous to the person trying to learn remote viewing unless a little warning is heeded.

The Learning Curve

The degree or percentage of success as compared to the number of attempts will not appear constant. This is sometimes described as the learning curve. Instead of a single plateau, there will be multiple plateaus, with long periods of what appear to be minimal successes in between. The mind, while trying to assimilate the new capabilities, is doing battle with itself. As the initial novelty wears off, the conscious mind tries to regain control over the process, thereby creating increasing levels of mental masking or overlay. There is a marked difference between a normal learning curve and one you might see from a new remote viewer. The normal curve may look like this (*Figure 45*):

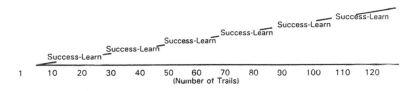

Figure 45. Normal Learning Curve.

The learning curve of a remote viewer will look more like this (*Figure 46*):

Figure 46. Learning Curve for a Remote Viewer.

Beginner's Luck

Psi-functioning takes place within the ancient brain/mind. What I mean is that, genetically that part of the brain/mind interface has always been there and has always functioned; it's just that we have never bothered to pay any attention to it. When we first set up our ritual (protocol), our first exercises are usually very successful. It's the first time we are able to see psi-functioning in ourselves, and it is exciting.

It works well the first few times because our conscious mind (rational self) and ego aren't prepared to deal with it. So there is no interference. We do exceptionally well, hence the term *beginner's luck*. Our conscious mind may be caught off guard initially, but it is quick to respond.

Soon, the built-in, automatic analysis systems kick in. They try to compensate for temporary loss of control. Once again, they take over and begin to override the more primitive sense inputs—the psi-functioning—and it is soon buried under tons of useless mental debris and overlay.

A picture of how this might look before and after is presented in Figure 47.

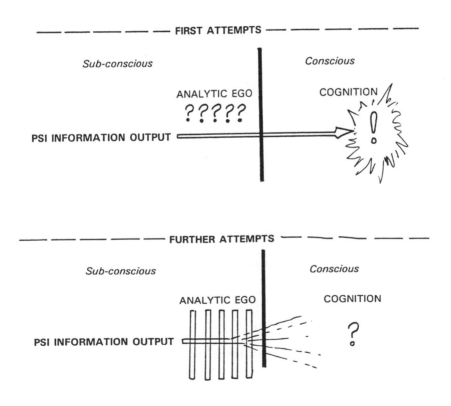

Figure 47. Before and After.

Guru/Technological Dependency

It is unavoidable that, during the discovery process, students of psi-functioning want to replicate the abilities of those who have gone before them, to become as good as their teachers. While there is some degree of replication necessary in the teaching of basics, once an understanding of why something is being done has been grasped by the student it is no longer necessary to develop in the teacher's footsteps. Somewhere along the line the apron strings require cutting.

This necessary separation is easily seen between parent and child. Once the child reaches an age where s/he can pursue her own ends and suffer her own consequences, specifically, carry the weight of her own decisions, there is usually a break in the parent/child relationship. Sometimes this is more difficult than not, but it must eventually occur. Within American society, this usually takes place around the eighteenth birthday, or when society as we understand it acknowledges the legality of partial adulthood. In some cultures it takes place much earlier, in some cases by age thirteen. In psi-learning, the break between teacher and student must come once the elementary basics have been transferred and understood.

In my own observation, watching psychics as teachers, I've noticed not only a great reluctance on the teacher's part to let go, but I've also seen the student doggedly hang on, refusing to leave the shadow of the instructor. Is it fear? Perhaps. My own thought is that it is a blend of a number of things, the following being a small list of possibilities:

1. Teacher ego. When the teacher relinquishes *control* of a student, the student might turn out better than the teacher.
2. Teacher need. The teacher has spent almost as much time trying to instill a feeling of *student need for the teacher* as she or he has in transferring the knowledge and talent. This is usually a direct result of the teacher's need for ego building.
3. Student responsibility. Complete severance from the teacher means the student must now take full responsibility for his or her actions or lack of action. This means accepting responsibility for right and wrong information.
4. Decrease in practice. The psi-functioning is no longer considered a learning modality; the student is now submersed in real-world applications.
5. No philosophic concept. The philosophic concepts and beliefs are borrowed from the teacher and cannot stand alone, or the student hasn't been taught how to develop them individually.

There are other problems, almost as many as there are relationships between student and teachers. The important thing to remember is that one of the goals in the teaching relationship is to eventually sever the strings between the teacher and student, which means the student must be given as much in support of independence as they are given with regard to technique or style. It is eventually up to the student to leave the teacher and develop an individual, unique style and methodology. If the student can't eventually do this, then s/he never really learned anything.

Learn, but learn to fly solo.

Too Much

Too much of a good thing can make anyone sick. There is an unfortunate belief that the more you do of something, the faster you learn it. This may hold true in some areas, but not in learning remote viewing. It is not how much you do; it is how well and how focused you do it. Overexertion, pressing on in spite of how you might feel physically, emotionally, or mentally can only lead to burnout.

What's appropriate? In my own case, I try to do no more than two remote viewings per day, practice or otherwise. In a rare case, when pressed for information on a critical subject, I've gone as high as five. How does that make me feel? Sometimes doing five isn't any more difficult than doing one. Sometimes doing two is more difficult than doing five. It depends on how I feel on any given day. It's like any other skill. If you feel good about what you are doing and you're up, then it's not a great deal of work producing the information. But, if you're down for any reason, low on energy, if it feels like you are really having to work to dig the information out, well. . .then it's going to be work, hard work.

My own recommendation is to prepare for doing three practice sessions a day; but stop on your first great success. In other words, if the first one you do turns out to be really good—a great session— then stop there. Quit on an upbeat. If it takes two to get a good result, then take two. If it takes three, then take three. If you do three but don't feel that you've done very well, go back over all three and look at the parts or portions that you know clicked, then skip a day.

It's important to stop on an upbeat if you can. This reinforces correct comportment, proper behavior, instead of underscoring the poorer performance. We are then able to remember what we did that *felt* right, versus what we did to *feel* wrong.

Personal Problems

Finally, in the beginning stages of learning to remote view, there are personal problems which can interfere with learning. Physical pains, colds, mental or emotional stress, menstrual cramps, anger, environmental noise sensitivity, and some natural interferences can make it more difficult to succeed.

While it hasn't been fully established, there is reason to believe that electromagnetic disturbances may have a deleterious effect on remote viewing. Extreme low frequency (ELF) and sunspot activity are two examples of these types of interference.

The Levels of Learning

As I mentioned in Chapter 10, there are a number of levels or separate degrees of proficiency that can be attained in remote viewing. For a long period of time I was convinced of four, possibly five levels. Later I agreed to a probable six. Somewhere around 1985 I learned there were at minimum seven; now. . .well, now I think there are a few more.

It is not surprising that the farther one progresses into the remote viewing experience, the more that becomes clear about it. This may have to do with the fact that, when learning to remote view, individuals never learn more than they are able to handle at any given time. In other words, a viewer will recognize the fifth level of learning only after somewhat mastering the four that come before it. Until that understanding has been accomplished, it is impossible to see what constitutes the fifth level.

While this aspect may be true in a thematic way, the rule breaks down somewhat when observed in application. You may observe a slight bleed-through from one level to the next at any level of application. This happens because the differences or boundaries between the different levels of capability are not as clearly defined as we would like to have them be. Also, the new remote viewer lacks the discipline necessary to insure that the different responses stay within their specific levels of learning. What the reader should understand is that this is all right. It's all expected in the learning processes.

What are the different levels? This question invites a very complicated and time-consuming response. However, at this stage of understanding it is only necessary to give a general outline of what each level may contain. The more detailed analysis will have to fall to individuals as they progress through their own stages of development. I will touch on, but not go into much detail about, some of the higher functioning levels. This is simply because I don't know if I fully understand them, and therefore I hesitate to make statements regarding them as yet. My experience is still going on, so all the data is not yet in. In any event, here are the levels as I understand them to be at this point in time:

Level One. Overwhelming major gestalts.

A gestalt, simply stated, is the *sum* of all the elements taken from the target. If you take a close look at most gestalts, you will find an overall representation of the target. It's like a silhouette of the target which captures its essence but doesn't usually provide sufficient information to name the target. Many new remote viewers have no difficulty in drawing the gestalt. They run into difficulty when they then try to define what it is. Usually they select something that is quite similar to, but categorically different from, the actual target.

Figure 48 illustrates this principle. It is a major gestalt or first-level impression of the Devil's Tower. While it might be drawn the same way by numerous beginning viewers, many will incorrectly identify it as the Eiffel Tower, a waterfall, a road, or an apron. Seeing the overall gestalt, it is not too difficult to understand how this might occur.

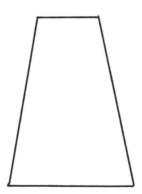

Figure 48. Level-One Example.

Sometimes a new viewer will processes the incoming gestalt and describe it by listing all of its pieces. These pieces won't usually be in order, so the impression will come in shattered or heavily corrupted. It generally takes some time before someone is able to correctly sort out major gestalts. Unfortunately, since it is the one major input, when you blow one, it is blown in a spectacular way.

Level Two. Information pertinent to the five senses, or sensual input.

This will be input that you perceive as coming in through your five senses. While it is not actually happening, you will be tempted to say that it is, with phrases such as "I *feel like* I can hear a clanging noise" or "If I could taste this, it would taste bitter." There may also be a lot of self-generated vision produced at this level.

This level, like the first, will not contain much detail about dimension. Most descriptive wording used will reference overall (gestalt) impressions of size or shape: it's tall, it's big, it's long, etc. Not until the viewer almost completes the level-two work will the area of target dimensions begin to open up. More complex descriptions might be "it's sweeping, it fills the front view" or "there are multiple approaches to this target."

Using the Devil's Tower as a further example, level-two details would be represented as drawn in Figure 49:

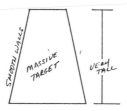

Figure 49. Level-Two Example.

Level Three. Aesthetic impact.

This is usually delivered by an overriding impression about the target, an idea about the target which you cannot discard. It has impact because it defines something about the target which makes it aesthetically appealing to us or is a distinct turn-off. Most of these impressions will be rather hazy at first, a little vague and indistinct. However, over time they will become stronger and the overall impact from a target will become easily defined.

The aesthetics of a target effect a change in our emotion regarding it. These changes are sudden, unexpected. Beauty, ugliness, joy, anger, and apprehension are some of the feelings that targets might arouse within us. The particular trick here will be to learn how to ferret out why the target does what it does to us.

Again, using the Devil's Tower as an example, a response that might be felt in level three is "target is absolutely massive, I feel as though I'm falling over backward while trying to look at it." Digging out why the target has generated such a gut response is difficult but not impossible.

Smaller portions of the target will also be represented. As far as dimensions, the viewer will begin to take parts or portions of the target and begin to tie them together. The "humped" part of the target will begin to be tied to the "smaller nodules," as in Figure 50, for example:

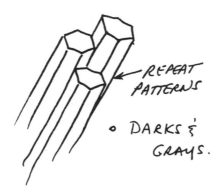

Figure 50. Level-Three Example.

Unfortunately, this is also the level at which we tend to become stuck on specific features about the target. We haven't yet learned to differentiate between recurring patterns and recurring overlay. In other words, we get an impression of many vertical lines. Is it overlay, a regeneration of the same incorrect bit of data, or is it a repetitive feature in the target? Since we haven't learned how to put all the parts together in their proper sequence yet, this problem can greatly affect the accuracy of level-three remote viewing.

Level Four. Emotional impact of the target, as well as target abstracts.

Remote viewers will begin to report on how the target affects themselves as well as others. Overall *feelings* about the target will surface. These feelings will guide the viewer with regard to decisions concerning the larger groups of details which have now begun to filter in. Abstracts about the target begin to make sense.

Examples of abstract statements which can be made about a target are "it's a high-tech building," "it's some kind of a medical facility," "illegal activity is going on here," etc.

Changes begin to take place which alter how dimensions at the site are reported. No longer is it just square, circle, cube, or line; now it acquires descriptions like "scalloped edges," "blocked off," "encircled," "framed in," etc., which begin to dominate. The viewer begins to insert correct proportional spacing between objects or designs of the target.

Level Five. Subject and Topic refined or underlying ideas presented.

If one looks at the preliminary information about a target as more of a gestalt picture, then the first question which comes to mind is what generated the gestalt. In other words, one can hypothesize that there must be a way of looking into the gestalt statement and finding the fragments that caused us to reach such a conclusion in the first place. By the time a viewer reaches level-four viewing, s/he will be providing information which is beginning to bring a picture together but which lacks definition. In the case of our example, the Devil's Tower, by the completion of level four we will have something like Figure 51:

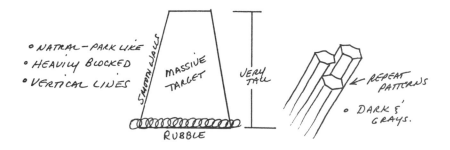

Figure 51. Level-Four Example, with Level-Five Comments.

Level-five information will begin to bring it all together into a consensus opinion about the target. The viewer will begin to present conclusions about the target but will not necessarily understand the reasons for them: "The target is a natural park, some kind of national or state monument."

So, in level five viewing, the viewer must begin to reverse the process of analysis. I call this "down analyzing" or trying to determine what made the viewer come to the conclusion in the first place. In the case of the "natural park" or "national or state monument," what made the viewer want to voice these descriptions? The underlying causes may have been a feeling of "it's a protected site, there are guided tours, many tourists, visitation trails, it's a famous place or object, a natural but unusual feature, etc." These are details about the target which will aid in fleshing it out.

Level Six. Time/space, size and proportion.

Everything in the previous five levels will come together and the viewer will realize the proper place for information in terms of size, proportion, and the target's place within time/space. A rotational view of the target becomes possible, and elements not previously brought together go into their respective positions.

Level six has sometimes been referred to jokingly as the "ah-ha" stage. Suddenly, within the viewer's mind, things come together in such a way that obvious features become apparent. A level-six understanding of the target will usually look exactly like the target from at least one perspective. What is interesting is that sometimes the perspective doesn't relate to anything we (the human race) might quickly or easily understand. The perspective, or *view*, may be unique enough to prevent subject or topic identification. But it will be dead-on accurate.

In the case of our example, the Devil's Tower will coalesce into something like Figure 52:

Figure 52. Level-Six Example.

While the final picture may not allow us to identify the target by name, it will certainly present a clear enough picture of what the target is.

Level Seven. Target history and abstract expressionism presented.

Usually, once we have reached the sixth level of remote viewing, we have obtained all that we reasonably require regarding scientific investigation or general information about a target. The experimenters aren't really interested in anything more abstract or obtuse concerning the target. However, for the viewer, it is only natural to want to progress to a seventh level.

Sometimes the information obtained at the seventh level is the most intriguing. For it is at this level that we begin to appreciate how or why our world *is* and why it works the way it does. We begin to gain a little bit of insight into the foundation or make-up of reality. We also begin to understand what makes us, as humans, tick.

If we continue with our examination of the Devil's Tower target, what we would see in level-seven viewing would be:

"Mysterious mountain used by space aliens to make contact with the human race. Formed of molten rock, vented upward into the base of a flat-rock layer, formed through erosion over six million years ago. A place of sacred worship to the Indians of northeastern Wyoming, where the sky and earth gods meet. A place so unique that it became the first of what are now hundreds of National Monuments." Or perhaps: "The future site of the Temple Zandar, in the year 2295."

As can be seen, the level-seven viewing can be quite surprising if it is carried out to its fullest expression. I've found that beyond level six, there is information available which can be both threatening and interesting.

I was having dinner once with a friend and scientist, after having done a few remote viewing sessions together. In the course of our discussion we happened to be talking about one of the targets we had done together—a primitive Indian burial ground. I innocently asked if anyone had ever determined whether or not the Indians who lived there were cannibals.

Shocked by the question, my friend emphatically stated that the Indians who had lived there in the period we had targeted were peace-loving grain eaters. I immediately dropped the subject.

Why would I ask the question? Well, back when we had done the targeting, the information produced dealt primarily with level-six details. How did they dress, what kinds of weapons and implements did they use, what did they eat, how did they process their foods, what did the terrain look like, etc., etc. Toward the end of the third session, I received a bit of information that didn't quite fit in with the rest. At that time, I understood only six levels of viewing, and so I was confused as to where the information came from or how it might fit in with the rest. I had what I called then an intuitive or gut reaction to what was essentially an off-the-wall concept. An image of ceremonial cannibalism popped into my mind. Knowing the scientist I was working with, and understanding his concepts and beliefs, I chose to not say anything at the time.

After the years went by, as we became closer, I had forgotten about my own caution and that was why I brought it up during dinner. He rejected it out of hand. Some years later, I was pleasantly surprised to be reading an article in *Scientific American* about the prehistoric Indians on whom we had done the remote viewing, in which it was stated that they are now known to have participated in rituals of ceremonial cannibalism. This had been determined by the unearthing of a number of pits containing human bones with human teeth imprints.

So, level seven is there and the information, while abstract in the extreme, can prove most interesting. Caution must be used in the voicing of such information, however.

Level Eight. Manifestations and apparitions.

Somewhere in my tenth year of remote viewing, I detected a subtle difference in my perceptions. At first I thought it might have something to do with what is generally referred to in the paranormal as "the reading of auras." The first experiences I had seemed to primarily center around people.

However, I'm not sure that I was actually seeing anything physically, so I dropped the aura concept early on. The effect simply began as a sort of knowing. Friends would introduce me to people and I would just simply *know* about them. What would I know? Well, that always varied. It was never anything general; it was more a knowing of something they probably didn't even know about themselves. One of the first examples occurred when I was introduced to a total stranger, a young man. I shook his hand and sensed intense pain, excruciating pain. He didn't appear to be in pain, but that was my sense of it—intense physical pain. I had to ask myself why. Why was I getting such an intense pain message? The response was—because he wasn't processing an old and deep emotional wound between himself and his father. I didn't know what to do with the information, especially since he didn't seem aware of it.

Over the course of a year I came to know him better and we became, if not close, at least acquaintances. One day, when I felt particularly open, I mentioned my first impression on meeting him sometime earlier. He chuckled and laughed the idea off, saying that I must have been tuned to something else at the time.

Almost another year went by before I heard from him again; this time a different story. He specifically called me to tell me that I had been more right than even he could have imagined. He had gone through an emotional breakdown and had spent some time in a hospital trying to get himself back together. It had all stemmed from an intense anger he had with his father over issues from childhood. What had precipitated the trip to the hospital was an intense stomach ailment which persisted and wouldn't go away.

It was also during this time in my remote viewing development that I began to see things out of the corner of my eye. Quite literally, I would be engrossed in some other activity—writing, typing, reading—and something would catch my attention over the edge of the typewriter or book, a movement perhaps, a subtle change in color, a dark object. I would then quickly look up to see whatever the object was, which would then quickly move out of sight, vanishing into a closet or moving rapidly out of the room. After a while these objects wouldn't leave the area; they would remain, sometimes staying in sight for some time, until they eventually moved out of view by casually walking or passing into the next room, the closet, or master bathroom. What is important here is to understand that I am not talking about vague impressions or flickers across the peripheral of vision. I'm talking about very solid, well-defined, objective *things* which one would not ordinarily see.

An interesting side line to this is that my wife and even my animals would sometimes see them. My wife and I have two dogs and four cats who share our home. We commonly refer to them as our fur children. Most of the time, when I am sitting up in bed and reading, at least one if not more of our fur children are lying there with me. On one occasion, I noticed a movement above the edge of the book over by the entry to the master bathroom and looked up. There was an unbelievable creature about a foot high looking at me; it then quickly turned and passed into the bathroom. It looked very much like a large lizard walking on its hind legs. The most interesting observation, however, was that my cat, Bing, was also watching it and growling in a low guttural way, all his hair standing up on the backside of his neck. Bing then got up from the bed and walked over to the entry of the bathroom. He wouldn't go in, but he lay down like a loaf of bread in front of the door and watched the room for nearly a half-hour before he eventually lost interest. What was it? I haven't the foggiest notion.

There have been other events which beg for explanation. In late 1984, my wife and I were visiting with a close friend at her home in Connecticut. She put us up in the guest wing of her house. It is a modern house, well-appointed with bright sunlit rooms and quality woodwork, not old with creaky floors, as you would expect a haunted building to be.

The third morning we were there, I was in the guest bathroom taking a shower when I heard the door slide open and closed. It was a pocket-style door, so it wouldn't have been possible for the door to partially close, or accidentally swing open. In fact, I felt the draft of cold air one feels when a door to a steamy bathroom has been opened for a moment. I heard it slide shut as I poked my head out of the shower curtains and asked "Who's there?" There was no one in the room, so I quickly stepped out of the shower, wrapped a towel around my body, and slid the door open, stepping into the outer hallway. At the end of the hall, where it made a right turn toward the main section of the house, there was an old Indian dressed in work clothes standing and staring back at me. I said, "Good morning," at which time he smiled, waved and disappeared on down the hall. I went back in and finished my shower.

Later, at breakfast, I mentioned the Indian to my hostess and asked who he was. She was surprised that I had met him. She brought me a stack of pictures and asked if I could pick him out, which I didn't have any trouble doing. She then explained that he wasn't there; he was a friend and lived some distance away. The last time she had seen him was some months before, at which time he had said that he would come to visit from time to time, to sort of check in on her. I guess he has a peculiar way of visiting his friends.

There have been numerous occasions where I've met and spoken with strangers who were later determined to be non-existent. Perhaps the veil between other realities is thinner than we suppose it to be. Or maybe it's the way we construct reality. When I've experienced the apparitions in the physical sense, I've never seen them appear or disappear. Perhaps the reason for this is that we are incapable of acknowledging or consciously accepting an event which won't fit into our rules for reality. So the coming and going part of the event we cannot process. However, once the apparition is here, well, it's with no great difficulty that we are able to process an interaction, provided of course that our minds are open enough at the outset.

It almost seems as if we are able to handle some disbelief, but not a great deal of it at one time. This would account for many people in a crowd not seeing the UFO that everyone else is seeing. They are just not able to process it as part of their reality construct.

Level Nine. Other reality information.

I've done a number of targets which would fall within this category, and describing these targets would be one of the few ways of providing a clear explanation for what I am discussing here. A viewer knows when s/he is working in level nine because there is a strangeness about the target that defies normal translation. The target just doesn't seem to want to fit within our physical reality constraints.

It is important to note that the protocol used is exactly the same as for any other target, so a viewer really won't know s/he is going to be in level nine until it begins to actually unfold in that way. Somewhere in the beginning of the remote viewing a sort of weirdness takes over which is hard to explain. On the surface, the target will appear to be normal, and somewhere into the collection of information there is a subtle shift of perspective which begins to twist the perceptions. It usually takes a well-trained remote viewer not to lose track of the destination in such a targeting scenario. It takes an even-better-trained interviewer to understand when this shift has taken place and to be able to go with the viewer.

Level-nine viewing seems to take place when the viewer has progressed to a point of understanding the possibility of other realities, or at least how they may interact within the physical world.

Example One

A picture of a target was placed within a double-sealed envelope. A specific date and time was written on the outside, which I was allowed to see. The place of viewing was an office in Washington, D.C.

For the first five minutes of the remote viewing session I described a winding road along a coast line, mostly hills running down toward the sea. The road wound its way up and down the hills, always seeming to keep what appeared to be cliffs off to the right. Direction of travel was perceived as generally south. The edge of the coast where the water met the sea was determined after a few minutes to be in California, probably south of the San Francisco Bay area.

I was beginning to describe the vehicle when I sensed a slight shift of perspective in the reality of the target. I even mentioned it at the time, stating that there was something that was different about the target, something that changed. The interviewer interrupted, asking me to describe what I meant.

I told him that it had to do with the driver of the car. I felt as if I were being blocked from any information about the driver. It was something that happened suddenly. At first I felt that I could get information on the driver, things like the fact that he was male, dark hair, businessman, etc., and then nothing was available. It was as if the information line was deliberately severed.

My next impression was that the driver was suspended in a black void and there were sheets of gauze being wrapped around him and strung up between myself and my perception of him. I was trying to penetrate the layers of gauze, but whenever I successfully got through one, two more would be put in its place. I then had an impression that the driver was drifting away from me and that I couldn't follow.

The interviewer suggested that I follow anyway.

At that point, my perception was that I was no longer alone. There was someone else with me, but it wasn't the driver. The other person, whoever it was, was blocking my path and telling me that I could go no further. I tried to ignore him, but he would respond even more persistently. His voice was soon the only information in my head. It was if the message were being yelled into both my ears. I stopped trying and my mind went blank. This I reported, so we terminated the session.

Who was the target?

The name in the envelope, which I won't repeat here, was a perfect stranger to everyone participating in the experiment. However, there was something unique about him which held great interest as to the probable outcome of the viewing. He was, in fact, the driver of a car along the coastal highway in California. He was driving south of Pescadero, on Route 1, when he fell asleep at the wheel and left the road. He was killed instantly in the resulting accident.

There is remarkable similarity between the description *sheets of gauze* and references to *beyond the veil* one finds in paranormal literature. Another item of interest is the number of minutes from the start of the session till the subtle shift in perception. The time targeted, that is, the time written down in the sealed envelope, was approximately five minutes prior to the known time of the accident. The duration of the remote viewing session from beginning to shift in perception was approximately the same length of time.

Example Two

On the 18th of June 1980, I was doing a remote viewing session for a private client. The specific target was a set of coordinates contained within a double-wrapped set of opaque envelopes. In this particular case, I knew where the envelope was being held but was not allowed to see or touch it. It is not necessary to describe the specific target here, since I have promised my client that I would protect its confidentiality. It is only necessary to know that I was able to both describe the actual target with great detail and draw a detailed ground representation.

It was during the requested remote viewing that another window of information became apparent. As I've discussed previously, there was a distinct shift in perception, a shift which was remarkable enough to be noted as it happened. At that point, I felt as if I had tapped into something else common to the target, but not actually a part of it.

Pictures speak louder than words, so I present an actual sketch of what I suddenly perceived (*Figure 53*):

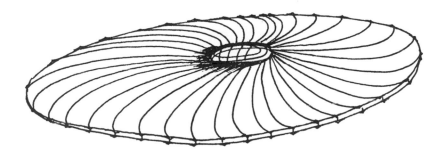

Figure 53.

In my own mind, there is no doubt as to this object's authenticity. Its presence at the target was as real as any other element I could have described. Was it really there? I, as well as my client, believe that it was. For those interested, the following are additional facts relative to the drawing:

— Object is hard and metallic.
— There are observation ports evident across the top as well as the underside.
— Its outer edges were rotating at high speed and the object was in the process of making a ninety-degree turn.
— It was traveling about forty-five hundred miles per hour and at about fourteen thousand feet altitude.
— Mode of power was a form of electromagnetically controlled fluid plasma.

Are there other levels of remote viewing? I'm sure there are. It almost seems as if I can just taste them on the peripheral of my mind. Are there dangers within any of these levels? Of course. But I believe these dangers are from the outside and not the inside. It isn't the remote viewing that's dangerous; it's the information and what people might do with it. As a viewer, I learned a long time ago to refrain from telling it all—especially beginning at about level seven.

20
Target Rules

I am sometimes asked the question "What can't be remote-viewed?"

This is actually an easy question to answer. My answer usually goes something like this: "You can view anything, anywhere, at any time. There is nothing that *cannot* be viewed."

But whenever I've responded with this answer, I've also always added: "However. . .there are probably some things that *should not* be viewed." Not because they can't be, but simply because to do so requires a sophistication of approach and understanding which most of us do not possess. It takes years of practice and an understanding of remote viewing functioning to recognize when information is good because it is a product of proper targeting and when it is bad because of a glitch in that same process.

A simple demonstration of this concept would be targeting an individual. Targeting an individual is no more difficult than targeting anything else. However, there are a number of problems inherent in the targeting that aren't easily recognized. Some of these are:

1. Does the viewer believe s/he is invading the privacy of the individual?

2. Does the viewer believe s/he can invade the privacy of the individual? Does the viewer also receive information as to why the privacy of an individual is being invaded?

3. Where does reality begin and end within the mind of the targeted individual?

4. Is there an inherent feeling that develops between the viewer and targeted individual and does that create a bias in the information obtained?

These are just a few of the questions that arise. Of course the answers lie in the mind of the viewer, and sometimes within the minds of the interviewer and the person analyzing the information.

Essentially, what we are talking about here is the morality or ethics of the viewing being done—how the viewer feels about the viewing and subsequently the impact of his or her feelings on the results.

We all create a self-righteousness about what we do. If we sell cars for a living, then we have to feel right about doing it. Car salesmen decide in their own minds just how far they are willing to go in order to make deals. How much real truth or how much real fantasy they are willing to blend into their statements to customers, or what they might strategically leave out, in order to encourage the sale of automobiles. The more scrupulous the salesperson, the more truth. The point is that there is a place, a line in the dirt which we all draw for ourselves, beyond which we are unwilling or unable to cross. It's what we will allow or will not allow ourselves to do.

The same holds true for remote viewers. Some can't remote view an individual because they are convinced that the information is an invasion of someone else's privacy. Actually, it's not that they can't do the remote viewing; it's simply that they won't. Reality shows that targeting individuals is easy. Sharing the information is something altogether different.

Likewise, there are individuals who believe that using psychic performance to make a lot of money is wrong. These people will always be poor but happy psychics. Unfortunately, I seem to fall within this category more than not. It's not that I believe making money by being psychic is wrong; it's just that I develop such an affinity for most of my customers and their problems that I can't bring myself to charge excessively.

Do I target individuals? Most assuredly. I can't help myself. When I reach out and shake the hand of a stranger, there is input. It can't be helped. Do I share the input with others? Most assuredly, no.

So there are some things that some viewers will do and others will not. Each viewer knows what those things are and therefore is the best judge of what s/he can or cannot remote view.

Aside from this consideration, there are some things which potential customers should also know about remote viewing or, for that matter, about being psychic, that most remote viewers and psychics will not tell them. These are things which have a direct bearing on the probability or credibility of the information and determine when information will be more correct than incorrect.

Viewers or psychics who do not advise their clients about these things are doing a disservice not only to the clients, but to the profession overall. It is one of the reasons there is a lot of muddy water when it comes to determining the validity of information that might or might not have been obtained psychically.

As an example, let's select a target to which we can apply some basic rules. Let's say a wildcatter (client) has just purchased six leases on properties which purportedly have oil under them. Let's further suggest that s/he can only afford to drill on two of them. It would be nice to know which two would make the best drilling sites. As we walk through the problem, I will address some things about remote viewing which apply to the target and with which the average client should be concerned.

The target has to be clearly identified, but the viewer doesn't need to know any information that will lead to logical conclusions. In our example, a good way to clearly identify the six targets would be to number them with randomly selected number patterns, perhaps five or six digits. Once identified this way, the number sequences should not be changed by the client. The targets would be marked and always referred to by the random digits.

(Targets: 23784, 18760, 88512, 98971, 10016, and 71272)

The wildcatter (client) should possess as much information from other sources as is possible about the target(s). Our wildcatter should possess available knowledge about the drilling sites which any oil prospector would be expected to know. S/he should know about any other nearby wells, how the oil-bearing strata lie under the surface, what problems other drillers might have encountered, grade or quality of oil expected, and any other information which would be available through standard existing tests and research.

It is only by knowing this information that the client can make a valid comparison with the information the viewer provides. If the client already possesses 70 percent of the information the viewer provides, it will give a picture of the probable accuracy of the information which is new and therefore previously unknown.

Even after the remote viewing information has been processed for feedback, the client should verify only the information the viewer had correct. The viewer doesn't need any additional information. The client may decide to have the viewer go back and look again at a later date.

An interviewer, if used, shouldn't know any more than the remote viewer. The client is dependent on the interviewer to ask the right questions. Providing these questions ahead of time will only cause the interviewer to unwittingly lead the remote viewer. Allow the system to work. Keep the interviewer as much in the blind as the viewer. Inevitably the interviewer will ask the appropriate question at just the appropriate moment.

If the psychic is too self-centered to share the limelight with an interviewer, then let him wing it on his own. Using an interviewer provides a great opportunity for essentially two psychics to work on the same problem from two separate perspectives. *One is trying to be psychic while the other is being psychic without trying.*

Any remote viewer or psychic who says he can provide you with all that you need, can't. There will inevitably be much that a psychic or remote viewer will miss. He may pick up on some of it with a re-look, but even then in all probability he will miss something. A viewer or psychic who claims to be able to do it all is going further out on a limb than is reasonable.

Remote viewing or being psychic is just one more tool among many for assisting in decision making. No one psychic or viewer is right all the time. Use one or many accordingly.

Depending on whom you talk to, estimates of my own hit successes range from 50 percent to far less. Making an honest appraisal of fifteen years of remote viewing, I would be very surprised if my percentage of "direct hits" were better than 20-25 percent. Also, if I reviewed only those projects which I know fell within the percentage of "hits" (20th percentile), they would probably range anywhere from 5 to 95 percent correct information. So there is a lot of room for variance.

It doesn't sound like much when stated in this context, but statistically it's way beyond chance. Knowing when someone is on the target or not is far more important in the overall analysis.

Information that isn't provided totally blind isn't totally psychic. In other words, if there is *any* information provided to the psychic or remote viewer directly, then s/he is getting a helping hand, or a slant if you will, on what is wanted. Maintain the double blind. If a viewer or psychic says it can't be done this way, find another psychic or viewer.

Ritual is ok as long as it doesn't offend the client. I like a certain ambient light and atmosphere when I do remote viewing. As long as it's within reasonable requirements, there shouldn't be any difficulty in providing a psychic or remote viewer with individual ritual requirements unless those requirements exceed good taste or the sensibilities of the client.

If a viewer or psychic makes extraordinary demands in order to perform, look for a replacement. A blood sacrifice, dancing naked on the lawn, getting drunk on the best wine, or embarrassing the client isn't necessary to good functioning.

Lying, cheating, or otherwise manipulating the results should never be tolerated. In this particular case there are no exceptions. Once the faith has been broken, it cannot be mended. Would you go to a cardiovascular surgeon who got caught taking short cuts, or maintain a relationship with a priest who disclosed confessional information? Probably not. I've always promised the best information my talent can provide, so the client deserves to get it from there. If my information is wrong or not up to the quality expected, then I must trust the client to understand that production isn't always an exact science.

A remote viewer or psychic should never violate his or her own integrity or that of the client. Remote viewers or psychics should have a clear idea of what they will or won't do and be honest about it with potential clients. Never promise more than can be delivered. Viewers should likewise respect the integrity of clients and never suggest anything which crosses the clients' boundaries of fair play. Confidentiality is an absolute requirement.

Anything can be targeted. Any person, group, association, thing, circumstance, object, event, occurrence, thought, place, belief, or concept can be targeted. Any derivative of these meanings within or without space/time can be targeted. All past, present, or future times, and all existent realities can be targeted. Even someone else's fantasies can be targeted. You only need to know the most effective methods to use to get to the information.

Remote viewing can't be blocked. To date, shielding or distance has had little, if any, effect on the information collected through the use of remote viewing. There has, however, been some effective masking of the target, by placing the target inside an area which contains objects of a similar nature or consistency. For instance, you could possibly hide a mechanical pencil with a few dozen mechanical pens, a nuclear device within a breeder reactor, or a psychotic inside a mental institution. However, eventually the appropriate object will be found if properly targeted. In fact, if there are singular differences between the target object and other objects located with it, it is sometimes easier to pinpoint.

21
Stargate

At the request of Congress, the Central Intelligence Agency (CIA) was tasked with considering the assuming of responsibility for the remote viewing program STARGATE in July, 1995. As part of its decision-making process, the CIA was asked to evaluate the research which had been conducted since the National Research Council's (NRC) 1988 report on *Enhancing Human Performance.* At the CIA's request, the American Institutes for Research (AIR) performed this review and published a document on September 29th, 1995, titled: *An Evaluation of Remote Viewing: Research and Applications;* by Michael D. Mumford, Ph.D., Andrew M. Rose, Ph.D., and David A. Goslin, Ph.D.

The review contained an Executive Summary, Background and History, Evaluation Plan, Research Reviews (which were essentially accomplished by Jessica Utts, Ph.D., Division of Statistics, University of California, Davis; and Ray Hyman, Ph.D., Department of Psychology, University of Oregon, Eugene, Oregon); an evaluation of the Utility of Remote Viewing for Intelligence Operations, and Appendices.

In brief, their conclusions amounted to the following:

Research

"Even though a statistically significant effect has been observed in the laboratory, it remains unclear whether the existence of a paranormal phenomenon, remote viewing, has been demonstrated. The laboratory studies do not provide evidence regarding the origins or nature of the phenomenon, assuming it exists, nor do they address the important methodological issue of inter-judge reliability."

Intelligence Applications

"Further, even if it could be demonstrated unequivocally that a paranormal phenomenon occurs under the conditions present in the laboratory paradigm, these conditions have limited applicability and utility for intelligence gathering operations. For example, the nature of the remote viewing targets are vastly dissimilar, as are the specific tasks required of the remote viewers. Most importantly, the information provided by remote viewing is vague and ambiguous, making it difficult, if not impossible, for the technique to yield information of sufficient quality and accuracy for actionable intelligence. Thus, we conclude that continued use of remote viewing in intelligence gathering operations is not warranted."

Sounds pretty cut and dried, doesn't it? The report then goes on for over a hundred pages noting all the reasons why they felt compelled to make these statements. Most readers, seeing only this report, would probably reach the same conclusions. However, there are some truths which were not mentioned by these esteemed AIR *scientists* that would imply otherwise.

I would initially like to address their ". . .review of the operational application of the remote viewing phenomenon in intelligence gathering."

My foremost objection would have to be their use of *scientists* to evaluate the applications methods used for the collection of intelligence material or its value.

If I, as an Intelligence Officer, were to evaluate a "scientific research project" for its *scientific* techniques, protocols, methods, accuracy and/or veracity, and then make public comment on them, I would be pilloried by the scientific community. Why? Because regardless of the extent of my background and expertise, I am still an Intelligence Officer and not a scientist. If I made a public assessment and concluded a "lack of foundation" for studies being conducted by Dr. Ray Hyman, regardless of subject matter, I would either be ignored outright, or challenged on the basis of not having the appropriate credentials for making such an evaluation. In the religion of science, there is no room for the uninitiated.

However, I am an Intelligence Officer. I am well versed in the collection, evaluation, and application of material in support of intelligence requirements. So, I must say that I find it incredible that scientists were used to evaluate something they know nothing about—that is, matters of intelligence.

This is not the only fly in the ointment. We can garner a great deal of information regarding the review from an article which was written by Dr. Ray Hyman for the *Skeptical Eye*, Vol. 9,. No.1, 1996, which underscores the very point I am trying to make: that a scientist has no business evaluating intelligence materials for their veracity. Aside from the lack of expertise, any scientist unfamiliar with the intelligence business is capable of being duped. As an example I offer the following as commentary on some of Dr. Hyman's statements:

1. *"In the spring of 1995, the CIA declassified all the documents related to a previously secret government program originated in 1973, involving psychic spying and parapsychological research."*

Not true. This may be what Dr. Hyman has been led to believe, but in fact 99% of the material (100 boxes of operational files—over 100,000 pages) is still classified.

2. *"After approximately five years, the CIA abandoned this program because they did not find it helpful."*

Not true. The CIA continued to task this program with intelligence requirements until its termination in 1995—a period of eighteen years.

3. *"Jessica Utts and I each received three large boxes of documents. These included all the reports and documents generated during the 20 years of the program."*

Not true. As I said previously, there were over 100,000 pages of classified materials generated, of which Drs. Hyman and Utts received probably less than 1%.

4. *"We did not try to evaluate the operational component because we agreed that the information available was impossible to evaluate."*

This is true. They did not evaluate the operational aspects. An interesting statement in light of their condemnation of the intelligence collection aspects of the project and the following statement made within the same article. *"For what it is worth, the conclusion is that the remote viewers did not provide information that was useful to intelligence or other governmental agencies."* He then goes on to argue the *scientific* aspects of the research as his basis for non-support of the collection effort.

There is room for numerous other complaints with regard to this *unbiased* evaluation of the operations. Rather than go into a long and drawn out detailing of these, I will simply list some of the more profoundly disturbing issues:

Of the dozens of departments, offices, and units within each of the dozen or so primary agencies that used remote viewing over eighteen years for operational purposes, they chose to interview only three. These were not selected at random, but were decided upon based on criteria which has not yet been made public.

The three interviewed had provided tasking only in the final year of the nineteen-year period. This was the single worst year in the unit's history, at least from an operational effectiveness standpoint. Low morale, inappropriate Congressional micro-management, and a lack of expertise across the board were just a few of the driving factors in the decision to shift management for the program back to the CIA. It doesn't take a rocket scientist to understand that singling out that specific time period (the last year) would be an effective way of quickly dismantling the program.

They did not speak with or interview any of the previous viewers, project managers, or other participants who could have shed light on the more productive periods of effort. In fact, they were directed not to consult with us, as a prerequisite for the review.

Finally, one of the comments made within the final report referenced the findings of the National Research Council of the National Academy of Sciences, a so-called blue-ribbon panel charged with evaluating the evidence bearing on the effectiveness of a wide variety of techniques for enhancing human performance. This review was conducted under the overall direction of David A. Goslin, then Executive Director of the Commission on Behavioral and Social Sciences and Education (CBASSE). "They noted that although the panel found some support for certain alternative performance enhancement techniques—for example, guided imagery—*little or no support was found for the usefulness of many other techniques, such as learning during sleep and remote viewing.*"

The NRC Report

What the public doesn't know, because it is not stated within the AIR Report, is that when the NRC study was made in 1988, they were *denied any access* to the classified remote viewing project—either its research laboratories, or its operations. The negative statement was based solely on the preliminary studies in remote viewing which were being carried out at a single laboratory not connected with the government project.

Likewise, the statistical evaluation methodology utilized by the NRC was faulty. Dr. Utts, a statistician and member of the evaluation panel for the AIR study, knew this and balked loudly at any reference to the NRC in the AIR report. Not only was she overruled, she was ordered not to include comment on the NRC report within her comments published in the AIR study. Aside from the inference that what she had to say was being censored, the comments made about the NRC study were made in such a way as to imply the NRC study was an effective one. A position not held by most serious parapsychologists.

What about the research? The CIA tasked AIR to address the following objective:

> A comprehensive evaluation of the research and development in this area, with a focus on the validity of the technical approach(es) according to acceptable scientific standards.

The following quote from one of the AIR investigators says it all. Under Review 1, *An Assessment of the Evidence for Psychic Functioning*, Dr. Jessica Utts, Division of Statistics, University of California, Davis, September 1, 1995, states:

> *"Using the standards applied to any other area of science, it is concluded that psychic functioning has been well established. The statistical results of the studies examined are far beyond what is expected by chance. Arguments that these results could be due to methodological flaws in the experiments are soundly refuted. Effects of similar magnitude to those found in government-sponsored research at SRI and SAIC have been replicated at a number of laboratories across the world. Such consistency cannot be readily explained by claims of flaws or fraud."* A remarkable finding, since even though she had been granted access to nearly all of the research material, she was denied access to virtually all of the operational data.

In her Commentary on the AIR study published in *The Journal of Parapsychology, Vol. 60, March 1996*, Dr. Utts responded to a query by Dr. Edwin May regarding the soundly criticized NRC review methodology and her failure to specifically address its faults by adding the following:

> "I would also like to explain another omission in my report (the AIR study) that occurred for much the same reason. [She

had previously stated that she was explicitly asked by the AIR staff *not* to mention the NRC report [or its faults.]] Despite the claims Ray Hyman is making in the media, we were shown very little of the 'operational' remote-viewing work. One of the few documents we were shown was a list of (the former DIA Project Officer's) 'best' remote viewing successes. Since the list provided almost no detail, you may recall that I asked you for names and numbers of individuals I could contact to get more information about those purported operational successes. In a memo dated August 1, 1995, you provided me with phone numbers for [a former DIA project officer, a former senior DIA official, a military General who had program responsibility], and Joseph McMoneagle. You sent a copy of the memo to the AIR staff.

"Shortly after you sent me that memo, I was contacted by the AIR staff and told that I was *not* to contact any of those individuals. Thus, I was unable to gain any details about the operational remote viewing work. I thought you should know that, in case you were wondering why I requested that information and then did not use it. Again, I am clueless as to why Ray Hyman is making claims in the media that we had access to the operational work for our review. I do not think he was given access to any information not shown to me. I don't know how he can substantiate the claims he's making about remote viewing being useless for intelligence. He may be correct, but he has very little data on which to base that conclusion."

She doesn't stop there. Within the AIR study itself, she goes on to talk about examples of *prima facie* evidence provided to the AIR committee, which is "evidence having such a degree of probability that it must prevail unless the contrary be proved," according to Webster's Dictionary. She states: "These are examples in which the sponsor or another government client asked for a single remote viewing of a site, known to the requestor in real time or in the future, and the viewer provided details far beyond what could be taken as a reasonable guess. Two such examples are given by May (1995) in which it appears that the results were so striking that they far exceed the phenomenon as observed in the laboratory. Using a *post hoc* analysis, Dr. May concluded that in one of the cases the remote viewer was able to describe a microwave generator with 80 percent accuracy, and that of what he said almost 70 percent of it was reliable. Laboratory remote viewings rarely show that level of correspondence." Further, "...the viewer who described the microwave generator allegedly knew only that the target was a technical site in the United States. Yet, he drew and described the microwave generator, including its function, its approximate size, how it was housed and that it had 'a beam divergence angle of 130 degrees.'"

What is interesting here, is that while the research effort provided conclusive statistical evidence for the existence of psychic functioning, it also provided *prima facie* evidence for **operational quality** viewing. Something not addressed anywhere else in the AIR study.

So that the reader might understand the importance of these statements by Dr. Utts, I've included a couple of these *prima facie* evidence targets, with the circumstances under which they were produced. As the remote viewer of record, I can emphatically state the following:

1. In all cases, the target location or site was known only by the tasking government agency. This data was not shared with anyone in the lab prior to targeting.

2. I was totally blind to the target, its location, or who the tasking agency was at the time of targeting.

3. I produced no additional information or drawings about these locations which were later thrown away or discarded because they didn't match the target.

I should also note, that while these few examples may appear to the reader as exceptional—having been done under laboratory controls—they *would not have been considered unusual* in the intelligence-collection side of the program. There were dozens of critical intelligence remote viewings that resulted in the same detail and accuracy against classified targets.

Example One

I was tasked with drawing and describing the actual location of an unknown person for a specific time and date. I was told this person could be anywhere in the Continental United States. The photograph represents where the person was actually located at that specific time and date. This drawing is the only material which I produced regarding this target.

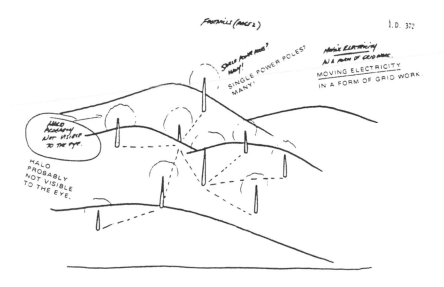

*Wind Generation Grid
(Courtesy of CSL)*

Example Two
(The microwave generator previously noted by Dr. Jessica Utts.)

I was shown the photograph of an unknown individual and told that he was currently working on a technical site somewhere in the Continental United States. I was asked to describe what he was working on.

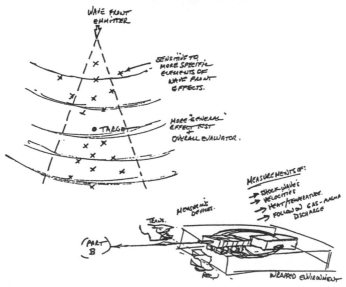

Microwave Generator (Courtesy of CSL)

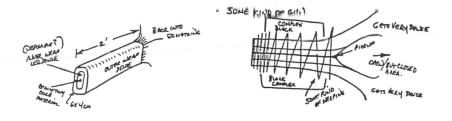

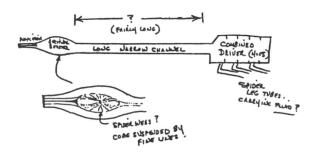

Microwave Generator (Courtesy of CSL)

A discussion of the effectiveness or non-effectiveness of remote viewing was presented on Ted Koppel's *Nightline*, in November of 1995. One of the guests was the former Director of Central Intelligence (DCI), from November 1991 to January 1993, Robert M. Gates.

During the show, he states: "In the 20 years, perhaps 25 years, that I was perhaps in a position to be aware, I don't know of a single instance where it is documented that this kind of activity contributed in any significant way to a policy decision or to even informing policy makers about important information."

A completely truthful statement. . .but, a very misleading one as well. Having been an intelligence officer in the United States Army for twenty years, I could essentially say the same about nearly all the other methods of intelligence collection. For a number of reasons, but primarily because:

No decision is *ever made* at the policy level by anyone based on a single method, fact, statement, photograph, or any other kind of intelligence data. Policy is based on stacks of *analysis*, based on raw data from many sources.

In the intelligence business, there is no such animal called "Stand Alone" intelligence. Decisions are not even made based on physical photographs of a site, because they could be staged.

In the analysis of raw data, great care is taken to purge the source or subject from that data. This was particularly the case when it came to *psychic* information.

As for twenty to twenty-five years of being aware, Gates was already acting as the DCI, when a dying William J. Casey resigned in February of 1987. President Regan nominated Gates as Casey's replacement, but Gates withdrew his name during the confirmation hearings after members of the Senate Intelligence Committee criticized him for not knowing about the Iran-Contra Affair. I for one would certainly have considered the Iran-Contra Operation as significantly more important to the DCI, whoever that might have been at the time, than the Army's project STARGATE.

It is interesting that Gates knew nothing about one, but knew all about the other. STARGATE must have had a much higher profile within the intelligence community than anyone has previously hypothesized. Such a high profile for so many years doesn't happen by accident.

Why, then, shut STARGATE down?

While I will always consider the AIR evaluation to be bogus, the reasons or decisions could have been based on very accurate and appropriate considerations. The reason for shutting down the project might have even been valid. But, no matter where I look, the strings of reality all lead back to the same specific point—FEAR.

No one wants to be crucified by the media for "believing" in the facts. Whether on religious, political, or scientific grounds, the issues surrounding psychic functioning, or in this case, remote viewing, are highly volatile. It is a subject for which there never seems to be a rational or middle ground. The subject matter alone polarizes people to one extreme or the other. By its very nature, belief in the paranormal requires a direct alteration to how one feels or thinks about reality, how it might be constructed, or how it might operate. It takes a strong and rational person to walk this middle line—to retain a healthy skepticism, and yet be open enough to the possibilities. It takes a person who is fearless and open minded, but not a fool. A very rare animal these days.

22
Delusions & Potentials

Since the release of information about the government's use of remote viewing, a direct result of the AIR study and report to Congress in November of 1995, I've been only mildly surprised by the number of stories and declarations that have been made concerning remote viewing and its capabilities. Some are fairly close to accurate, most are exceptionally misguided, and nearly all are a mix of fact and fantasy.

Many of these stories appear to stem from incomplete or slanted stories in the media, accusations and counter-accusations being made by the those who have polarized to the extreme, and disinformation produced by the misinformed. While most of these perceptions are probably not deliberate attempts to mislead, many are certainly born of ignorance to the facts as historically supported by the both the applications as well as the scientific study of remote viewing.

It is not my intention in addressing some of the more major issues, to establish the time-table or technical history of remote viewing, or decide who did what first, or why. I simply want to bring to bear my viewpoints on certain issues that seem to be the most perplexing to those who are trying to understand what is going on.

PREDOMINANT DELUSIONS

• Remote viewing works all the time.

In fact, remote viewing doesn't work all the time and no one knows why. Both within the applications and in the scientific study of remote viewing, there are times when a remote viewer will not make contact with a target, for any of numerous reasons. Hindsight evaluations of the target or the remote viewing session may sometimes point to obvious mistakes or technical errors made during targeting, but in the majority of cases, when a remote viewer has missed the target there is no way to establish the cause. A number of hypotheses can be established post-session that may indicate a "probable" reason, but it is nearly impossible to establish a "cause and effect" relationship for failure.

Why this is so difficult for some to accept is beyond me, but there are those who refuse to accept the inevitable consequence of failure. At present there is no such thing as a 100% success rate with remote viewing, nor does there appear to be one predicted for the near future.

There is some indication that we may have a foot in the door with regard to understanding some of the base-line mechanics of remote viewing, but until sufficient research has been completed, we are not even sure about that. There is no formula for success.

- Anyone can be trained to remote view.

Surprisingly, this is probably true. But, some insist on adding ". . .with 100% accuracy and expertise." This is certainly not the case.

Evidence suggests that the remote viewing technology (protocols, etc.) can be easily transferred to most people who have an open mind and a desire to try remote viewing. People thus exposed can sometimes produce results which show some psychic connection with a target. However, the vast majority of people who learn the remote viewing technique will not pass beyond a rather rudimentary display of this capability.

Many have argued with this position, but both the applications project (STARGATE) as well as the research and development side of remote viewing have established otherwise. Arguing about it won't change the facts. As mentioned in earlier chapters, an individual's natural psychic talent—what they bring to the table—has everything to do with the outcome during training—any form of training.

That doesn't mean that someone who has never shown a "psychic flair" can't be trained to be an expert remote viewer, or someone who considers himself or herself to be "very psychic" will succeed where others fail. It means, no one knows how good or how bad someone will be until they have been exposed to the technology. Anyone who guarantees expertise prior to training is simply deluding themselves and others.

- Remote viewing is good for locating things.

In fact, it is just the opposite. Remote viewing is *not* good for locating things. One of the most elusive and difficult targets in the applications arena deals with finding a lost person, object, or thing.

Very detailed descriptions of a person's location, the location of a lost object or thing, may assist in solving a problem, but only when combined with an evaluation of many other factors relative to a specific target. There is evidence that dowsing in combination with remote viewing will produce a significant increase in success, but for the most part, remote viewing is not well equipped to deal with such problems.

In the past, when remote viewers with sufficient expertise were able to locate missing persons, objects, or things, it was apparent there was a whole lot more going on than just remote viewing. Again, the natural talent of the individual probably has a lot to do with these successes.

Statistically, remote viewing alone is significantly less successful in finding locations than it is at other types of remote viewing problems. This does not mean that remote viewing won't locate something, it just means that as a general rule, one shouldn't expect it to.

A number of experimental designs may offer solutions to this problem in the future, but these are currently under evaluation.

• Teaching methodologies are remote viewing protocols.

Over the past two decades a number of methods have been designed to teach remote viewing, to address specific problems faced or encountered by remote viewer trainees, or to polish the natural psychic talent someone brings to the table.

These methods are used for *teaching*. They should not be mis-construed as representing appropriate protocols for applications of remote viewing. Teaching methods nearly always violate appropri-ate applications or research protocols, a direct result of the teacher or instructor's requirement to maintain absolute control during train-ing, in order to facilitate learning.

In teaching, the need for immediate feedback requires the teacher or instructor to know something, if not everything about the target. This is called *front loading*. A teaching session, wherein the instruc-tor knows about the target, is not valid remote viewing and should never be considered one.

Some would argue that some front loading is essential to appli-cation types of targets. This is not the case. While the person who sets up the targets may know something about the target, the monitor and the remote viewer do not. There are sophisticated variations to this which were developed within project STARGATE that go well beyond the scope of this book. They were designed very carefully over a period of 18 years and were used only in the rarest of cases (in other words, they were specifically target related and/or designed).

Within research, there is *never* any front loading. All targets are blind to *whomever* is participating in the experiment. Hence, while there may be multiple *teaching methods* for remote viewing, there are no multiple-protocols. There is only one remote viewing protocol and that protocol dictates *all* people in the room during a remote viewing are blind to the target.

- Remote viewing is the same thing as out of the body experiences or astral travel, bi-location, crystal ball reading, tarot card reading, channeling, automatic writing, etc.

In a sense this statement is both true and not true. If someone chooses to use a crystal ball or channeling to produce information while operating under the established remote viewing protocol (blind to the target), then that crystal ball reading or that channeling could technically be considered remote viewing. How they choose to produce information is solely dependent upon the training methodology employed to polish their psychic ability.

However, whatever the method chosen—if it is used or performed outside of the approved protocol for the collection of information—it does not validate the person as a remote viewer. This is true even if the information they produced is found to be correct. The stringent requirements for doing remote viewing only under the approved protocol was developed for a reason. It is to prevent front loading, fraud, and numerous other possibilities from clouding or diluting the results.

Since the public disclosure of project STARGATE in November, 1995, hundreds of psychics, channelers, card readers, and other types of mystics or mediums have now claimed "remote viewing" prowess. If what they are doing is within the approved protocol, this is fine. But unfortunately, this is usually not the case. Many are simply attempting to use remote viewing as a validation for their own work. Not only is this unconscionable, but it denigrates the validity of other well known and effective psychics, channelers, card readers, mediums, and mystics who have spent years building a reputation with their clients.

- Remote viewing can only be used for the good of mankind or it won't work.

Unfortunately, this is not true. Remote viewing can be used to target individuals, companies, institutions, governments, secluded places, etc., regardless of motivation. If someone chooses to use remote viewing for less than honorable purposes, they can.

The concept that remote viewers need be "good" people in order for it to work is false. A well-trained remote viewer with a high degree of natural talent can provide information on whatever target for whatever purpose.

I am reminded of the movie series *STAR WARS* when I make this statement. Remote viewers can actually pick which side of the "FORCE" they want to play in. However, as in *STAR WARS,* there may be consequences.

An individual may believe him or herself to be "evil" and able to deal with it, when in fact, they can't. We are all subject to our subconscious mind and how we personally define "evil." Since we really have no idea to what degree our subconscious affects our physical or mental well-being, some may pay a heavy price for playing on the "dark side."

It has been my observation, however, that most remote viewers have gravitated to the positive or constructive side of the issue. This is usually born out of the remarkable philosophic growth that occurs as a result of their exposure to the unique changes in reality taking place within them as individuals. They recognize that their abilities exceed those commonly thought of as normal and react by assuming more responsibility towards the human race. This does not automatically make them correct in their actions, but it does act as a governor on the psychic engine. Over time, they come to recognize that playing in the mud will make them muddy.

- Remote viewing can be used for anything.

Remote viewing is not a panacea or solution to problems. It is simply a tool like many other tools. Its value is in how it is wielded. It cannot stand alone as a method for producing answers to anything.

However, when used properly, in conjunction with other tools that are available, it can help to eliminate or reduce wasted effort or time in arriving at an appropriate answer. The zealots would have you believe that remote viewing can provide answers where it can't. On the other side of the scale, the hard core disbelievers would have you believe that it is simply a "sleight of hand" magic trick. In both cases, fear rules.

It takes a strong and rational mind to see the narrow limits of its ability, as well as recognize the inappropriate and irrational attitudes of the bigot. Remote viewing is a small but finite crack in the door to how we may interface with reality. It would be irresponsible to slam the door shut or step through it without caution. Mankind should carefully tread where no one has trod before. It is okay to be open to the possibilities, but care should rule our actions.

- Remote viewers who were part of Project STARGATE were under military control and therefore haven't matured spiritually.

Some of the most moral individuals I have ever met are military personnel. It is insane to assume that because someone wears a uniform and has sworn allegiance to a country or government, they are not spiritually developed.

In fact, the armed services of our nation are established for the sole purpose of defending our nation and sometimes taking a life in doing so. This is a conscious thought in every man and woman serving in our military services. While many (who have not served) can hypothesize how they might think about killing, taking, or affecting a human life, the soldier, airman, or sailor has to live with it in their every action. They are chartered and ordered by the civilian population of America to provide the first line of defense. They are usually placed in a position of having very little latitude to decide whether or not they agree with the actions they are forced to take on the behalf of Americans in general. To say they lack a spiritual nature as a result is preposterous.

Regarding military remote viewers, I have known quite a few over a course of twenty years and they have always taken remote viewing, and their participation in it, very seriously and very personally. While I cannot speak for these individuals, I can say it has affected each one of them spiritually. In my own observation and experience I find they are as tuned to the reality of life, the spiritual nature of man, and the consequences of their actions than anyone could be. This is not to say there aren't exceptions. There are many within the military rank and file who have no direct relationship with the consequences of their acts.

However, unique to the military, there also seems to be no secure platform on which to voice a concern one way or the other. So the issue of personal spirituality resides within the individual. We are taught from the beginning to accept responsibility for our actions. Under these circumstances, the military individual is constantly making decisions most civilians are not faced with. We learn very quickly to make these decisions and suffer the consequences. These consequences are borne silently and courageously, usually without complaint. But, because they are issues which usually do not surface publically, does not mean the military individual is not reckoning with them or paying the price.

The same holds true with military remote viewers. Their religious or spiritual convictions are very personal, very real, and are the very strength upon which they make their decisions, and upon which they depend.

- One individual is responsible for the development of remote viewing.

I've been involved in the remote viewing effort from its conception within the Department of Defense. In the course of the effort— nearly eighteen years—contributions towards the understanding of what is going on have been made by dozens of individuals. Some of those contributions may appear to be small or insignificant to the uninformed. Some of those contributions may even go unnoticed by the system.

All the participants within the GRILLFLAME, CENTERLANE, STARBURST and STARGATE programs have contributed to our understanding of remote viewing and what it represents. Time will establish which contributions are valued and which are forgotten. For every success there were hundreds of failures. For every failure there is a fragment of light, knowledge, or understanding that didn't exist prior. It would be wrong to point a finger or make a statement that so and so did such and such, without acknowledging the efforts of others. There are those who initiated, those who modified, and those who tested. No one individual was capable of achieving what we know today about remote viewing without the contributions of others. Do not misconstrue arguments about remote viewing, in particular the philosophic or personal perceptions, as demonstrative of the right or wrong of it. It is out of these very arguments that much of what is known about remote viewing today was birthed. Such arguments or disagreements are the breeding grounds of the open mind. I like to think we all are capable of learning something new.

IMPORTANT POTENTIALS

It would be impossible to list all of the potential uses for remote viewing. To do so would require printing an entire book as an addendum to this one. How many of these have been addressed? Very few, but there are reasons for this. Before I talk about what I consider to be the three greatest potentials and why, I must address why things appear to be moving so slowly.

Research and Development

If one reviews the research and development side of the issue, it is easy to see that only a small segment of what can be addressed, has been. There are many valid reasons for this, but the all-encompassing problem is: time, money, and expertise.

- Time

It takes a great deal of time to perform the necessary number of experiments required to establish something as fact. This is particularly true in paranormal research. Believe it or not, most parapsychological labs are still dealing with "proving" the existence of psychic functioning. Any competent meta-analysis of the last fifteen years of research in remote viewing alone will show an effect size and distribution that exceeds most required effect sizes for any other field of science. In fact, it will probably exceed the requirement for proof by four or five fold.

Over the years remote viewing has been assaulted by the skeptics for its targeting methodologies, how the results were assimilated or evaluated, the statistical methods used to determine the effect size, even how the papers were stacked when they were handed to an independent judge. Following each assault, whether real or not, the researchers have made changes which in effect have eliminated these complaints piecemeal. Unfortunately, since each response changes the experimental procedure, all of the experimental requirements must be re-addressed in order to provide proof. Unquestionably a burden usually not found in other areas of science. It's called moving the goal posts. You can never score a goal if they keep moving the goal posts.

- Money

The extraordinary burden of proof placed on paranormal researchers means they need more money to do what less money will do elsewhere.

If a year's worth of experiments costs $100,000.00, it doesn't take a rocket scientist to figure out that redoing the protocol three or four times will drive the cost beyond most researcher's pocket book or support. Skeptics will be quick to complain that it isn't their fault if paranormal researchers don't get the protocol right in the first place. In some cases this would be a valid complaint, however, from my own observation and experience, this is usually not the case. In fact, paranormal researchers are usually more precise and detailed in their scientific approaches than people within other more accepted scientific areas.

- Expertise

It takes years of expertise for a paranormal researcher to assimilate the tools necessary for studying human potential. One must garner all of the knowledge available on the normal aspects of mental science, in order to address the paranormal aspects.

This garnering of tools is heavily impacted by the two previously discussed problems, time and money. Since there is actually very little money spent in the paranormal area on a year-to-year basis, it is difficult in the extreme to get someone to commit to the deprivation necessary to develop their expertise.

I harbor a great love for any researcher who sticks it out long enough in the paranormal to be respected for their expertise. I know the kind of sweat, blood, and privation they suffered to get there.

These are just a few of the reasons the science side appears to move so slowly. When it comes to science, there are no short cuts, nor should there be. Finding appropriate firms, companies, or individuals willing to provide funds to endow a paranormal laboratory for twenty-years isn't impossible, but it is exceedingly difficult.

Applications

The primary applications remote viewing has been used for is espionage. There are a number of people who might claim they have cornered the market on the use of remote viewing, but none could ever hope to compete with the twenty-five years of intelligence collection accomplished by the military unit at Fort Meade.

Even so, the areas that were focused on usually depended upon a very narrow array of departments and offices within various agencies who could see a use for remote viewing in responding to their specific problems or issues. It is my observation that a lot of time was wasted in providing "proof in principle" to the heads of each of those offices or departments, in spite of the existent "proof" amassed by those who came before.

The specific targets selected for remote viewing within the military were almost exclusively those against which all other forms of collection had failed to make any headway. This is not unlike being a doctor with a new approach to cancer who only gets to work with patients medical science has given up on. The expectation for success is already near zero when the patient first walks through the door. Consequently, when significant successes are experienced, this is truly phenomenal.

However, there is no reason to suppose that had the military project continued, it would have extended its capability beyond that which it had previously displayed.

THREE GREATEST POTENTIALS
FOR REMOTE VIEWING

I've decided to present three primary areas where I believe remote viewing can best be utilized for the good of mankind. Due to differing views of morality, religion, or politics, some might question my three choices, but I have chosen these areas primarily based on the following assumptions:

* These will benefit the greatest number of people, regardless of nationality, religion, or race.

* These areas appear to be the most vulnerable to the use of remote viewing both from an applications as well as a research and development point of view. In other words, we can have a higher expectation of success in these areas.

* These areas are where we can expect the biggest bang for the buck, both in the applications as well as research and development sides of the program.

* Finally, we can expect by focusing on these areas to open doors quickly to the mechanics of remote viewing—what makes it tick—thereby producing an exponential rise in new application areas of equal importance. Sort of a short-cut to the future.

Nuclear Non-Proliferation

There is a very strong indication within the scientific literature concerning remote viewing, that targets which emit large amounts of energy actually produce more information, which increases the probability of success many-fold.

In my own experience, I have seldom missed targets which have nuclear material associated with them. If one were to extract nuclear types of targets from the thousands of controlled experimental and application types of sessions that I have done in the course of eighteen-plus years, there is probably something less than one percent that I have missed. This is also true with other remote viewers who have developed the same level of expertise.

There is a reason for this. Nuclear material, even in a static state (while stored under shielding), is generally releasing more energy than most other things in our universe. To a remote viewer, this translates as more information. This also holds true for other high energy targets, such as electric power stations, machines that create large emissions of X-rays, etc. However, nuclear targets are the best. So, nuclear targets are the targets we can expect to have the highest degree of accuracy within remote viewing.

In this current era of détente, many nations are dismantling their nuclear weaponry. As a result, the availability, storage, and security requirements for bomb-grade material has increased ten-fold. Within the rapidly changing and chaotic political structure of some nations, it is not only possible but probable that security will be lax at some time or another. It is only a question of time until someone walks off with or buys sufficient bomb-grade nuclear material to construct what I call a suitcase bomb.

There are numerous technologies which have been or are being developed to contend with this problem. But even with the best technology, you have to know where to point it.

Let's suppose for a moment that someone has bought or stolen sufficient material to construct a bomb. Let's further suppose that we might even know the four or five terrorist organizations that might be receiving it. Assuming we've narrowed the search area to approximately 1/8th of the world's surface, that is still tens of thousands of square miles which will have to be methodically searched. An accurate description of the location of that material could reduce the search parameters by conservatively 30 percent, or in the case of unique features being collocated with the material, by 90 percent. This translates to "time saved" in recovering the material.

If you have someone walking around with a suitcase bomb, say half a megaton, wouldn't you want to know where they were in the fastest possible way?

Let's examine a worst-case scenario. Let's assume that remote viewing is only half as effective and we have only a fifty/fifty chance of reducing the area of search. Would you want to "not" employ remote viewing? Given you would have to search the entire area anyway, the 50 percent chance of knowing where to begin still looks awfully good.

While I believe there is sufficient scientific evidence existent today to show the effectiveness of remote viewing, regarding the location of nuclear material, many may still require a personal "proof in principle." If that is the case, I wonder why there is currently no effort to even pursue this. With what is at stake, I find it preposterous, even criminal, that such a capability continues to be ignored. Especially given the cost in comparison to the billions being spent elsewhere.

Anti-Terrorism

What few Americans know is that between 1980 and 1987, there were 9,301 terrorist organizations existent across the world. Virtually every continent, nation, island, protectorate, or zone on the face of the earth dealt with terrorist acts of violence that took human life, usually the innocent (*International Terrorism in the 1980's, A Chronology of Events;* Volumes I and II; Edward F. Mickolus, Todd Sandler, and Jean M. Murdock).

The acts of these terrorist organizations are probably the single greatest threat to human society that have ever existed in the chronology of human events.

Police and governmental agencies have made minimal advances against only the largest of these organizations. One only has to look at how they operate to understand why we are so unsuccessful in combating their strategies. They operate from individual cells containing five or fewer members, and they are extremely secretive in how they operate, communicate, or interact. As a result, they are nearly undetectable prior to, or even after they have struck. Almost without exception, most intelligence apparatus are stymied by their very *modus operandi.*

But, they are vulnerable. Remote viewing offers at least a minimal percentile of success in addressing this plight. In other words, it is better than nothing.

Very little has been done toward applying the remote viewing methodologies against these terrorists. Where it has been used, it has sometimes proven to be successful. If used properly in conjunction with the other methods currently being employed, one could expect at least a small percentage of increase in the current success rate. But, not even trying to use it for this purpose is slamming the door on a possible and significant advantage.

Again, I find it reprehensible and immoral not to at least try to develop remote viewing approaches to this growing problem. Especially in light of the damage one could expect from a terrorist group armed with a dirty nuclear bomb in a suitcase.

Specific areas where remote viewing might prove to be of benefit are: establishing money trails, descriptions of covert locations or training and assembly areas, communication and encryption methods being employed, and establishing and detailing the vulnerability areas within potential target sites.

Creativity

The first two suggestions address potential hazards. But there are also areas which have only been touched on lightly during the years I've been associated with remote viewing. Since the program was usually inundated with threat-oriented targets and research questions regarding these military types of applications, very little was done to address the peaceful or civilized aspects of performance. I would consider these performance aspects as falling within the cutting edges of technology.

A lot of mystique has developed around the visions of Jules Verne and his ability to predict the future. There is evidence within much of his writing that demonstrates his ample ability to envision many things that have since come to pass: the computer, the FAX, the television, the automobile, to name a few. Remote viewing expertise, as displayed within the research and development portion of the project, has established the same capacity for envisioning or conceptualizing that could be found in a Jules Verne.

It is beyond my ken that research and development (R&D) departments within leading edge corporations have not sought to capitalize on these abilities to foresee the robust possibilities for future development. A good remote viewer, operating under the stringent controls established within a qualified laboratory, could put such potentials within easy reach of those bold enough to take advantage. I am not talking here about a fly-by-night or slip-shod approach to the future. I am talking about a well-financed and knowledgeable division within such an R&D facility that would deliberately target the future to bring back sufficient information to possibly enable building or constructing the machines not yet extant.

In the current age of technology, where companies must create to survive, remote viewing can provide an edge to those willing to risk such an attempt at application.

Many companies compete on an international basis with other companies or corporations with predominantly national or self-serving interests. There is little doubt in my mind that many of these companies are already using forms of psychic functioning to target other companies, what they are doing, or where they are going. Such activity, even psychic in origin, is called industrial espionage. I am not a supporter of psychic industrial espionage, as I believe it is morally and ethically wrong. However, remote viewing at a minimum could be the singular method available that might protect a company against such espionage. The more we learn about it and the mechanisms which drive it, the better we can defend against such assaults. The bottom line is, a company could still honestly develop an advantage over another by simply targeting the future.

I honestly believe there are corporations in other countries who have already begun to develop their own remote viewing departments and capabilities. It is not a band-wagon which will remain in one place. Now is the time to get on.

CONCLUSIONS

These are only three suggestions for what I consider the most positive aspects for the use of remote viewing. There quite literally are hundreds more. Each problem unique to the human race is a fertile field for the future use of psychic functioning.

If anyone reading this book has a desire to pursue any of these three areas of applications or research, they should contact me directly through the publisher. Serious inquiries regarding the possible endowment of such a lab will be brought to the immediate attention of my colleagues at the Cognitive Sciences Laboratory (CSL), California. We possess the infrastructure and expertise of nearly twenty-five years of research and applications in remote viewing. The CSL web site can be reached at: http://www.jsasoc.com/~csl/index.html/

23
Questions & Answers

As with any book, there are a number of questions which never seem to be answered. In my travels and presentations before many different groups of people, I'm usually asked a plethora of questions. From these experiences I've selected a number of questions. In this fashion, I hope to address those which are most frequently asked.

How long did it take you to develop your remote viewing capability?

I began to involve myself in remote viewing in mid-1978. I didn't reach a level of proficiency that would allow me to participate in formal research studies until the end of 1980. It must be remembered that I sort of had the skids greased as a result of my near-death experience in 1970. I didn't have to break down any cultural barriers that might have prevented my learning or might have gotten in the way of my experiencing remote viewing.

Over the years, experience has shown that the minimum amount of time required to become proficient in the art of remote viewing would be a period of something in excess of eighteen months. That is assuming that almost every day was spent in the effort. It is a full-time job, changing one's entire perspective on reality.

Is there any such thing as spontaneous remote viewing?

Probably not. Remember, remote viewing is differentiated from psychic functioning in that it is always done within an approved protocol. "Spontaneous" implies without a protocol, so it probably can't happen. You can have spontaneous psychic functioning, but not spontaneous remote viewing.

What confuses the issue is that there are people who claim to be remote viewers who are actually psychics. They may be very good as psychics, but have no real claim to remote viewing. They are doing a disservice by claiming both. People who claim remote viewing must be able to replicate what they do in a lab within an approved scientific protocol.

Have you ever had a UFO experience?

Yes. Aside from any experiences that I've had while doing the remote viewing targeting of UFO events or incidents, I had a classic UFO experience while stationed in the Bahamas in 1965 and 1966. I was assigned to an Air & Sea Rescue unit on Eleuthera, near Governor's Harbor. The event occurred sometime in October of 1965, but I cannot recall the exact date. I remember that it was a Tuesday night, and a friend and I had watched a feature movie at the outdoor theater run by Pan American at the down-range tracking facility (part of the Cape Canaveral launch and tracking system). We had a few drinks in the club afterward and were walking down the sidewalk to my apartment; the time was approximately 1:15 A.M.

The entire area lit up like high noon. Very bright light. So bright that you would expect it to hurt your eyes, but it didn't. I looked for the light and found it directly over my head. It was coming from a large circular discus-shaped object. It appeared to be approximately three hundred feet across and hovering four or five hundred feet above my head.

I remember thinking I should be hearing some kind of noise, but it was absolutely silent. In fact there was no sound at all, no wind noise, no night crickets, no frogs, nothing. It was moving in quick stop-and-start jumps, a hundred yards at a time, from due west to due east. After six or seven starts and stops, it shot over the horizon and everything went back to normal darkness.

The following morning I had what felt like a severe sunburn on my front side and face and gritty eyes, and I felt as though I had a case of the flu. I stayed in bed for most of the day. I didn't feel right again for almost a week. My friend suffered the same effects. We agreed never to speak of it with anyone because we liked being in the Bahamas.

Do you go out-of-body to get your remote viewing information?

No. The out-of-body experience and remote viewing are two distinctly different experiences for me. My remote viewing information comes in numerous ways: symbols, sounds, feelings, tastes, fragments, pictures (accurate and inaccurate), and holistic impressions.

My view of a target in the out-of-body sense is just as if I were standing there in the flesh. Only the view is much more pristine. You can see what appears to be the molecular energy fields within objects, both animate as well as inanimate. While it's probably not actually the molecular movement, it is most certainly something like it.

What are some of the other differences between an out-of-body view of a target and one by remote viewing?

While out of body, you know that you have gone somewhere and left your body behind. You see exactly what you would have seen with your physical eyes, only it looks clearer, sharper; there is more color. In order to see something on the other side of a wall you must move through the wall to see it. There is a lot of information available in the remote viewing state that is not available in the out-of-body state. For instance, in the out-of-body state it is impossible to see what language a person speaks at the target, you can't tell someone's nationality unless it's obvious by dress, you can't tell how someone feels. In the remote viewing state, you can discern all of that without "seeing" it.

For me, achieving the controlled out-of-body is extremely difficult. I was successful at the Monroe Institute lab, but only after thirteen months of effort. I personally prefer the remote viewing access to a target over the out-of-body. It's far easier to control and manipulate.

What kind of scale is there? Can you see energy transfer, feelings, or concepts?

The scale in remote viewing is dominated by the type of target. If the expected target is a room in a building, then that is the scale in which the viewer responds. If it is the insides of a watch which are being targeted, then the viewer will describe the workings as if he is inside the watch with the parts. There are no limits to scale in remote viewing. Anything can be viewed and described in detail, from the sub-atomic structure of an atom to the deck of an aircraft carrier.

You can perceive energy transfer, feelings and concepts. In fact, the most interesting targeting which can be done deals with concepts. For example, Jules Verne was probably doing some excellent remote viewing when he described the drive unit for his submarine in *20,000 Leagues Under the Sea*. All we have to do is emulate him and look ahead to about the year 3000 to pick out all the miracles of technology. The only problem is that, while we can describe what's there, it takes a lot of work to put it all into an acceptable concept.

What kind of school background do you have?

I went into the Army after finishing high school. I attended an all-boy Catholic school in Miami. In fact, all of the schools I attended were Catholic. I currently need fifteen hours to complete my degree in sociology. That has taken me the better part of twenty-six years. I'm still working on it.

Unfortunately, there aren't a lot of schools awarding majors in remote viewing. One day there will be.

What kind of a job did you have while you were in the Army?

I spent my entire career, twenty years, in Army Intelligence and Security. Most of my assignments were overseas and all of my jobs were classified. My participation within the Army remote viewing project now known as STARGATE extended from 1978 through my retirement in 1984, after which I continued within the project as a research consultant and sub-contractor to SRI-International, and Science Applications International Corporation. My early retirement from the Army was predicated by my desire to participate in more than just the applications or collection area of remote viewing.

You mean you didn't do remote viewing in the Army?

Previously I responded to this question with, "That would imply the United States Army has an open attitude regarding psychic functioning, which it doesn't. There is very little in the Army which is conducive to remote viewing or its function. It would be nice if there were more government interest in remote viewing, purely from a research and development standpoint, of course. I believe any investigation into expanding the human ability is of importance."

While the above evades a direct answer to my participation within the Army's remote viewing project, the response is still accurate. While the project existed, the Army *never* had a truly open attitude regarding psychic functioning. There was then, and still is, very little within the Army that is conducive to remote viewing or its function. There should be more government interest in remote viewing, purely from a research and development standpoint, for the following reasons:

A. There are few if any private sector investors who are willing to fully support or properly endow continued research.

B. A lack of open minds, insight, or vision may result in the termination of government support within the United States, but it certainly isn't the case in many other countries, where the acceptance of the possibilities of super-human functioning is taken very seriously. I still consider information collection through psychic means a direct threat to the security of my nation, whether the government does or not.

C. At a minimum, not using remote viewing in support of other intelligence collection methods, particularly within the areas of anti-terrorist or nuclear-threat scenarios is unconscionable, particularly given its statistical reliability.

D. I believe any investigation into expanding our understanding of the human condition and/or capabilities is of importance, and will have ripple effects throughout many other areas of investigative research.

How are you generally treated by other cultures and people who are first introduced to the paranormal through your perspective and your viewing?

Fear—that is, fear of the unknown—knows no boundaries. I'm still greeted by some who don't know me, or what it is that I actually do, as if I were Dracula risen from the grave. So, it is not the sophistication of the people which determines whether or not they have open minds, it's their entire attitude toward the subject.

Ten years ago the average physicist wouldn't have given paranormal research a second glance. It's a lot different now. While many scientists still refuse to even look at the subject, there are many more who are willing to concede that there might be something to it.

I believe that it is important here to understand that looking into it doesn't mean you believe in it. A good scientist is a skeptical scientist. Healthy skepticism is perfectly all right; that's what you want. Flat rejection, however, comes across exactly as what it is—ignorance and fear.

Those who allow me to demonstrate what remote viewing is all about usually treat me very fairly. I have some close friends who still give me that look whenever I talk about what I do. I believe they have decided to humor me in my idiosyncrasy, and that's all right. The other perception you have to be careful about is not to misinterpret a lack of interest as lack of belief.

Do you continue to have what many call *abnormal* experiences since your near-death experience in 1970?

I continue to have experiences, yes. I don't know if I would call them abnormal. The statistics that I've read regarding spontaneous out-of-body events in other people would tend to substantiate the experience as more normal than abnormal. But yes, I've continued to have spontaneous out-of-body experiences. It's usually when I least expect it to happen: dozing on the couch during an afternoon nap, when I'm waking from sleep in the morning, or even out of a uniquely clear dream, a lucid dream.

It should be reiterated here that I've never had a "bad" out-of-body, either. There have been some which were very entertaining, very bizarre if you will, and I wasn't sure what was going on. But none have ever appeared to be nightmarish.

Are there differences in the OBE associated with the near-death experience (NDE) and those which are spontaneous?

Yes, there are marked differences. The OBE associated with the NDE was at a different reality or level of existence. The OBEs that are spontaneous almost always occur in the physical world. In other words, I've always seemed to go to places that I recognize as the physical. There have been a couple in which I've found myself in places or times that either couldn't really exist or exist somewhere outside of time and space. Could they be hallucinations? Of course they could be, but then I believe there are many points within normal living that are hallucinations. We are constantly fooling ourselves; that's why things always appear to blend together so smoothly. I can't imagine everything being as coordinated as it is, if that weren't so. Most would reject such a concept, simply because God can't make any mistakes. But I'm not talking about God here; I'm talking about our fragile ability to make sense out of all the mish-mash of input we consciously and unconsciously try to process.

Can you control your OBEs now?

Only if I go back into a rigorous training cycle with control of OBEs being the focus point. I spent the better part of thirteen months in the lab at the Monroe Institute in order to learn to do just that. We were ultimately successful, but only at the sacrifice of my efforts to remote view. It's just too hard to try to control both. So, I gave up trying to control the OBEs and went back to trying to control the remote viewing.

I can pretty much control the OBE once I'm into it. I don't get as excited about it anymore. Initially, the excitement is so overwhelming that you can't maintain the state once it's established. After you get burned out on the excitement, well, that's when everything seems to work well.

Why didn't you want to come back into the physical after your NDE?

Because, in comparison, this physical reality we live in is most primitive. There are many people who share our world but have no respect for it. They don't even respect themselves, so it would be futile for us to expect them to show respect for others.

I wanted to remain in the Light and become part of it because it felt as if all knowing and feeling were contained there. It was like swimming in nothing but pure and unconditional love. I was accepted, not for who or what I was, but simply because I was a part of the whole. I argued to stay, but lost the argument. There is probably a reason for it, but I haven't a clue as to what it might be.

Is there good and evil? Can evil exist on its own, or does man invent it?

This question actually requires two responses. First I need to say that yes, I believe that evil can exist on its own. However, it takes human interaction to give it a place for expression. In other words, good and evil stem from humans and our judgments of what is right or wrong. We determine what good and evil are according to how much control we exercise, one upon the other.

Following the termination of World War II, our consensus was that what Hitler did to the Jews, the gypsies, and other minorities was an atrocity; it was absolutely evil. We were able to exercise this belief because we were successful in defeating Hitler and his henchmen. But what if they had won? By now we would all be speaking German and history might have painted an entirely different picture.

I am not berating the Germans here; I am simply pointing out that judgment goes with the strong, the winners. So judgment is a transient view, a view which is subject to change by whomever carries the strength, holds the cards, or decides what is right or wrong. New rights and wrongs are being established every day.

Unfortunately, mankind isn't always right. As capable as we think we are, we are unable to identify evil in all of its manifestations or cope with it wherever it might spring up.

Recently, a large segment of mankind stood by in silence while millions have been put to death in Kampuchea. We virtually ignore what is going on in parts of Africa, where disease and starvation are at such epidemic proportions that human beings are dying wholesale, by the tens of thousands. Is this any less an expression of evil than the Hitler example? I think not. So yes, evil can manifest without any great effort of humanity; in fact, it would seem to do so best when we pay the least attention. It's only when mankind decides that it can't live with the outcome that something is done about eliminating it.

The other problem is that morality itself gets in the way of a solution. Morality is so different between one segment of mankind and the next that we can't seem to arrive at an agreement in definition.

By looking at things from a different perspective, let's say constructive versus destructive, we can make a more effective decision about what should or shouldn't be done. I find it far more constructive to pursue the preservation of life than to support its destruction, and I act accordingly. In other words, I try to invest my energy into the positive or constructive side of issues.

Some would say this is an argument in semantics, but it's not. In the case of Kampuchea, when the situation is looked at as good or evil, people automatically bring in their Judeo-Christian background or perhaps their political view—"they are brown-skinned heathens—they are communists." It's unavoidable. If democracy is good, then communism is bad; if being a God-fearing Christian is good, then being a Buddhist is bad. You can see it in our own country as well; being rich is good, being poor is bad—ergo, being a street person is "evil."

When the same problem is approached from a constructive versus destructive viewpoint, everything changes. The loss of valuable human life through political programs (Kampuchea), starvation (Africa), or insensitivity (street people), is not constructive. It is destructive to the spirit of mankind. Constructive input is energy expended to prevent continued destructiveness.

Remember, one of the most effective exercises in free will is being able to choose where we might invest our own limited supply of energy, in the constructive or the destructive. It is always our own choice.

How many remote viewers are there?

There are probably hundreds out there who are actually practicing the art. I know of only ten or so who participate through the same labs in which I participate. You should be careful here not to assume that all viewers are alike, that all viewers believe the same things. In fact, there is evidence to suggest that each viewer is remarkably different from the next, in both approach as well as philosophic viewpoint. Viewers are iconoclastic in every sense of the word.

The most common traits shared by viewers are a willingness to look at any input or process any possibility, a willingness to accept change at a moment's notice, a willingness to step off into the unknown, and the strength to do any of the above, alone if necessary.

Can remote viewing be used for political or military ends?

Of course. It is just like any other tool that might be used to bring focused energy to bear on a problem. This includes political or military needs as well. There are numerous constructive projects within the political or military structures. It is unfortunate that so many people think of the political or military part of our society as only a necessary evil. There are far more constructive than non-constructive uses of our political and military system.

Remote viewing will work within the system just as well as it does from the outside. However, problems will arise when a viewer is asked to do something that goes against the grain; e.g., when s/he is asked to do something destructive. Of course, the terms constructive versus destructive are just as individual as the terms good or evil. So, it depends on the time, place, and circumstances.

Does the Hemi-Sync™ system used by the Monroe Institute have any effect on remote viewing?

Yes. It doesn't necessarily improve the quality of the remote viewing result, but it does considerably shorten the cool-down period before an experiment. Prior to using the Hemi-Sync system, my cool-down periods were sometimes hours long. It was very difficult trying to get into the necessary frame of mind. After using the Hemi-Sync tapes for about a year, these cool-down periods were virtually eliminated, or at least cut down to three to five minutes.

In addition, the Hemi-Sync system is good for learning many forms of meditative study. I benefited a great deal from attending one of the Monroe Institute's seminars.

Can you tell us about some of your most important remote viewing targets?

Unfortunately, there is insufficient room within this book to describe them in detail. Some of the more interesting remote viewings have covered such topics as how the Great Pyramid was built, the Crucifixion, the assassination of President Kennedy, UFOs, and life in the year 3000. I am currently in the process of constructing a second manuscript which will contain a compendium of remote viewing targets with the details of information produced in those sessions.

How do you think remote viewing works?

Simply put, I think that I am sending myself information from the future. In other words, at some point in the future I will come to know the answer to whatever question has been put to me in the past. Therefore, *whenever* the information is passed to me in its accurate form, that is when I send it back to myself in the past.

I know this sounds a bit like over-simplification, and to some degree it is, but that's quite simply how I believe it works.

Epilogue

What about the future? How far into the future can we go?

It is impossible to know. Obviously, this Joe won't be around in the year 3000, but I believe that some form of Joe will be. So, if I'm properly tuned into whatever rendition of me might be present then, I should be able to make some pretty good predictions.

If you can accept a concept that we inform ourselves by passing information into the past, then you need only carry it one more step to understand how much a part of one another we might truly be.

Perhaps most of you out there are renditions of Joe, at least as much as I am a part of you. As far-fetched as it might sound, it makes perfectly good sense. In order for us to fully experience an event in physical reality, we would need to see all perspectives or views of it. Therefore, at a minimum, within each event, I would have to be the observer as well as the observed. Of course, if there were other witnesses to the event, then I would have to be them as well. All renditions of us would be actively passing information into the past.

This creates a whole different view of the world, doesn't it? It automatically puts us in charge of the *cause* as well as the *effect*. It makes us truly responsible for all of our actions.

Sort of underscores the act of free will, don't you think?

Predictions, whether they are about climate, earth changes, or mankind's future achievements, stand in a category all on their own. There is nothing wrong with knowing them ahead of time, because the adventure isn't in knowing what they are; it's in the getting there.

We are designing our future as we've decided our past, and we all share in the responsibility. Let's wake each other up and work on it together.

Appendix

Live Target Protocol—Using an Out-Bounder Team

a. A pool of targets is selected by an individual who will not directly participate in the experiments.

b. A sufficient pool of targets may consist of six, ten, twelve, or more. The number of targets probably shouldn't exceed thirty.

c. Targets should be within reasonably close driving distance.

d. Once the targets have been selected, their addresses, locations, and titles should be printed on small cards and placed within double-wrapped or opaque envelopes.

e. Targets selected should stand alone and be unique, different from one another.

f. Targets with an overall ambiance or gestalt make the best beginning targets

g. Target envelopes should be assigned random three-digit numbers and be stored away from all participants until required for use.

h. Never store more targets than you plan to use within a reasonable length of time.

i. Once the targets have been selected and placed in a pool, the out-bounder team must generate a three-digit code to obtain a directions envelope. This can be done by throwing a single-digit die of ten sides (0-9) three times, or three of the same ten-digit dice once.

j. Once the out-bounder team has obtained the envelope, they then drive around until fifteen minutes prior to the set target time. At this point, they open the envelope and follow its instructions, by going directly to the target of interest. On the way, they should avoid looking around as much as possible, so as not to confuse the real target with other possible targets within the area.

k. At the set time, the remote viewer and interviewer (if required) generate both a verbal as well as pictorial representation of the target location where they believe the out-bounder team may be located.

l. The out-bounder team is asked to interact as much as possible within the target, keeping their curiosity focused only on the target selected.

m. When the time designated to be spent interacting with the target is up, the remote viewing is terminated and all notes and tapes put away.

n. The out-bounder team then returns and picks up the remote viewer (and interviewer if present) and all participants of the experiment then return to the target area for feedback and to discuss the remote viewing information obtained.

Pictographic Targeting Mechanism

a. Same as above, except that it doesn't require an out-bounder team. Instead of using locally selected targets, the person making the target selection selects them from a magazine. Appropriate magazines from which to select targets are *National Geographic, Smithsonian, Scientific American, Travel and Leisure, Life,* or any other periodical which features photographs of distant places with unique scenery. Selection of a target is just as critical here as it is for the out-bounder team.

b. Once a target has been selected, it is cut from the magazine and pasted back-side down onto a white sheet of paper. This is then placed within a double-wrapped or opaque envelope for use as a target.

c. Specific target selection is still made randomly through the use of a single ten-digit die thrown three times or three ten-digit dice thrown once.

d. After the remote viewer (and interviewer, if required) have finished putting the information on the tape and have completed the drawings, they then open the envelope and compare the accuracy of the remote viewing description to the photo.

Coordinate Targeting Methodology

a. Same as the above, except that the person selecting the targets provides the coordinates of the targets to degree, minute, and second.

b. These can be either read aloud to the remote viewer or placed within a double-wrapped or opaque envelope.

BASIC RULES

1. Targets are always selected and put together by someone outside of the experiment.

2. Targets should be uniquely different within the same target pool.

3. Targets should always stand alone, or be as separate from their surrounding as they can be.

4. An interviewer can be used, but is optional.

5. The interviewer should be as blind to the target as the remote viewer.

6. Minimum and maximum times spent working on a target are fifteen to thirty minutes, respectively.

7. A specific date and time for targeting must be established up front.

8. Take plenty of notes; you'll need them later.

9. Don't cheat!

Books of Related Interest

The Stargate Chronicles
Memoirs of a Psychic Spy
Joseph McMoneagle

McMoneagle is now known as the best Operational Remote Viewer in the history of the U.S. Army's Special Project—Stargate. He was the only remote viewer who worked one-on-one with the out-of-body pioneer Robert Monroe, and who has achieved intelligence-collection results that have never been surpassed and rarely equaled. Was it his unsuspected psychic ability, which helped keep him alive in Vietnam and aided in his invaluable contributions to the cold war effort, that made McMoneagle a first-class remote viewer? Were his abilities a natural gift, or taught? How much did he owe to his near-death experience in the 1970s? This is his story.

Hardcover * 368 pages * ISBN 1-57174-225-5

Remote Viewing Secrets
A Handbook
Joseph McMoneagle

Remote viewing is not simply using psychic ability to obtain information. It is using scientific protocol to develop and extend that ability, so that ordinary people can learn to do what psychics do. This book teaches you how to teach yourself. McMoneagle uses examples, exercises, and anecdotes to share what he has learned, and gives you everything you need to begin developing your own abilities. *Remote Viewing Secrets* is easily the most complete, authentic, and informative guide to remote viewing published to date.

Paperback * 320 pages * ISBN 1-57174-159-3

The Ultimate Time Machine
A Remote Viewer's Perception of Time, and Predictions for the New Millennium
Joseph McMoneagle

McMoneagle explores the questions that philosophers have debated for centuries: Does time really exist? Do our actions today really affect our future? Can we change the past? Do we slip between alternate realities? McMoneagle delivers new insights into these mysteries, including firsthand information on the origins of humanity, the crucifixion of Christ, and the building of the Egyptian pyramids; a detailed picture of the future through the year 2075; a vision of the year 3000; and more.

Paperback * 280 pages * ISBN 1-57174-102-X

Captain of My Ship, Master of My Soul
Living with Guidance
F. Holmes Atwater

Atwater—who, as an army lieutenant, took the initiative that resulted in the creation of the remote viewing intelligence program now known as Stargate—looks at the "coincidences" that led him from childhood out-of-body explorations to army counter-intelligence operations to sessions with consciousness pioneer Robert A. Monroe. Included in this volume is a CD-ROM containing declassified government documents pertaining to remote viewing, audio recordings of remote-viewing sessions, slide presentations on remote viewing workshops, audio recordings of Atwater's altered-state explorations at The Monroe Institute, and the original audio recording of the remote viewing of Mars performed by Joseph McMoneagle.

Paperback w/ CD-ROM * 256 pages * ISBN 1-57174-247-6

Voyages into the Unknown
Volume 1 of the Exploring the Afterlife series
Bruce Moen

This fascinating book recounts the story of some of Moen's voyages past the edge of life using techniques learned at The Monroe Institute. Moen says, "I sailed out and back many times, returning with more knowledge through my own direct experience." He describes for the reader how to access this knowledge, and says he hopes that "at least bits and pieces here ring true to your own experience, and that finding those bits and pieces will encourage you to continue."

Paperback * 256 pages * ISBN 1-57174-068-6

Muddy Tracks
Exploring an Unsuspected Reality
Frank DeMarco / Introduction by Colin Wilson

Muddy Tracks is a record of what one man found when he went looking to find out "what is real" from firsthand experience. Keeping strictly to what he has experienced, DeMarco shows how many aids we may find in life, including selected reading, dream analysis, and interaction with others, as well as more unusual resources such as The Monroe Institute. Most important, he demonstrates that we all have our own internal guidance, which is reliable and is willing and able to come forth when welcomed—and he shows how to contact it. The meaning of your life can be found, DeMarco says, but only by you yourself. Muddy Tracks was written to help you learn to do that.

Paperback * 328 pages * ISBN 1-57174-362-6
Hardcover * 400 pages * ISBN 1-57174-257-3

Photo by
Nancy McMoneagle

About the Author

Joseph W. McMoneagle was born January 10, 1946, in Miami, Florida. He voluntarily joined the U.S. Army and was recruited by the Army Security Agency for classified assignments. He spent mid-1964 through 1978 on various overseas missions within the countries of The Bahamas, South Vietnam, Germany, Italy, Thailand, and others, eventually being assigned to the headquarters of the U.S. Army Intelligence and Security Command (INSCOM) in Arlington, Virginia.

As a result of many unusual events in his life, a near-death experience, a UFO sighting, and numerous spontaneous out-of-body episodes, he was one of the original Intelligence Officers recruited for the top-secret Army program now known as STARGATE. While there, he earned a *Legion of Merit* for providing ". . .critical intelligence reported at the highest echelons of our military and government, including such national level agencies as The Joint Chiefs of Staff, DIA, NSA, CIA, DEA, and the Secret Service, producing crucial and vital intelligence unavailable from any other source."

Following his retirement from the Army in 1984, he maintained his association with the STARGATE program through his own company, Intuitive Intelligence Applications, working as a remote viewing consultant to the Cognitive Sciences Laboratories at SRI-International and Science Applications International Corporation until the program's closure in November of 1995.

Joe is currently a Research Associate with the Laboratories for Fundamental Research in Palo Alto, where he continues to seek more effective answers to questions concerning the applications of remote viewing, its underlying mechanisms, and the paranormal. He is now acknowledged as one of the best remote viewers in the field.

Hampton Roads Publishing Company
. . . for the evolving human spirit

Hampton Roads Publishing Company
publishes books on a variety of subjects including
metaphysics, health, complementary medicine,
visionary fiction, and other related topics.

For a copy of our latest catalog,
call toll-free, 800-766-8009,
or send your name and address to:

Hampton Roads Publishing Company, Inc.
1125 Stoney Ridge Road
Charlottesville, VA 22902
e-mail: hrpc@hrpub.com
www.hrpub.com